44 C

D1759569

 University of Hertfordshire

Learning and Information Services

Watford Campus Learning Resources Centre
Aldenham Watford Herts WD2 8AT
Renewals: Tel 01707 284673 Mon-Fri 12 noon-8pm only

This book is in heavy demand and is due back strictly by the last date stamped below. A fine will be charged for the late return of items.

ONE WEEK LOAN

WITHDRAWN

Subversive Heroines

Subversive Heroines
Feminist Resolutions of Social Crisis in the Condition-of-England Novel

Constance D. Harsh

Ann Arbor

THE UNIVERSITY OF MICHIGAN PRESS

UNIVERSITY OF HERTFORDSHIRE
WATFORD CAMPUS LRC
WATFORD WD2 8AT

BIB
0472105663

CLASS
823.8093520042 HAR

LOCATION
OWL

BARCODE
4405020306

Copyright © by the University of Michigan 1994
All rights reserved
Published in the United States of America by
The University of Michigan Press
Manufactured in the United States of America
⊛ Printed on acid-free paper
1997 1996 1995 1994   4 3 2 1

A CIP catalogue record for this book is available from the British Library.

Library of Congress Cataloging-in-Publication Data

Harsh, Constance D., 1960–
    Subversive heroines : feminist resolutions of social crisis in the
    condition-of-England novel / Constance D. Harsh.
        p.   cm.
    Includes bibliographical references and index.
    ISBN 0-472-10566-3
    1. English fiction—19th century—History and criticism.
    2. Feminism and literature—England—History—19th century.
    3. Literature and society—England—History—19th century. 4. Women
    and literature—England—History—19th century. 5. Social problems
    in literature. 6. England—In literature. 7. Women in literature.
    I. Title.
PR878.F45H37   1994
823'.809352042—dc20   94-31064
                                                                CIP

Acknowledgments

This book began its life as a dissertation under the direction of Nina Auerbach, to whom I owe a great debt of appreciation for her astute guidance and unflagging support. David DeLaura always gave my work careful and helpful readings for which I am grateful. Malcolm Laws also provided a useful reading of my initial study. Rosemarie Bodenheimer and Richard Maxwell gave generous and incisive criticism that helped me reshape many of my arguments. Part of the research for this study was conducted with the support of an Annenberg Fellowship at the University of Pennsylvania.

Special thanks are due to Susan Cerasano and Michael Coyle for their advice and encouragement; I am grateful as well to Margaret Maurer and my other colleagues at Colgate University. I would also like to thank the following people for their suggestions and assistance: Victoria Carchidi, James K. Chandler, Paula Giuliano, Jill Rubenstein, and the members of the National Endowment for the Humanities (NEH) Summer Seminar on Walter Scott. I wish to acknowledge as well the Philomathean Theater Guild, which brought an earlier version of this piece vividly to life.

I owe the shape of my scholarly career to James L. Rosier, an unfailingly sage counselor who went to bat for me when I most needed help.

Finally, no list of indispensable people would be complete without the following names: Margaret J. Harsh, M. Duffield Harsh, and Edward D. Harsh.

Contents

Introduction

> How true, for example, is that other old Fable of the Sphinx, who sat by the wayside, propounding her riddle to the passengers, which if they could not answer she destroyed them! Such a Sphinx is this Life of ours. . . . Nature, like the Sphinx, is of womanly celestial loveliness and tenderness; the face and bosom of a goddess, but ending in claws and the body of a lioness. There is in her a celestial beauty,—which means celestial order, pliancy to wisdom; but there is also a darkness, a ferocity, fatality, which are infernal. She is a goddess, but one not yet disimprisoned.[1]

Thomas Carlyle, in *Past and Present*, warned that English industrial society could not hope to survive unless it learned the answer to the riddle of human existence—a question posed in this case by a female figure implacably guarding the road to the future. This figure is in one sense all too familiar: the personification of nature as a stereotype of womanhood, with scant intelligence and limitless malevolence. But the Sphinx is an intriguingly positive figure as well: a powerful force underlying all petty contemporary activities, a goddess waiting to be loosed upon a world that badly needed sources of energy and value. Carlyle did not explore the transformative possibilities of a myth of powerful womanhood, but he did clearly define the terms of a fictional debate that would. For the novels that consider the "condition-of-England question" that Carlyle crystallized explore the potential power of feminist myth to resolve imaginatively the social crisis of the day.

In the 1830s English society had become urgently concerned with the condition-of-England question that Carlyle addresses in such works as *Past and Present* (1843) and *Chartism* (1839). Discontent with the human consequences of the Industrial Revolution had spread from the working class to the middle and upper classes only in this decade.[2] Politicians such as Richard Oastler and Michael Sadler began to address the treatment of workers with their call for a Ten Hours Bill, and the publication of the Sadler Committee's report in 1833 created widespread outrage at the horrifying conditions it described.[3] But, while the Sadler report and the bluebooks that would follow it did much to set an agenda for the improvement of industrial working conditions, the increasing belligerence of the working class was perhaps more responsible for convincing the upper classes that social crisis was imminent. The working-class enthusiasm for politics that had been aroused by the agitation preceding the First Reform Bill[4] did not subside after 1832; if anything, as James Epstein notes, passage of the bill increased tensions in English society by "sever[ing] the working class from the middle class politically."[5] Lower-class radicalism grew throughout the decade; it took on greater intensity with the onset of economic depression around 1837[6] and the implementation of the New Poor Law. The decisive proof of unrest in the laboring classes came with the rise of Chartism in 1838; its troubling demand for universal suffrage and its often fiery rhetoric convinced the ruling classes that violent revolution was a real possibility and that a genuine crisis already faced the nation. Even several months after the anticlimactic Chartist rally of 10 April 1848, a reviewer in the *Edinburgh Review* could write of the potential for violence in English society: "We are fully aware of the danger of delaying any urgent and desirable reform; and even admit the consequent *possibility* of revolution, as the result of frustrated hopes operating on human passion and infirmity."[7] In 1839 Thomas Carlyle expressed the general feeling of the privileged with his ominous forebodings in *Chartism*:

> [T]his matter appears, and has for many years appeared, to be the most ominous of all practical matters whatever; a matter in regard to which if something be not done, something will *do* itself one day, and in a fashion that will please nobody. The time is verily come for acting in it.[8]

Among those who assessed the contemporary condition of England, Carlyle was at once the most trenchant and the most influential. As Steven Marcus has observed, Carlyle offered "insights of a kind, formulated with a force, passion, and penetration that were not . . . to be found anywhere else at that moment";[9] Philip Rosenberg has argued for his status as the first English intellectual to become as well virtually a political actor.[10] By the late 1830s he was considered sufficiently important to merit lengthy journal reviews of the body of his work (although it was as yet uncollected); Jules Paul Seigel asserts that he had a particular appeal for the young.[11] Even after his ultimate fall from public favor with the publication of *Latter-Day Pamphlets* (1850), George Eliot would affirm his intellectual significance for the age.

> [T]here is hardly a superior or active mind of this generation that has not been modified by Carlyle's writings; there has hardly been an English book written for the last ten or twelve years that would not have been different if Carlyle had not lived.[12]

Carlyle, then, brought to his subject matter in *Chartism* and *Past and Present* a striking power of thought and expression and a growing reputation as England's foremost sage. His formulation of the condition-of-England question provides the most focused explanation of those issues that preoccupied his generation. So hostile a reviewer of Carlyle's work as William Sewell was in agreement with him on the nature of the contemporary problem; more typical was Peter LePage Renouf's stronger affirmation—Carlyle's "most vivid and frightful picture of the present state of things . . . [is] the more frightful because it is undeniably a true one."[13] By setting the tone of the condition-of-England debate, he would provide not only an outstanding attack on society's shortcomings but also a particular way of seeing the contemporary crisis—an imaginative filter for those novels that would create a largely self-consistent myth in the course of their own fictional contributions to the debate.

Carlyle's analysis of the condition-of-England question offers two general principles that prove crucial to the formation of this fictional genre. Early in *Past and Present* he turns to rioting workers in Manchester and declares that they articulate "the first practical form of *our* Sphinx-riddle" by asking "their huge inarticulate question, 'What do you mean to do with us?'"[14] The first sentence of *Chartism* states the same central tenet more clearly—that the chief problem of modern English life is class relations: "A feeling very generally exists that the condition and disposition of the Working Classes is a rather ominous matter at present; that something ought to be said, something ought to be done, in regard to it."[15] Throughout his wide-ranging discussions of such issues as English history, statistics, religion, and the Irish situation, Carlyle maintains an underlying interest in the working class and its relationship to the upper class. As he sees it, unlike the world of medieval St. Edmundsbury he extols in *Past and Present*, his own society is characterized by a large-scale disorder in class relationships that has grown out of the upper classes' foolish allegiance to a laissez-faire political philosophy. The old rulers of the country, in abandoning their responsibility to the ruled, have created an anarchic situation out of which lower-class demagogues may arise with disastrous results.[16]

Carlyle's second major contribution to the fictional condition-of-England debate is his characterization of the solutions required in this time of emergency. The language that he uses, both in its biblical diction and its calls for a new priesthood, has strongly religious overtones that emphasize his concern with the mystical, mythological dimension of human reality. The sort of change he calls for, moreover, is not a painless and meretricious "Morrison's Pill" but a profound reorientation in attitudes, as this passage from *Past and Present* indicates:

> A total change of regimen, change of constitution and existence from the very centre of it; a new body to be got, with resuscitated soul,—not without convulsive travail-throes; as all birth and new-birth presupposes travail![17]

Carlyle's proposed resuscitation of the soul requires a complete transformation of the organization of English society. John D. Rosenberg has noted "his fear of anarchy"; Carlyle throughout his career demonstrates an apocalyptic sensibility, a fascination with "cataclysmic upheaval" that makes him "the instinctive partisan of revolution."[18] In the two works at hand Carlyle expresses this sensibility by calling for change in a contemporary world that is not simply sick and in need of some invigorating tonic but utterly corrupt. His vision entails revolution rather than a superficial tinkering with the system.[19]

Carlyle produced a compelling indictment of what was wrong in English life and a convincing appraisal of how far-reaching reform would need to be. He did not, however, provide a solution to the problems he saw that would be equal in influence to his analysis. Even he admits, in *Past and Present*, that drawing blueprints is not his forte.

> Of Time-Bill, Factory-Bill and other such Bills the present Editor has no authority to speak. He knows not, it is for others than he to know, in what specific ways it may be feasible to interfere, with Legislation, between the Workers and the Master-Workers.[20]

Chartism offers particularly meager specific proposals that elicited reservations from contemporary critics and open scorn from William Sewell: "[R]eading and emigration!!! . . . We can assure him, from our own knowledge, that many of his readers doubt if he is serious."[21] Although *Past and Present* provides a clearer set of suggestions, what John D. Rosenberg goes so far as to call a "programme" for a "strong, paternalistic government,"[22] this essay too proves more successful in evoking an emotional response than in outlining measures to be taken. Carlyle's solutions always come as a disappointment after the fiery rhetoric of his social analysis; his first readers recognized the limits within which he could offer guidance to a troubled age. William Henry Smith observed: "It is not by teaching this or that dogma . . . that Mr. Carlyle is doing his *work*, and exerting an influence, by no means despicable, on his generation. It is by producing a certain moral tone of thought."[23] In a sense the very vagueness of Carlyle's formulations is part of his power. Philip Rosenberg, while noting that "Carlyle's activism [in *Chartism* is] almost contentless," also points out that "the virtue of Carlyle's activist ideology lies precisely in this ability to call for revolutionary struggle . . . while at the same time remaining remarkably free of dogmatism about the outcome of that struggle."[24] Yet such a strategy leaves the matter of satisfactory solutions to the problem at hand disturbingly unresolved. Carlyle crystallized the terms of the contemporary debate, but he failed to establish a standard for its resolution. Those novelists who found in his work a means of focusing their analysis would need to discover their own means of concretely embodying plausible answers in fictional modes of social analysis.

By the end of the 1830s the novel had developed an interest in contemporary issues and the self-confidence to deal compellingly with them. Elliot Engel and Margaret King observe that the decade saw the emergence of the "contemporary-realistic mode" as "the normative fictional mode" in England.[25] An increasing concern with realistic representations of everyday life, however, was not the sole component of fiction's interest in things as they are. As Richard Altick has recently observed,

> Never before had the novel been so tightly and extensively involved in the events of the day. It was not simply a matter of a new didacticism appearing to replace the one that had languished. . . . When ideological concerns of various sorts increasingly animated the public mind, the art of fiction was prepared to express and debate them in imaginative frameworks. Fiction, in short, met the social needs of the hour.[26]

One result of this increasing preoccupation with the present was fiction that approached directly those problems in industrial society that were beginning to come to the attention of the English middle and upper classes. Although many earlier novels had conducted social criticism, for the first time fiction felt it could compete with nonfictional genres such as essays and sociological documentation; it claimed to have as much authority as they did in the representation as well as the analysis of social reality. As Patrick Brantlinger has put it, "Victorian fiction aspire[d] to the condition of bluebooks."[27]

My concern is with a particular group of novels that claimed fiction's new authority—works that specifically addressed the contemporary English crisis. Critics have often called them industrial novels or social problem novels, but the label that seems most appropriate is condition-of-England novels: they belong to the time in which the condition-of-England question was widely debated, and they make a contribution to the version of the debate that Carlyle had crystallized.[28] They appeared throughout the years in which the working class was perceived to be a revolutionary threat—from the time of the first Chartist Petition in 1839 to the aftermath of the Preston strike of 1853–54. There are seven of them: Frances Trollope's *The Life and Adventures of Michael Armstrong, the Factory Boy* (1840), Charlotte Elizabeth Tonna's *Helen Fleetwood* (1841), Benjamin Disraeli's *Sybil; or, The Two Nations* (1845), Elizabeth Gaskell's *Mary Barton* (1848) and *North and South* (1855), Charles Kingsley's *Alton Locke* (1850), and Charles Dickens's *Hard Times* (1854). (All dates given for novels are years of publication in volume form.) These novels share an understanding of the contemporary situation similar to Carlyle's: they locate the fundamental difficulty of the age in class relationships, and they acknowledge the need for visionary solutions that will radically transform the face of English society. But they move beyond Carlyle by presenting coherent solutions, and they make use of a potential source of power that Victorian society commonly ignored and to which Carlyle would only allude: women.

There are notable omissions from my list of condition-of-England novels—works that deal with contemporary difficulties but do not belong to the analytic community of which Carlyle and these seven novels are members. The existence of such divergent fiction underlines the remarkable intellectual coherency of the genre I survey. The early work of Charles Dickens frequently highlights social inequities and systematic exploitation, but only in *Hard Times* does he anatomize a particular contemporary moment of potential class warfare. Charles Kingsley's *Yeast* (1848) examines the condition of England without ever focusing on a single underlying problem. Lancelot Smith, Kingsley's hero, bounces from issue to issue—from the condition of agricultural workers to the state of the young aristocracy to the Church of England to modern art. Where *Yeast* has no center of gravity, Disraeli's *Coningsby* (1844) has an idiosyncratic center: in this novel the greatest problem facing England is not the state of the working class but the state of politics and Parliament. Harriet Martineau's "A Manchester Strike" (1834) in *Illustrations of Political Economy*, on the other hand, rejects Carlyle's analysis of the gravity of the current situation. This short piece sees no need for radical change because it denies the existence of any real problem. Martineau argues that, if only workers would understand the relentless, inevitable operation of the free market system, they would stop complaining about wages and go back to work. Since human pigheadedness, rather than any unique historical exigency, lies behind the brief hiccup of revolt in Martineau's England, her story clearly does not partake of the Carlylean interpretation of the condition of England.

The seven novels that are central to my study vary widely in style. But, unlike the works I have not included, they present an essentially unified analysis of the condition of England. In my first three chapters I examine this analysis in detail and bring to light the covert feminism of these novels—their empowerment of women to bring about the resolution of the national crisis. Chapter 1 discusses how women come to power in the imaginative worlds of these novels. Because the authors establish domestic life as their central reality, the female figures who dominate the home are able to take a commanding position in public life. Chapter 2 examines one role women play in this fiction: as significant victims, they are uniquely important to a delineation of the inhumanity of industrialization and paradoxically powerful. The more obviously active role of women comes into focus in chapter 3: those women who are the foremost initiators of reform assume an almost sacramental importance in society and point the way toward an England reorganized on principles other than the patriarchal ones of aggression and exploitation.

Having brought to light the feminist solutions of condition-of-England novels, I describe how subsequent novels of social criticism are unable to continue the genre's feminist analysis or make use of its imaginative power. The attitudes of the age, which Carlyle at once clarified and encapsulated, may have led inevitably to the empowerment of women, but this empowerment could not survive the age of English social crisis. My chapter on Charlotte Brontë's *Shirley* (1849) reveals the limitations that can operate on female power even when the criteria for a condition-of-England novel are met. Brontë's novel may agree with the other books on the problem, and on the solution that would be most desirable, but it cannot envision the successful intervention of women. In my final chapter I go beyond the boundaries of the condition-of-England genre to trace the fate of female empowerment. I focus on one novel by a newcomer to the genre of industrial fiction, George Eliot's *Felix Holt, The Radical* (1866), and two later novels by writers who had earlier produced condition-of-England fiction, Dickens's *Little Dorrit* (1857) and Gaskell's *Wives and Daughters* (1866). This section explores the nature of and the reasons for the failure of condition-of-England powers to survive the occasion for their emergence. The ultimate aim of my analysis is to provide a chart of the imaginative territory within which Victorian women were able to gain a significant though temporary fictional role in the public affairs of English society.

Until very recently, the industrial novel has been taken seriously as a sign of its times or not at all. Traditional critics in search of literary value have historically been reluctant to examine this genre with much care. Philip Collins's damning assessment is outstanding in its vehemence but not in its essential valuation of these books:

> [This is a] remarkably sparse and feeble literary response to a phenomenon so evident and momentous as England's becoming the first predominantly industrial and urbanized community in the history of mankind. For, like the Great American Novel, the great industrial novel never got written.[29]

One result of this rejection on aesthetic grounds has been a dearth of criticism that holds to old-fashioned values of transcendence and universality.[30] Industrial novels have been most readily assimilated into these critics' intellectual framework on an individual basis, when the issue of membership in a genre of questionable merit can be more or less overlooked.[31]

Given the nearly peremptory dismissal literary critics have generally given to the industrial novel, it is not surprising that most modern critics have tried to find a more productive point of view for investigating this genre by taking a sociological approach in their criticism. It has at least never been suggested that the industrial novel lacks importance in the historical tradition of the novel. Analysis of the genre's relationship to its time promises to afford this fiction whatever dignity is possible.

The first of the three strands that compose sociological criticism of the industrial novel is what I will call class-based criticism. This critical approach, often allied to a Marxist analysis, holds that the social class of an author inevitably determines the character of a work of literature. In this view the industrial novel is an attempt by the bourgeoisie to describe and explain the world of the worker in a way palatable to and reconcilable with the ideology of their class. Although writers may show discontent with aspects of the contemporary scene, they invariably endorse the oppressive political and economic order that caused the problems in the first place. The second strand, the history of ideas approach, values the genre for the insight it gives into the minds of Victorians. Critics in this tradition are interested either in broad philosophical trends and how they are reflected in fiction or in what was thought about particular social doctrines or groups of people. The final strand, documentary criticism, uses these novels as possible sources of factual information about Victorian life and judges them worthwhile to the extent that they reflect social reality. All three downplay questions of aesthetic value in their approaches to the industrial novel.

The earliest class-based criticism of the industrial novel tended to be openly dismissive of its subject matter.[32] Raymond Williams's widely influential study of the genre in *Culture and Society* (1958) inaugurated an era of greater critical complexity and sympathy.[33] While Williams, like earlier critics, condemns the political timidity of the novelists and their failure to depict the plight of the working class, he also praises their compassion (particularly Elizabeth Gaskell's for John Barton). Subsequent class-based critics have more or less maintained this balance between disparagement and praise.[34] John Lucas, for instance, in his noteworthy essay "Mrs. Gaskell and Brotherhood" (1966) argues that the best of the industrial novels begin as imaginative explorations of their subject and are only forced into making pernicious "recommendations" for the solution of social problems when the frightening truth about working people and society shocks them back into conventional class loyalty.[35] Lucas's analysis epitomizes a recurrent problem in class-based criticism by suggesting that industrial novelists at times suspend their ideological premises and perceive the truth. Critics who are usually keenly sensitive to middle-class prejudice become curiously confident of an author's perceptiveness when they agree with the novelist's understanding of social relations.[36]

With *The Social Novel in England, 1830–1850* (1903), Louis Cazamian began the history of ideas strand of criticism. For Cazamian the industrial novel holds interest primarily in its reflection of the age's dominant doctrines of idealistic interventionism and utilitarian individualism.[37] Although some work in the tradition of Cazamian tends to evaluate a novel by the coherence of its political philosophy,[38] this strand has also produced less judgmental studies. Patrick Brantlinger's *The Spirit of Reform* (1977), for instance, provides an invaluable contextualization of Victorian fiction between 1832 and 1867 and intelligent readings of individual novels; Joseph Kestner's *Protest and Reform* (1985) offers helpful insights into women writers' special role in exploring industrial issues.[39]

A third strand of critical thought dominated the analysis of industrial novels in the 1970s—a documentary criticism that focused on the relationship of these works to verifiable historical reality.[40] Although this school established a number of interesting connections between industrial novels and their nonfictional sources, all too often it made verisimilitude its foremost criterion of literary worth. Sheila Smith's *The Other Nation* (1980), for instance, is highly critical of novels about the poor for not ringing true but has little appreciation of their genuine accomplishments.[41] Documentary criticism leads too easily to the treatment of literature as an inferior form of sociological data and masks the subjectivity of its aesthetics of verisimilitude with appeals to the supposed objectivity of historical reality.

While conventional literary criticism has labeled the industrial novel artistically unsuccessful, sociological criticism has sought to find value by avoiding the question of artistry. But, as Arnold Kettle observes, "to dismiss the effect as not art is to beg half the questions of practical aesthetics."[42] In recent years literary critics have begun to fill the gap in assessments of the industrial novel that Joan Kirkby perceived as early as 1972: "It is time, then, that Victorian social and humanitarian novels be re-examined in the light of modern critical theory to see if a study of their form will indeed reveal something new about what it is that they have said."[43] The developments of the last nine years have demonstrated that a fresh engagement with these texts can offer productive insights into their interest as literary works.

Catherine Gallagher's *The Industrial Reformation of English Fiction* (1985) has led the way in recent critical reappraisals. Gallagher draws upon a wide variety of fictional and nonfictional texts to argue brilliantly that these novels precipitated "the 1860s discovery of an independent realm of representation"[44] by revealing, through their engagement with the "Condition of England Debate," the contradictions of realist literary practice. While I find Gallagher's argument enormously impressive, her different critical interests and her evaluation of the importance of the private sphere in these novels distinguish her views sharply from my own. Unlike Gallagher, I confine my analysis to fictional considerations of a condition-of-England question I define more narrowly. Gallagher's chapter on *Hard Times* and *North and South* provides the clearest indication of how her analysis and mine diverge. Where she asserts that these novels ultimately separate the private and public realms they ostensibly link, I argue that it is more useful to emphasize connections between private and public that promote social change. For her, both here and in earlier chapters, a plot resolution by private action represents an antisocial retreat rather than a socially significant gesture. While Gallagher's keynote throughout her book is disjuncture, paradox, and contradiction, mine is successful integration. Although I find her approach a very suggestive one, it leads in very different directions from my own.

Rosemarie Bodenheimer has also provided an extremely productive approach to the genre with *The Politics of Story in Victorian Social Fiction* (1988), which considers "the shape and movement of narrative" in a wide variety of social-problem novels. Part 1 of her work examines the role of heroines in, among others, *Shirley, Michael Armstrong, North and South,* and *Felix Holt.* In particular, her first chapter, "The Romance of the Female Paternalist," approaches some industrial novels written by women from a perspective fairly close to my own. Bodenheimer observes the active role women play in these books and remarks that "some of these novels exploit [women's] exemption [from the marketplace ethos] in order to challenge images of domestic tranquillity, endowing their heroines with a power to act in the public realm."[45] To my mind, however, she does not do full justice to the genuinely subversive power of heroines and (more generally) of women's sphere in Victorian culture. Bodenheimer examines a broader phenomenon, the social-problem novel, than I do, and she sees a variety of narrative patterns; in contrast, I see a single pattern in a smaller array of texts by both men and women. In the study that follows I have attempted wherever appropriate to position my analysis with respect to the contributions Gallagher and Bodenheimer have made.

My own argument contends that, by paying to this genre the sort of close attention traditionally reserved for canonical Victorian fiction, we discover a surprising level of agreement among these authors on the kind of transformation the condition-of-England crisis demanded. Ultimately, the condition-of-England novel calls upon contemporary cultural beliefs about women to create its own feminist myth of social salvation.

To appreciate this myth we must first interrogate the realist impulse in industrial fiction. As I mentioned earlier, the Victorian novel often aspired to the condition of bluebooks, but it did not expect to reach the bluebook's status of unquestioned truth through precisely the same means. In the dissemination of information about social abuses, Roger P. Wallins has pointed out, the earliest industrial novels "were as much as six years behind the periodicals."[46] Although writers incorporated incidents from contemporary life into their narratives, then, the primary goal of their fiction was not the exposure of unfamiliar wrongs. Their own literary procedure was not a purely sociological one: George Levine observes that "there was no such thing as naive realism—simple faith in the correspondence between word and thing—among serious Victorian novelists."[47] Even the stridently mimetic assertions of the uncanonical, un-"serious" Charlotte Elizabeth Tonna, who claims to have "set forth nothing but what has been stated on oath,"[48] run up against the powerfully unnaturalistic elements of her fictional practice. The more theoretically sophisticated of the condition-of-England novelists would have acknowledged that their project was to comment on their society by transfiguring social fact. "Fiction," Carlyle's fictional Herr Sauerteig disparagingly observes, "partakes . . . of the nature of *lying*";[49] the only justification for using this form to reach the truth is to make use of the freedom a lie can offer.

Kenneth Burke has observed that literature must be seen as the strategic encompassment of a particular set of cultural circumstances. It is therefore inappropriate to focus on a text's accuracy of representation; instead, one should be concerned with the "motives" (in Burke's sense) that underlie the text's form of engagement with reality.

> Here there is no "realism for its own sake." There is realism for promise, admonition, solace, vengeance, foretelling, instruction, charting, all for the direct bearing that such acts have upon matters of welfare.[50]

Indeed, Burke has suggested that literature has a proverblike quality, both in its ability to find a name for "typical and recurrent" situations[51] and in its hortatory dimension. Winfried Fluck has usefully elaborated upon Burke's ideas about symbolic action to propose a way of understanding the relationship between literature and culture.

> Literary texts are distinguished from other forms of communica-
> tion by their status as fictions. Simply put, they respond to real-
> ity by inventing stories. . . . In its freedom to arrange, to con-
> struct and to correct reality according to our own norms and
> interests, fiction permits us tentatively to reformulate, comple-
> ment or oppose the social and cultural constructions of reality,
> and it is exactly in this tentative, playful nature that one unique
> value of literature as a symbolic strategy can be found.[52]

It is fiction's capacity for tentative reformulation that the condition-
of-England novel exploits in its implicit utopian promises of reformation. It is not necessary that these promises be hard-headedly practical or that the authors should have been aware of the changes they
were espousing. What is significant is that the social constraints of
the particular historical moment and the ideological constraints of
their culture produced a shared reconception of society's ordering
principles.

To come to terms with this shared perception of and symbolic
response to the condition-of-England question, the most effective
means of approach would seem to be a formalist one. Fluck observes:

> To what extent a fictional text can be said to have drawn success-
> fully and with imaginative resourcefulness on its own potential
> as a testing-ground . . . can only be decided in the process of a
> detailed reading and discussion of the text itself. In this sense,
> the concept of literature as symbolic action leads straight back
> to the text itself, for it creates a renewed interest in the complex
> interaction of its thematic and formal strategies as the logical
> place in which the symbolic materials of a culture, its theoretical
> claims and constructs are put to a test.[53]

My own analysis of these novels does focus on texts rather than their
sociological underpinnings or competing modes of cultural discourse.
With my approach I hope to understand the shared myth of this
fiction as something akin to an "orchestra score."[54] To this end I have
considered these books for the most part as a single text with numerous significantly repeated motives: the object will be to arrange this
"score" so that it is possible to understand it both in terms of develop-

ing plot and in terms of the relationships between individual exem-
plars of a particular motif.

This analysis of the condition-of-England novel's feminist myth
shares with Sandra Gilbert and Susan Gubar's work an appreciation
for the imaginative communities that can exist among writers under
the pressure of shared social circumstances and anxieties.[55] Much
recent feminist criticism has perceptively explored the qualities literature by women uniquely possesses, but I believe that common features in men's and women's writing can also be usefully examined
from a feminist point of view. While I explore and in some degree
celebrate the values associated with women, I detail as well the appeal those values would have for both sexes. Male as well as female
writers of this period can be said to belong to an imaginative community whose members all experienced the stress of class tensions and
had equal access to the submerged myth of powerful womanhood
that Nina Auerbach has identified in Victorian culture.[56] For both
sexes a covert feminism would have offered an attractive resolution
of their culture's social dilemma.

By emphasizing the mythic consistency of the condition-of-England novel, I hope to offer a new perspective on the ideology that
underlay it. The pattern of myth that emerges tells us something
about the bases of Victorian thought and the sources of its utopian-
ism. But it reveals as well intellectual connections where they might
superficially seem least probable. Kenneth Burke has also observed
that "[e]very question selects a field of battle, and in this selection it
forms the nature of the answers."[57] One of my arguments will be
that the particular definition of the condition-of-England question
these authors provide makes inevitable the ascendancy of women in
the novels' fictional solutions. But surely this initial definition is itself
not random. The struggles in class relations that dominate the condition-of-England novel may have an ineluctable affiliation to other
contested sites within nineteenth-century culture. It may not be a
coincidence that the 1830s and 1840s marked a crucial moment in the
consolidation of both bourgeois power and the ideology of separate
spheres; both middle-class women and workers took on new roles
in middle-class ideology.[58] In the condition-of-England novel considerations of class and gender unite to create a utopian fiction: it may
be that cultural instabilities within both terms play a mutually rein-

forcing role in enabling the creation of a radical social vision out of apparently conservative materials.[59] Millenarian ideas of radical change would have been available throughout the century, but only in this time of extraordinary unrest could they find an incarnation that would seem an apt solution for a radically disturbing set of problems. The emergence of visionary heroines within a situation of class crisis may therefore reflect the confluence of two powerful English social anxieties, and this itself may reveal the inextricability of class and gender in the Victorian imagination.

Chapter 1

"If she gave way, who was to act?": Feminocentrism and the Road to Female Empowerment

At the onset of the riot scene in *North and South*, Margaret Hale is safely stationed with the Thornton family on the second floor of their home. But, as the crowd grows increasingly wild, she shames Thornton into confronting his workers directly and then ventures out into the mob herself. She takes it upon herself to provide the conciliatory words that Thornton is too stubborn to utter: "You shall have relief from your complaints, whatever they are" (234).[1] When he in turn undercuts her efforts at mediation, she uses her body to protect him, ultimately with success, from the strikers' anger. "I choose to believe," Thornton tells her with more than a lover's fancifulness, "that I owe my very life to you" (252).

How does Margaret obtain the authority to take such dramatic action? As the daughter of a poor, newly arrived private tutor, she is of no social importance in the town of Milton. Yet she suddenly steps with complete self-assurance into the public world of labor relations and attempts to direct the course of Thornton's industrial policy. She assumes that with her words and actions she can have a greater power over his workers than he could himself. Although this is not Margaret's last or most successful assumption of power, it is perhaps the most striking.[2] But it is no more surprising than the ascription of wide-ranging power to women in each of the other condition-of-England novels.

The nature and consequences of this power will be the subject of a later chapter; my concern right now is to explore the means by which this empowerment occurs. Margaret Hale's own explanation is deceptively simple: "[A]ny woman, worthy of the name of woman, would come forward to shield, with her reverenced helplessness, a man in danger from the violence of numbers" (253). In her attempt to demystify (and desexualize) her actions, she cloaks her political presumptuousness with an appeal to "natural instinct" (252).[3] In this process, however, she is invoking a deeper mystery than her personal attraction to Thornton: a notion of powerful womanhood, rooted in nineteenth-century social ideology, that provides a philosophical framework not only for *North and South* but for the other novels in the condition-of-England genre as well. This orientation, what I will call *feminocentrism*, puts women in central or decisive roles in these works and defines the world and the industrial threat in terms of female experience. The result is a linkage of the public and private spheres that proves crucial to the ascription to women of significant power.

The condition-of-England novelists' depiction of women and female roles depends upon the distinction middle-class ideology drew between public and private spheres. Leonore Davidoff and Catherine Hall, in their study of the formation of the English middle class between 1780 and 1850, have identified the increasing rigidity with which women were associated in this period with the domestic and men with the actively economic. In the course of this heavily gendered class formation, occupational opportunities for respectable women perceptibly narrowed, so that, whenever possible, "the energy, organizational skill and sense of commitment which middle-class women had put into economic activity were deflected into domestic affairs."[4] Women were expected to tend to the home rather than pursue directly remunerative activities. Naturally, the ideology of femininity that allied women with the domestic was never uniformly enacted across English society either in theory or practice;[5] for example, Anna Clark has noted that (at least initially) Chartist rhetoric offered a different version of domesticity that provided an explicit politicization of the family.[6] Davidoff and Hall observe that, even within the middle class, "[p]ublic was not really public and private not really private despite the potent imagery of 'separate spheres.' Both were ideological constructs." Yet, as they point out, the notion of separate spheres became, by the 1830s and the 1840s, "the common sense of the English middle class."[7]

The ideology that relegated woman to the home gave her a set

of responsibilities for the physical and moral well-being of those under her care. Sarah Stickney Ellis, the best-known proponent of domestic ideology, outlined an arduous daily schedule of self-effacing
support: assisting the sick, preparing meals, atoning for past lapses
in kindness, doing work others might be too tired to perform, and all
in all jollying the household along.[8] Through such activity women
were to exert a moral influence that would counterbalance the competition and acquisitive materialism of the public sphere. The home was
to be, in Barbara Corrado Pope's words, "the source and repository
of all affections and virtues," with woman presiding as "its guardian
angel," a morally superior being.[9] Although domestic ideology was
suspicious of the values of capitalism and respectful of female potential, its apologists advised women against any direct attempt to
change the contemporary state of affairs or to act publicly for themselves. In the midst of acknowledging women's power, Ellis warns
women against letting her words go to their heads:

> [I]t is not easy to award even to her quiet and unobtrusive virtues
> that meed of approbation which they really deserve, without
> exciting a desire to forsake the homely household duties of the
> family circle to practise such as are more conspicuous, and con
> sequently more productive of an immediate harvest of ap
> plause.[10]

In America Catharine Sedgwick promised her audience of schoolgirls
that the pressure of their good example alone would sufficiently guarantee rights for themselves.

> Now, my young friends, be "what a sister should be," what
> Mary Bond was, *is* to her brother, and then you will be compe
> tent to exercise all the rights which your friends claim for you;
> and when you are thus competent, they will not, as I have said
> before, long be withheld from you. *Your might will enforce your
> right.*[11]

The drawbacks for women of domestic ideology are obvious. The
division of the world into separate spheres had apparently detached
women from any possibility of political significance; reduced to a
supportive, influential role in the home, they could only hope that

men would grant them respect and somehow take their moral lessons back into the marketplace.[12]

But, just as "Your might will enforce your right" echoes with a vague threat, domestic ideology offers more than passive detachment and political inconsequentiality. American historians have argued for some time that an incipient feminism lurks within this apparently oppressive ideal. Daniel Scott Smith first argued for the presence of a "domestic feminism" in women's increasing ability throughout the nineteenth century to exercise control over family size.[13] Mary P. Ryan has usefully summarized Smith's central point: "[S]ince it offered honor and relative autonomy to women as homemakers, [the cult of domesticity] fostered a positive consciousness of female gender identity, which could lead to demands for further autonomy and even to overt feminism."[14] My second quotation from Ellis above reveals the dangerous temptation to further action even the most modest assertion of women's power offered. As Barbara Welter has observed, the nineteenth-century definition of woman implicitly raises the issue of her involvement in the world outside the home.

> The very perfection of True Womanhood . . . carried within itself the seeds of its own destruction. For if woman was so very little less than the angels, she should surely take a more active part in running the world, especially since men were making such a hash of things.[15]

Despite the reluctance of those who promoted domestic ideology to endorse women's public action, the tensions and inconsistencies within their ideal of womanhood opened up a subversive possibility—that the power women held in so innocuous a sphere as the home might not always be contained by the limits of domestic life.

According to the historians who have propounded the theory of domestic feminism, real American women of the nineteenth century turned an oppressive ideology into a means of obtaining freedom and power. In Jane Tompkins's estimation, writers such as Harriet Beecher Stowe achieved similar ends within the genre of domestic fiction: "Instead of rejecting the culture's value system outright, they appropriated it for their own use."[16] I argue that condition-of-England novels similarly appropriate the potential power of domesticity by building upon the opportunities provided by the ideology of womanhood.[17] Their starting point is the idea that women have a peculiar proprietorship of the domestic sphere and therefore naturally exert great power within the home. But the novels' ability to use domesticity to justify social action outside the home depends upon their insistence on locating the public world within the private sphere.[18] Because these novels always see the public world in the context of the private world, women are able to extend their power to the sphere of public affairs to which they did not in actuality have such ready access. As Rosemarie Bodenheimer has observed in a somewhat different context, "The focus on womanhood is a powerful way to locate a space for alternative activity and social criticism in the midst of the social order itself."[19] Ultimately, this type of fictional domestic feminism enables women to play an enormously influential role in public affairs. But to reach that point at last I must first explore the details of the characteristic feminocentrism that is so important to these novels' definition of society.

The most obvious evidence of this feminocentrism is the centrality in each novel of a female character. Because *North and South* shows an exemplary adherence to this and other patterns I shall be describing, it will constitute the foremost point of reference in my subsequent arguments. Margaret Hale clearly provides the focus and dominant consciousness of the novel. She is the instrument by which we come to understand Milton: the fullness of explanation accorded her as a newcomer gives us a good understanding of the local inhabitants and an overview of the industrial situation. The relationships she establishes with Thornton and the Higginses are crucial to this exchange of information, and they also result in a dialogue between employer and worker that would not have taken place without her. Margaret plays devil's advocate in her discussions with both sides of the labor question: with Thornton she argues the case against the masters, while to Higgins she presents the economic considerations the masters must weigh. Her role as go-between makes her a sine qua non of the discussion and gives her a central position in the elaboration of the industrial question.

But her importance in the narrative goes beyond the purely structural to the interpretive. She is not a colorless medium by which arguments are merely transmitted; she is instead a dominant consciousness that leavens arguments and individuals. When Margaret discusses economics with Higgins, for instance, she does not put

forward Thornton's notion that employers have no obligation to account for their actions but suggests the possibility that workers may
learn what she has learned about supply and demand:

> Ask some of your masters [why your wage is to be lowered].
> Surely they will give you a reason for it. It is not merely an
> arbitrary decision of theirs, come to without reason. . . .
> . . . [T]he state of trade may be such as not to enable them to
> give you the same remuneration. (183)

Here she is not simply relaying information but transforming the
terms of the debate so that dialogue is possible. And, interestingly,
she plays such a central, interpretive role early in the book, before
she comes into the full economic power that makes her a public force
to be reckoned with in her own right.

Margaret interprets individuals as well; Gaskell often presents
her characters with the heroine's consciousness as a filtering agent.
The insight Margaret offers into the personality of each individual
influences our attitude to the abstract arguments espoused by each.
Her ambivalent appraisal of Thornton lets us know that his economic
theories are at odds with what is most humane and appealing in his
nature:

> She saw [his understanding of her mother's illness] in his pitying
> eyes. She heard it in his grave and tremulous voice. How recon-
> cile those eyes, that voice, with the hard, reasoning, dry, merci-
> less way in which he laid down axioms of trade, and serenely
> followed them out to their full consequences? The discord jarred
> upon her inexpressibly. (205)

Nicholas Higgins provides an implicit contrast that gives us reason
to respect his intense partisanship—Margaret has observed a consistency in his vehement approach to both the strike (182) and the welfare of his daughter Bessy (133). Margaret's personal reactions can
even do much to offset the force of more empirical evidence: although
Bessy and Higgins observe that Boucher is a shiftless father and a
less than competent worker, our heroine's reaction to him carries
greater weight—"The man turned round . . . a face so white, and
gaunt, and tear-furrowed, and hopeless, that its very calm forced

Margaret to weep" (207). We do not see events in Milton objectively; Gaskell so frequently makes use of a third-person limited perspective in *North and South* that Margaret's reactions and feelings attain a status almost equal to those of the author herself.

For the novel is concerned with Margaret not only as a reliable observer of the contemporary industrial scene but also as a character who compels attention by the force of her personality. While the novel does not begin to consider industrialism until the seventh chapter, her personality and development constitute one of Gaskell's concerns from its opening. Although Dickens insisted on giving the novel the misleadingly schematic title of *North and South*, Gaskell's own preferred title, *Margaret Hale*, would have better suggested what Angus Easson calls her concentration "on a central human drama— the mental and emotional conflict of a single person, whose fate is bound up with her experience."[20] Once Margaret does arrive in Milton, her interactions with Higgins and particularly Thornton hold interest on two levels: as communications about the condition of England and also as stages in her personal odyssey. Margaret's actions in the riot scene with which I opened this chapter are attempts to assume power in a time of crisis; however, they are also attempts to defend a man to whom she is deeply (though subliminally) attracted. Gaskell is concerned with both aspects of the scene, but Margaret and her personal motivations provide the context for the political action, and not vice versa. Margaret's feelings, observations, and reactions are the means by which we understand this fictional world; because Margaret is not only the defined, but the definer, all the issues of this novel eventually lead us back to her. It will be no surprise when she finally attains a position of explicit public power in Milton, for the narrative has given her implicit power from the start.

The centrality of the female role, best exemplified by the figure of Margaret Hale, also informs other condition-of-England novels. Just as Margaret dominates her novel, Mary Brotherton comes to dominate Frances Trollope's *Michael Armstrong*. Unlike Gaskell, Trollope does not give her central figure any substantive role until several chapters into the novel. But, once Mary takes an interest in the condition-of-England question, she becomes the only person actively opposed to the evil influence of Sir Matthew Dowling and the means by which we reach an intellectual understanding of the horrors of industrialism. Indeed, Mary's significance comes to overshadow that of the ostensible hero, Michael Armstrong, whose brief disappearance from the novel and apparent death cause no noticeable hitch in the narrative. Tonna's *Helen Fleetwood* and Gaskell's own *Mary Barton* are more closely akin to *North and South* to the extent that they maintain a constant focus on the female title characters. But both differ from the model text in the diminished consistency with which they keep that focus. Helen Fleetwood does not provide the dominant consciousness of her narrative, but her history does best exemplify the bitter confrontation with industrialism that immigrants from the countryside experience.[21] Mary Barton plays a more dynamic role, although she too is less of a general interpretive agent than Margaret Hale. Mary is the linchpin of Gaskell's depiction of society: she is at once the focal point of Harry Carson's personal attentions and a victim of his family's public policy of economic oppression.[22] Like Margaret, she provides in herself a convergence of public and personal interests.

Louisa Gradgrind of *Hard Times* more nearly provides a central consciousness to her novel than do Helen and Mary to theirs.[23] Like Margaret Hale, Louisa befriends the workers who suffer the most obvious negative consequences of industrialism; at least part of our understanding of Stephen's and Rachael's goodness is due to her favorable interpretation of their demeanor. Moreover, Louisa incisively analyzes the invidious effects of her father's and Bounderby's doctrines on her own private life as a daughter and wife. But by the end of the novel Sissy Jupe has insinuated herself into the role of heroine and central consciousness: it is she who advocates a social doctrine opposed to Gradgrind's utilitarianism and she who is given the power to appraise and rebuke Harthouse. A similarly insinuative and influential role is assigned to Eleanor in *Alton Locke* and the eponymous heroine of *Sybil*. Although Sybil captures Egremont's attention because of her personal charms, she gives their relationship a political dimension by guiding his subsequent activities. It is, after all, explicitly because of her that he begins to crusade in Parliament on behalf of the poor. Their marriage provides not only the inevitable resolution of the romantic plot but also a necessary ratification of his Young England schemes. In this novel, as in *North and South*, it is difficult to separate public motive from personal motive.

The character of Lady Eleanor in *Alton Locke* provides fewer difficulties, if only because she becomes a figure of romantic interest to the hero only very late in the narrative (and then fruitlessly). Eleanor is the heroine of the Christian Socialist movement that emerges as the proper ideology for those who would improve the condition of England. She assists Alton at several points in his career and ultimately steers him away from Chartism and into safer intellectual waters. If she is not the dominant consciousness of the novel (Locke is that), she is at least the presiding genius, the one who provides the underlying standard of right thought and conduct for English society. Like Sybil and Sissy, she is a more indirectly influential authority than Margaret Hale but, like Margaret and the rest of the condition-of-England heroines, she stands at the very center of her novel's social concerns.

The feminocentrism of these novels finds expression not only in the centrality of female roles but also in a domestication of reality that takes two forms: a definition of the world in terms of female experience and a definition of the industrial threat in terms of the endangerment of domestic values. This feminization of reality gives primacy to the private sphere, but it does not lead to the retreat from reality of which the industrial novel is so often accused. Public life is subsumed by private life without excluding the contemporary crisis that initially generated these books: despite their private focus their goal remains the illumination of public life. The issues of the day—class, industrial relations, poverty—are matters of primary concern to the condition-of-England novel. As we shall see in a later chapter, the narrative of each work leads up to a proposed solution—not just to private problems but to generalized social ills as well. It is precisely because the avenue of approach to these issues is domestic life that the destination of the world of public affairs can be meaningfully reached.

Margaret Hale becomes acquainted with the world of Milton as she is performing conventional domestic duties similar to those she carried out in rural Helstone. She has taken over from her mother the responsibilities of being her father's hostess; this role provides the framework for her relationship to Thornton. Her first meeting with the industrialist opens their relations on this social, domestic basis:

> She felt no awkwardness; she had too much the habits of society for that. Here was a person come on business to her father; and,

as he was one who had shown himself obliging, she was disposed to treat him with a full measure of civility. (99)

And indeed their subsequent discussions of the industrial situation
take place within a framework of domestic scenes and social interaction. Margaret's first introduction to Northern attitudes comes in the
middle of a tea (for which, incidentally, she has performed most of
the necessary homely tasks). She obtains further information in the
course of making and receiving social calls as well as at a dinner
party. There is no need for Margaret to diverge from her accustomed
pattern of life to learn about Thornton's beliefs and views: he conveniently appears within her sphere of influence.

Gaskell presents the other side of the industrial question within
a similarly domestic context. Although Margaret has no quasi-pas-
toral obligations in Milton, she acquaints herself with the Higgins
family out of an impulse to perform traditionally female duties. Her
request for Bessy's and Nicholas's names is part of a convention—"at
Helstone it would have been an understood thing . . . that she intended to come and call upon any poor neighbour whose name and
habitation she had asked for" (112–13). She is informed about the
plight of the working class in Milton during her visits to the Higgins
home; significantly, she learns of particular cases of suffering as well
as abstract theories. Hearing these case studies will be her closest
approach to the daily reality of the poor. For Margaret almost never
experiences events herself: the strikers' riot at the mill is the only
occasion on which she directly witnesses important labor-related activity. Typically, one of Margaret's interlocutors describes a situation,
as when Higgins talks of the sufferings engendered by an earlier
workers' strike (182) or when Boucher details in her hearing the agony endured by his family (206–7). This distancing of nondomestic
action is particularly notable in Gaskell's presentation of Boucher's
death. As Higgins sits at home with Margaret recounting that hapless
worker's recent activities, Boucher's lifeless body is brought to the
house and becomes the subject of their conversation (367–68).
Boucher's activities could easily have been accessible to Gaskell's
occasionally omniscient third-person narration, but she will not re-
move her focus from private, domesticated life. Teas, hearthside con-
versations, and internal musings, rather than public or political ac-

tions, provide the building blocks of *North and South*'s reality. In so presenting its material, the novel demonstrates that its deepest, most fundamental reality is located in the private life: working life is a subsidiary reality significant for its effect on the private sphere.

The other novels maintain a similar focus on domesticity through their use of domestic settings for action and their concentration on issues of private life. *Alton Locke* represents an exception to this rule in its use of such settings as a tailors' workroom, a prison, and the Dulwich Gallery, but it is fair to add that the novel begins in a disordered domestic sphere and progresses toward the Christian Socialist household Eleanor has founded. Despite *Helen Fleetwood*'s occasional glimpses within the mills, the novel takes place for the most part within one home or another; we learn of Helen's persecution at work, for instance, only when she tells Widow Green the story one evening at home (548–49).[24] Gaskell's *Mary Barton*, like *North and South*, establishes domestic life as the fundamental reality upon which all else is built. As Terry Lovell has commented, "[T]he novel is remarkably lacking in any scenes which are set in the public world of paid work and politics. . . . The book is almost entirely enacted in terms of the effects of this relationship [between masters and men] upon personal and family lives."[25] All industrial injustice and human suffering are deviations from the life of genial hospitality and personal friendship evoked by the first scene of the novel, in which the Barton and Wilson families take a companionable stroll followed by a hospitable tea.

Frances Trollope creates a similar effect by setting the opening section of *Michael Armstrong* almost exclusively in domestic locales, as Michael is introduced into the household of Sir Matthew Dowling.[26] Although the novel strongly implies that working conditions for Michael's family and neighbors are horrendous, scenes of private life form the basis of the narrative and provide the backdrop for the characterization of the leading figures. Even once we get a glimpse into the lives of the poor, we see them at home rather than at work; when Trollope describes that miserable sweatshop, Deep Valley Mill, she favors us with scenes of the domestic life (such as it is) of the children rather than with any description of what work they are compelled to do. Although Disraeli's description, in contrast, does take a brief glance at the working conditions of miners, neither Egre-

mont nor Sybil experiences these: they learn of such matters in brief
and impersonal reports. Even among the miners, discussion centers
most extensively and vividly on the evil of "tommy"—the difficulty
of buying good, cheap groceries. Again we see an emphasis on the
domestic lives of the working class in those set pieces by which
Disraeli illustrates the state of the poor. Egremont himself becomes
acquainted with the plight of the Other Nation by placing himself
among some of Its members, but this by no means entails the direct
experience of poverty: like Margaret Hale at the Higginses' home,
he hears of the injustices committed against the poor at the cozy
fireside of Sybil's cottage.

   Hard Times makes for a useful transition between the two ways
in which these novels domesticate reality. Like many other condition-
of-England protagonists, Louisa Gradgrind learns about the sad life
of a worker (Stephen Blackpool) in both her home and his. However,
Dickens provides a consistent intertwining of setting and characterization that makes the home not only the literal backdrop for events
but also the figurative basis for character assessment. Domesticity
provides the framework for understanding such characters as
Thomas Gradgrind. He may be an avatar of utilitarianism, but we
come to know him chiefly through his abject failure as father to Tom
and Louisa. Similarly, Tom reveals himself largely through his inadequacy as a brother to Louisa, which he enacts primarily though not
exclusively in the arena of the home. Josiah Bounderby offers a particularly strong example of an individual offender who is characterized in terms of domestic malfeasance. Bounderby is presumably a
cruel employer, but he is hateful because of his inadequate performance of domestic roles. As Louisa's husband, he fails in kindness
and compassion; as Gradgrind's friend, he fails in understanding at
crucial moments. Even his villainy as Stephen Blackpool's employer
first emerges as a lapse in domesticity: Bounderby, eating lunch at
his own fireside while Mrs. Sparsit malevolently presides, refuses to
provide Stephen with helpful information about divorce. Bounderby,
as both a man and an industrialist, comes to judgment within this
context of his lack of homely virtues, for he is simultaneously an
industrial threat and a domestic threat.

   Just as in *Hard Times* domestic values become the touchstone for
all characterization, other novels make the home the focus of all

assessments of English society. These novels measure industrial society's failure by its imperilment of the private sphere; the industrial threat is a domestic threat. Margaret Hale's acquaintance with the Higgins family leads her to an understanding of the domestic lives of the poor and, consequently, to a recognition of the dangers threatening society. Gaskell depicts the evil of which industrial capitalism is capable primarily in terms of its disintegration of the family unit. Certainly Bessy's occupationally induced consumption and Boucher's impecuniousness cause suffering in their own right, but the framework within which we always see these and other misfortunes is the implication they have for the domestic circle. The Higgins family is already a damaged organism when Margaret encounters it. Because Higgins's wife has died, elder daughter Bessy has had to go to work in a factory. What the sickly Bessy fears most is the further fragmentation of her home that may arise from the factory hands' strike:

> I knew I ought for to keep father at home, and away fro' the folk that are always ready for to tempt a man, in time o' strike, to go drink,—and there my tongue must needs quarrel with this pipe o' his'n,—and he'll go off, I know he will,—as often as he wants to smoke—and nobody knows where it'll end. (185)

What Nicholas might do while away from home is unclear—Bessy offers no specifics beyond her subsequent observation that striking men will "maybe ha' done things in their passion they'd be glad to forget" (186). What is clear is that he will become divorced from his home and that to alienate people from the moral influence of the domestic sphere is to destroy the possibility of civilized behavior. When Bessy dies, her younger sister and Margaret fear that Nicholas, deprived of the dead girl's filial influence, may turn to drink and, implicitly, violence. Only Margaret's force of will and her invocation of Bessy's last words—"Keep my father fro' drink" (283)—prevent the dissolution of the family from effecting the dissolution of the individual. The bonds between family members, and in particular the influence of female family members, ensure stability and sanity; as Nicholas declares to his daughter's corpse, "thou'st been a blessin' to thy father ever sin' thou wert born" (284). The living conditions that are the focus of the novel's depiction of industrialism have a pernicious influence on these bonds. Without action to deal with the sources of industrial injustice, the clear danger is that the family unit may decay beyond restoration.

This fear for the family unit is so intense that extreme measures are taken to salvage even the most apparently hopeless unit, the Boucher family. Boucher, a weak and polyprogenitive man, is torn apart by the conflicting demands made on factory workers during a labor disagreement. Unable to deal with the union on the one hand and the difficulties of feeding his family on meager funds on the other, he resorts in turn to whining, violence, disloyalty, and suicide. His initial complaints to Higgins center on the disruption in family relations engendered by the strike and by his wife's consequent ill health (206). The domestic anarchy that results from his death and the weakness of Mrs. Boucher disturbs Higgins so much that he makes himself into a substitute father for the Bouchers. In his anxiety to reconstitute the family unit he swallows his very considerable pride to ask for work: "I would na ask for work for mysel'; but them's left as a charge on me" (380–81). The impending death of Mrs. Boucher makes Higgins's plans only partially successful. Although the family, threatened by the faulty industrial order, must evidently be propped up at all costs, more wide-ranging solutions than Higgins's are called for. The domestication of the problems of industrialism may reduce the scale of the issues involved, but it does not trivialize them: partial remedies for individual difficulties still do not substitute for fundamental reform.

The nature of the industrial threat is particularly clear in *Helen Fleetwood*, since Tonna focuses her narrative on the fate of one Christian family. Unlike Gaskell, Tonna articulates a primary concern for the effect of factory town life on religious belief; the vehicle for this theme, however, is again the partial but irreversible disintegration of a family unit. In spite of the economic hardships they face in the country, the Green family remains both faithful and cohesive as long as its members dwell in their rural home. But, once they arrive in the city, they immediately encounter in their cousins' family a unit that has been corrupted by industrial life. The Wright household is anarchic: full of disdain for one another, they are united only in their contempt for the naive newcomers. The only remnant in the Wrights of the mutual love and respect that characterizes the Greens is the affection of the son Charles for his crippled sister, Sarah. Some families in this town descend even farther, into a savagery that Tonna passionately condemns:

> [T]housands of delicate little girls were habitually oppressed, overworked, starved, beaten, and that by men, frequently by their own fathers. . . . [I]t is an awful fact, that under the hardening influence of covetousness or the cravings of wretched want, more barbarous usage awaits the girl at the hand of a father or brother than that of a stranger. No tyranny is so dreadful as domestic tyranny: and he who sacrifices natural affection at the shrine of mammon, becomes a monster among God's works. (581)

Here Tonna interestingly characterizes the most seriously diseased homes as those in which matriarchal power is wholly absent: men brutally abuse young girls, and mothers or older sisters are nowhere in sight.

Once the Green family falls under the influence of the industrial town, its members, too, begin to fall from grace. The headstrong Mary becomes a victim of her own wrath and pride, Widow Green becomes ever more hopeless and ineffectual, and the almost saintly heroine herself falls prey to self-righteousness. The deleterious moral conditions promoted by the grasping, unchristian proprietorship of the Z.'s cannot help but endanger the strongest family unit: even the Greens, with what should be an all-conquering faith, do not escape. As we have seen before, what Tonna fears in English society is not so much the physical suffering of the poor (extensive though that is) as the terrible spiritual consequences of the moral atmosphere of the industrial town. *Helen Fleetwood* measures those consequences in terms of their significance for the family unit. After Richard has rescued his brother Willy from the snares of the city, the latter observes that the nature of the family's bondage was spiritual: "I am sure it was the wickedness of the place, more than the work, that killed Helen" (643). Even Helen, who represents both firm Christian faith and the best impulses of the family that took pity on her helpless orphanhood, cannot survive. Although Richard is able to take some steps to salvage his brothers and sisters, it is clear that the Green family has largely been destroyed. This wanton crushing of such a mutually supportive Christian unit emerges as the novel's greatest tragedy. Tonna's Evangelical project—to provide examples of continued commitment to Christianity in the face of great trials—has by the novel's close become disengaged from the secular, industrial issue. The Christian ideals of which Tonna is so protective emerge unscathed but ineffectual from the debacle as the characters evince continued devotion to them. Although Tonna has placed these ideals in constant opposition to industrialism, it is ultimately the family unit, exemplifying through its destruction the horrors of M., that offers the greater critique of the contemporary scene.

In *Hard Times* industrialism's threat to domestic life is made more alarming by the position of home and family, rather than Christianity, as the basis of all moral behavior. Where Gaskell's Milton and Tonna's M. have destroyed domestic life, Coketown has distorted it so that the family does nothing to foster the good cheer and love that figure so prominently in Dickens's ideal of humanity. Utilitarianism has turned the Gradgrind family into a bloodless facsimile of genuine human relations; in his ruthlessly selfish industrialism Bounderby has disowned his own family so that he may brag about his lack of conventional domestic ties. What we have in this bastion of industrialism are not the mutually supportive, usually matriarchal families that are such sources of strength in *North and South* and other condition-of-England novels but, instead, almost farcical perversions of family life. Bounderby, in the meanness of his devotion to the capitalist myth of the self-made man, has exiled his nurturing mother from his life, founding first with Mrs. Sparsit and then Louisa twisted families that are remarkable for the paucity of affectionate understanding between their members. Bounderby's malevolent distortion of family ties extends its influence to his hands: Stephen Blackpool's legal wife is battered down by the pressures of industrial life and turned into a demonic obstacle to his dreamed-of happiness with Rachael.

Hard Times's perverted families do irreversible damage to individuals, but Dickens does not preclude the renewal of the family unit. The utilitarianism that Thomas Gradgrind espouses discourages natural affections between family members and leaves Tom and Louisa so without guidelines for the direction of human feeling that the one is driven into utter selfishness and the other into marital disaster. The tragedies of Stephen, Tom, and Louisa result directly from the failure of the industrial environment to provide sufficiently strong models of familial support. But, unlike the Boucher and Green families, the Gradgrind family at least proves to be ultimately salvageable.[27] The projected salvation of some of the Gradgrinds is to be accomplished through the agency of Sissy Jupe, who is, significantly, the product of the only true family in the novel—the circus.[28] Nevertheless, Sissy's domestic magic cannot transform the lives of those most twisted by industrial society. The exiled Tom dies without having rejoined his family, and Louisa is denied the possibility of establishing a family of her own. The great tragedy of *Hard Times* is that the inhumanity of industrialism has engendered family groups that do not operate for the benefit of individuals; to Dickens, domestic tyranny is more dreadful than any other sort because it extirpates the natural resiliency of the individual.

Other condition-of-England novels, while subscribing to *North and South*'s definition of the industrial threat, are often somewhat less insistent on the irreversibility of the damage done. *Alton Locke, Mary Barton, Sybil*, and *Michael Armstrong* provide their own interesting, though slightly less emphatic, versions of destroyed or perverted family life. In *Alton Locke* the unjustly low wages given tailors force Crossthwaite and his wife to forgo sexual intimacy because they cannot afford children. And the book's most harrowing scene does provide a horrendous vision of irreversible familial destruction: Jemmy Downes's discovery to Alton of the rat-eaten corpses of his wife and children. Of these three *Mary Barton* provides the most extensive consideration of the domestic destructiveness of industrialism. As Bodenheimer has observed, "All of the major threats in the novel are rendered in terms of their potential to destroy family life. Factory work for women, a subject discussed at several points, is just such a threat."[29] The novel clearly associates John Barton's moral disintegration with the breakup of his family: the death of his son embitters him against the masters (60–61), and the death of his wife loosens "[o]ne of the ties which bound him down to the gentle humanities of earth" (58). Once more the family is crucial in determining the behavior of its members, and the culprit in this unit's decay is again industrialism: we learn that John Barton's mother and son died from "absolute want of the necessaries of life" (60); we learn that, because he was a factory worker, he was unable to obtain the prompt attendance of a doctor at his wife's deathbed. Barton's later murderous actions are the direct consequence of the fragmentation of his family that a callous social system perpetrated.

Because the figure of Sir Matthew Dowling is so closely associated with the industrial menace in *Michael Armstrong*, Trollope's characterization of him becomes a characterization of that threat.[30] Like Bounderby in *Hard Times*, Dowling is marked by a complete lack of domestic virtue; Dowling, however, shows an even more violent antagonism to domestic life. He is, of course, responsible for breaking up the Armstrong family by his removal of Michael from his mother and brother. But Dowling's venomous character becomes most apparent in the twisted and unnatural charade of family life he offers his protégé. In public, he seeks the community's approbation by welcoming Michael into the bosom of his own family; in private, however, Dowling cruelly reviles and tortures him. Trollope's evident fascination with this domestic mistreatment, described in nearly obsessional detail, is only the most baroque manifestation of the condition-of-England novel's intense concern with what happens to families in an industrial age.

Sybil's variation on the theme reveals most clearly the feminocentric basis of this critique of industrial society. When the enlightened cleric St. Lys describes the plight of the working class, he traces all difficulties to a tampering with women's matriarchal power.

> We have removed woman from her sphere; we may have reduced wages by her introduction into the market of labour; but under these circumstances what we call domestic life is a condition impossible to be realised for the people of this country; and we must not therefore be surprised that they seek solace or rather refuge in the beer-shop. (109)

In contrast to most of his colleagues, Trafford, the benevolent factory owner, understands the importance of the family to a stable society and takes care that it flourishes—"one of his first efforts had been to build a village where every family might be well lodged" (182). If industrialism primarily poses a threat to the integrity of the family, then one of the foremost goals of those who would ameliorate the situation is ensuring the strength of the domestic sphere by providing for women's freedom to manage it.

So, the feminocentrism of the condition-of-England novel finds expression in these three strands of the fictional presentation of society: the central positioning of women, the domesticating of experience, and the domesticating of industrialism's threat. The feminocentric element common to all is the explanation of the world in terms of female experience. The dominance of a female consciousness in *North and South* and *Michael Armstrong* serves particularly to emphasize this, since events and people are filtered through a woman's mind. But the other novels as well maintain this focus by insisting that all needful information about industrialization can be acquired in the course of one's private, domestic life. These fictions do not need portrayals of trade union meetings or factory brutalities to communicate an understanding of the current situation—through private talks and domestic ceremonies they arrive with equal assurance at an analysis of the situation. Their attention remains on the home, even when they consider the ravages of unfair labor policies, for the tragedy of industrialism here is the impoverishment of domestic life rather than the exploitation of workers' energies. The fundamental reality of English life, these novels suggest, will be found in the private sphere rather than in the public, working world. And this orientation on what many writers other than Disraeli called "woman's sphere" necessarily gives women particular importance in these visions of society. Condition-of-England novelists present reality in those terms of which women are conventionally masters: the activities that take place and the relations that are endangered belong to them.

Feminocentrism has led to a seemingly paradoxical outcome: based in an ideology that kept the public and private spheres scrupulously separate, it has created a situation in which those spheres are closely connected. For female characters have gained a stake in the public realm from which real women were excluded. Indeed, since the public world of work and politics is defined only within the context of private life, the public world has become women's responsibility. Other connections between public and private buttress this primary linkage of spheres. These novels express a deep concern with the employer's responsibility to his workers, but they enunciate this in terms of a responsibility for private lives. *North and South* is not alone in demonstrating the fallacy of an attitude such as Thornton's: "I choose to be the unquestioned and irresponsible master of my hands, during the hours that they labour for me. But those hours past, our relation ceases" (171). As Margaret notes, masters and men will find that in all respects their "lives and [their] welfare are . . . constantly and intimately interwoven" (169). Such an understanding of this connectedness both supports and depends upon the establishment of the overarching significance of the private sphere—its control over all aspects of life. Moreover, public and private life are joined in the characterization of those individuals, such as Bounderby and Dowling, who are both domestic and industrial villains. In identifying their actions in both arenas as similarly oppressive, the novels set up an analogy between home and workplace.[31] This association suggests that the same dynamics operate in both areas, while the domestication of reality ensures that the predominant relations are those of the home. The interconnectedness of public and private worlds has important implications for these writers' analysis of society. For other characteristic patterns in the condition-of-England novels join this linkage of spheres to make the ascription of power to women possible and meaningful.

No one can even begin to meet the domestic threat divined by these novels if English society is not a comprehensible, manageable organism. Indeed, the complex problems of labor relations, economic forces, and industrialization were more than a match for those Victorian social theorists who considered them. But the heroes and heroines of the condition-of-England novel encounter fewer difficulties when they approach these problems because of the novelists' characteristic miniaturization of English society. In these books a few characters and events stand for a far greater number of social facts and interrelationships. Other nineteenth-century fiction employs a similarly drastic reduction in scale; the condition-of-England novel, however, combines it with feminocentrism to increase its usefulness: in these novels it has great significance for the prospect of social amelioration.

The world of industrialism in *North and South* is narrowly circumscribed. The only manufacturing town we see is Milton; the only manufacturer we see at any length is Thornton (although there are glimpses of Hamper, Nicholas Higgins's previous employer). From what Higgins says, it seems that Thornton is an unusual factory master; unlike the others, Thornton will give the union "an honest up and down fight" (184). Nevertheless, there is no direct description of other mill owners who are presumably less amenable to Classical Studies and extended considerations of the rights of labor. The absence of a broad spectrum of industrialists in *North and South* leads inevitably to the assumption that Thornton is representative. There is no way to avoid making generalizations about mill owners and the situation in industrial towns from Thornton's experience and personality. In the same way, the limited depiction of the working class expands the significance we accord to each of its members whom we see. Despite the appearance of a mob at Thornton's mill, there are really only two working-class families in Milton: the Higginses and the Bouchers. Each is representative of a certain type of industrial worker, with the former typifying the responsible and intelligent and the latter the indolent and querulous laborers. Once Margaret has become aware of their various problems, she seems to have reached an adequate understanding of the situation of all industrial workers, since she shows no inclination to probe further into working-class life (and indeed neither Higgins nor the Bouchers encourage her to do so). She gains from Thornton and the two laboring families all the information she needs to make a shrewd assessment of the condition of England. Thornton's mill, its owner, and these two families constitute a pared-down version of English industrial society that is nonetheless a fully functional closed system: all elements necessary to the operation of society are represented; nothing of importance is omitted. Gaskell may refer to other economic forces such as foreign trade and supply and demand, but they are essentially extraneous to the dynamics of society. What matters is the constellation of personal and business relationships formed by Thornton, his workers, and (ultimately) Margaret. Since all the component parts of this self-contained system are present in the novel, it becomes possible to solve the problems inherent in the system within the novel's scope and in its feminocentric terms.

As a result, when the problem of Thornton's relations with his workers is solved, it seems possible that a solution may be found for all, implicitly similar, industrial problems. Consequently, the condition of England becomes more manageable in fiction than it could ever be in a considerably more diverse English society. Although the complex and varied problems of contemporary society cannot be understood and dealt with by a five hundred–page sociological tract, Thornton as a bullheaded but fundamentally sympathetic individual can be reformed in a novel of similar proportions.

The use of a model conceived as a microcosm of society is not confined to *North and South*. Other novels create similar small-scale versions of England. Several of them are characterized by the extensive presentation of only one industrialist and only a few workers: in *Helen Fleetwood* the Z. family operates the factory, and the only workers are the Greens, the Wrights, the Malonys, and Tom South; in *Mary Barton* the Carsons own, and the Bartons and Wilsons serve; in *Hard Times* Bounderby is owner and Stephen and Rachael workers. *Sybil*, with its multifarious collection of social problems, provides a greater number of representative figures, but only because there is a greater variety of social roles in the novel. There are actually only a few of each of the following figures: oppressive rural landlord (Lord Marney), industrial oppressor (tommy shop–owner Diggs), brutal leader of the masses (Bishop Hatton), oppressed workers (Devilsdust and his friends; the Gerards). The spectrum of problems is broader, but the technique remains the same: only a few representative figures are depicted. When it comes time to draw together the threads of this analysis of society and point the way to an improved future, the various oppressors can be disposed of with relative ease.

In *Michael Armstrong* it is especially easy to eliminate the source of trouble, for there is only one central social offender. Trollope declares that problems are widespread in English industrial life, but the book's depiction of evil is almost entirely confined to Sir Matthew Dowling. His tentacles seem to extend throughout the countryside and inflict all the suffering the principal characters undergo in the course of the novel. Here there is hardly any pretense that external economic or political factors play a role in industrial society: injustice is the result of personal malfeasance, and so the plea Trollope makes for the Ten Hours Bill seems completely beside the point. To the extent that personality as much as policy becomes the problem, miniaturization effects its own connection of public and private sphere: how can one separate the social evil Sir Matthew represents from his personal malignity toward Michael Armstrong? Certainly Dowling's individual downfall provides part of the satisfactory resolution of Trollope's condition-of-England crisis; as in the other novels, to deal with the representative of industrialism is to deal with industrialism itself. Without the convenient miniaturization of society, such small-scale victories over evil would have no larger significance for English society: they would simply be individual, anomalous events in the private sphere.

While feminocentrism provides the fundamental orientation of the condition-of-England novel, and miniaturization opens up the possibility of solving the problems the novels present, yet another characteristic pattern deals with the question of *how* problems are to be solved. For these works use a process of elimination to approach the issue of means; by making inroads on a variety of conventional sources of authority, they reveal the desperate need for some new form of social management. As Martin Dodsworth remarks, the first six chapters of *North and South* may seem a "leisurely, almost hesitant" beginning, but Gaskell is striking "a very calculated false note. . . . Because the story and its heroine are to be unconventional, she begins by setting up the conventions against which she will offend, and dismisses them expeditiously, almost savagely."[32] This section clears away some of the traditional pieties of Victorian culture, as various sources of value are shown to be bankrupt. The respectable marriage that opens the novel is not a stereotypical ratification of the maturation of complex characters but only the latest banal event in Edith's shallow life. Once Margaret has had the chance to reject her own opportunity for such a purposeless though socially acceptable match, she must confront an upheaval in her customary form of life.

Her family must leave their rural community, another traditional fount of values, because her father has found himself unable to participate fully in the communal beliefs that supposedly hold society together in mutually reinforcing bonds. So, even though Margaret has not lost her own beliefs, she has seen the myth of social coherence given the lie. She can no longer have her old confidence in the working together of all things for good: even the proximity of a poacher, who was once a symbol of innocent freedom to her, now fills Margaret with dread (90). Their forced removal from Helstone and their confrontation with the challenges of a new life reveal with ever-increasing clarity that her mother and father are fundamentally weak people. When Mr. Hale decides to leave his ministry, he is too much of a coward to inform his wife himself and gives his daughter the onerous task; even the loyal Margaret realizes that "it was an error in her father to have left [Mrs. Hale] to learn his change of opinion, and his approaching change of life, from her better-informed child" (79). Further evidence of this weakness appears at Milton, as Margaret becomes head of the household when her mother falls ill; she observes that her father is unable to face the fact of this terminal sickness. Yet another traditional source of value, the parental and more especially the paternal, is gradually undercut.

More and more, Margaret plumbs the depths of her own resources as she recognizes that she must bear all the burdens of her family because authorities other than herself have been pared away. She must begin to find a new, self-defined basis for her actions. Although she initiates her friendship with the Higgins family on the grounds of traditional assumptions about the duties of a clergyman's daughter to the poor, she soon needs to reorient herself. As Easson observes, "She is no longer the vicar's daughter . . . ; such roles have broken in this society. She has no clear social position"[33]—she is compelled to create her own. She shoulders this burden in all areas of her life because she recognizes the inability of others to do it for her: "[I]f she gave way, who was to act?" (89). In the rubble of her old intellectual and emotional supports, Margaret finds the responsibility of self-definition and action thrust upon her.

A similar stripping-away of conventional values operates in other condition-of-England novels. Often this process emphasizes the ineffectuality of fathers: *Hard Times* establishes almost at once the inadequacy of those placed in traditional positions of paternal power. Certainly Bounderby and Gradgrind provide the clearest examples, but it is worth mentioning that Sissy's father has also been a failure, both in the deterioration of his professional skills and his sudden abandonment of his daughter. The Green family of *Helen Fleetwood* is forced into industrial servitude when the local authorities of their rural village prove callous and irresponsible; subsequently, figures of authority such as the industrial town's judge and clergyman prove inadequate. Eventually nothing remains but family bonds and Christian faith. *Michael Armstrong* most clearly offers a debunking of traditional authority similar to that of *North and South*. The first few chapters unmask the moral bankruptcy of two standard repositories of English social value: the paternalistic ruling class (Sir Matthew Dowling) and the aristocracy (Lady Clarissa Shrimpton). Even more interestingly, the novel indicts Martha Dowling's ineffectual kindness;

this dutiful, loyal daughter has attempted to aid Michael within the framework provided by her father's authority over the household, but she ultimately fails. As soon as Martha's assistance begins to falter, Mary Brotherton enters the fight against Michael's mistreatment. Martha is an insufficient character because of her subservience to a father who ought to be rebelled against.[34] Only Mary Brotherton, with her independence from paternal tyranny, is capable of fighting against that authority that, though thoroughly malevolent, retains power in society. The plucking of the humanitarian mask from the face of the powers that be is a precondition for Mary's charge into battle against the evils of industrialism. Once this unveiling occurs, she is freed to develop, like Margaret Hale, her own way of managing a society that is in need of leadership.

Clearly, the stripping away of possible sources of authority has often involved a particular focus on the inadequacy of paternal authority. This is part of a pattern by which these novels reject the nineteenth century's favorite model of reform—social paternalism. Although the roots of paternalism lay in the Middle Ages, after industrialization English writers began to transform general ideas and common practice into increasingly formal doctrines that, according to David Roberts, "called for the more conscientious practice of paternalism as a social remedy for new and frightening problems."[35] Paternalist ideology held that English society operated most efficiently and justly when those who held power in its hierarchical structure responsibly ruled, guided, and assisted those in the lower classes. But this ideology was articulated not only in terms of class but also of gender, for its operative social metaphor of governance was the benevolent yet controlling relationship of a father to his wife and children. On the one hand paternalism's use of the home as a model for the public world bears obvious affinities with domestic ideology's sense of the potential power of familial relationships.[36] Yet on the other hand paternalism is incompatible with the domestic feminist appropriation of the domestic cult.[37] While domestic feminism emphasizes the authority women had over the household and its morals, paternalism underscores the final authority of the father. Both ideologies employ familial models, but the latter locates the essence of the family in its patriarchal hierarchy rather than in the fostering of values antithetical to those of the marketplace.[38]

Condition-of-England fiction generally raises the possibility of paternalism only to reject it as an appropriate model for change. *Sybil* and *Alton Locke* constitute the exceptional cases here, for they envision the continuing usefulness of paternalist activity. Egremont lectures Sybil on the pivotal role the aristocracy must play in English society (276–77), and Eleanor urges Alton Locke to continue with his poetry so that it may "awaken some rich man to look down and take pity" on the gifted among the underclass (387). Even here, as chapter 3 will show, reform is most significantly enacted by the heroines. Yet the more typical pattern of this genre involves an explicit rejection of paternalist ideology. The Chartist delegates of *Mary Barton* set out for London in the belief that Parliament cannot know and be indifferent to the workers' misery: "[A]s who should make domestic rules for the pretty behaviour of children, without caring to know that those children had been kept for days without food" (127). Their confidence in the validity of the paternalist metaphor proves tragically ill-founded. Similarly, in *Helen Fleetwood* Widow Green appeals hopefully for relief to each of the Z. brothers in turn not merely because they are owners but because they are fathers (556, 559). Both dismiss her rudely in a demonstration that there is no valid analogy between their domestic benevolence and their industrial performance.

North and South confronts paternalism more explicitly than most of the novels. Thornton explains his own approach to governing his workers in typically paternalist terms:

> In our infancy we require a wise despotism to govern us. Indeed, long past infancy, children and young people are the happiest under the unfailing laws of a discreet, firm authority. I agree with Miss Hale so far as to consider our people in the condition of children, while I deny that we, the masters, have anything to do with the making or keeping them so. I maintain that despotism is the best kind of government for them; so that in the hours in which I come in contact with them I must necessarily be an autocrat. (167)

But Mr. Hale responds to these remarks with the observation that the hands are no longer children but "already passing rapidly into the troublesome stage which intervenes between childhood and manhood" (167); Margaret herself suggests that attempts to keep workers in a state of childish subjection may stunt their development (168). Moreover, Bodenheimer has observed, Gaskell extends her critique by "overturning the paternalist model from the working-class point of view" by Nicholas Higgins's "refus[al of] the role of beneficiary."[39] Paternalism is simply inconsistent with the facts of life in Milton-Northern. Dickens develops his own theories on this matter in *Hard Times*, in which paternalism is avowedly part of the problem that faces England.[40]

> [T]here happened to be in Coketown a considerable population of babies who had been walking against time towards the infinite world, twenty, thirty, forty, fifty years and more. These portentous infants being alarming creatures to stalk about in any human society, the eighteen denominations incessantly scratched one another's faces and pulled one another's hair by way of agreeing on the steps to be taken for their improvement—which they never did.... Still, ... they were pretty well united on the point that these unlucky infants were never to wonder. Body number one, said they must take everything on trust. Body number two, said they must take everything on political economy. Body number three, wrote leaden little books for them, showing how the good grown-up baby invariably got to the Savings-bank, and the bad grown-up baby invariably got transported.... But, all the bodies agreed that they were never to wonder. (38)

Here paternalism provides a mechanism for the suppression of Fancy that is one of Coketown's chief ills: like obedient infants, the inhabitants of the town are expected to bow to the higher authority of the governing class rather than think independently. The imposition of this morally bankrupt authority on the working class is part of what Dickens vehemently protests; paternalism for Dickens is merely the philosophic equivalent of Bounderby's and Gradgrind's illegitimate assumption of control over the working people of Coketown.

Although condition-of-England novelists are rarely as insistent as Dickens on the ludicrousness of the infancy metaphor, they typically do not embrace paternalism. Instead, they use imagery associated with the family to establish a conception of society that, in its respect for the autonomy of workers, is inconsistent with paternalism. They emphasize in the first place that it is crucial for employers to gain, as does *Sybil*'s Mr. Trafford, "a correct conception of the relations which should subsist between the employer and the employed. . . . [B]etween them there should be other ties than the payment and the receipt of wages" (181). This relationship should be personal and humane, as the relationship between Thornton and Nicholas Higgins becomes. The foundation of their wary friendship is Thornton's early realization that "my interests are identical with those of my workpeople, and vice-versâ" (166). This, rather than any assumption of fatherly power, provides the basis for his gradual understanding that Margaret is right to say he is morally responsible for his workers' private lives (169). Mr. Carson in *Mary Barton* also learns, in part by listening attentively to Job Legh, that he bears personal responsibility for his workers and that he cannot ignore them once the working day is done.

Like Margaret Hale, Job Legh argues that employers have a duty to the poor. This responsibility is in part based on the higher social and economic station of the employer, yet it is not paternal. The upper class has the duty to provide the lower class with the physical, moral, and emotional support that was the ideal of domestic ideologues. The role envisioned for them is not an authoritarian paternal role but rather the role of a more successful sibling who helps draw together and sustain a family—the role, in fact, that Richard Green imperfectly fills at the end of *Helen Fleetwood*. In *Mary Barton* these duties become explicitly those of a nineteenth-century mother. John Barton complains that rich people do not perform any of the actions that might fill him with genuine respect for them:

> "And what good have they ever done me that I should like them?" asked Barton . . . "If I am sick, do they come and nurse me? If my child lies dying . . . , does the rich man bring the wine or broth that might save his life? If I am out of work for weeks in the bad times, . . . does the rich man share his plenty with me . . . ? When I lie on my death-bed, . . . will a rich lady come and take [Mary] to her own home if need be, till she can look round, and see what best to do? No." (45)

In this passage Gaskell envisions a role for the rich in society that is maternal rather than paternal, compassionate rather than dictatorial. Interestingly enough, in *Mary Barton* the critique of social paternalism leads us right back into those feminocentric terms that, I have argued, form the backbone of these novels' social analysis. These writers are seeking not a social paternalism that looks back to the Middle Ages but a new way of structuring class relationships. The new system will not be democratic and egalitarian, but it will entail the mutual respect of upper and lower class; it will be familial but not coercive.

We have seen that the condition-of-England novel's critique of social paternalism is part of a pattern of discrediting many traditional sources of value. This stripping-away process creates a power vacuum: English society requires some new authority to provide moral leadership. Despite the absence of coercion in the familial model I have described, these novels do not argue for the elimination of all social hierarchy: there is no hint, for instance, of a class revolution that would put workers on a basis of equality with the middle and upper classes. With the debunking of paternalism, however, the matter of who is to take on the mantle of social authority becomes a serious concern. It is at this point that condition-of-England fiction can safely put women in positions of significant power. Women are the logical candidates for the leadership role left vacant by the failure of conventional authorities; alone among Victorian cultural forces, women's authority over the private sphere has been consolidated rather than undercut. Since the private sphere provides the fundamental reality of these fictional worlds, this power is no trivial one.

So, to address the question I posed at the outset of this chapter, the reason Margaret Hale takes charge in a time of crisis is that she, the central female figure, is the only character who can draw upon sufficiently strong and authentic sources of power to manage the novel's crisis: if she were to give way to passivity, there would be no one strong enough to act. When condition-of-England heroines take action, the full implications of the novels' feminocentrism become apparent. Where domestic feminism gave women a power that was derived from their traditional roles in the home, these works give female characters power that grows out of the centrality of women's role in this depiction of society. Because the world of these novels is rooted in female concerns, a society in trouble must turn to the preeminently important female sphere for help in transforming public life. Reform must be based on this domestic bedrock of society and must be accomplished under the leadership of those who are most powerful in the private sphere—women.

When women do seize power their actions are not always so overtly radical as Margaret Hale's; not every female character rushes in to mediate labor disputes. But even women's attempts to counter the industrial threat within the private sphere gain significance in the public sphere because of the linkage effected between these spheres. Because the two arenas are so closely associated by these novels, to act in private is also to act in public. Moreover, the fictional miniaturization of society suggests that solving social problems is a matter of dealing with representative individual offenders—sometimes simply by privately thwarting a single evil man, such as Sir Matthew Dowling. Hence, in the terms the novels define, the benevolent actions that women take on a small scale are appropriate for dealing with the larger scale of industrial society.

The feminocentrism that makes all this possible may be a natural epiphenomenon of fiction's increasing turn toward the personal and the domestic. But it may have at least as much to do with the novelists' subconscious appropriation of what Nina Auerbach has identified as the nineteenth-century myth of woman as a subversively powerful creature of astonishing capabilities.[41] This myth may explain why, as we shall see, the women who begin by operating safely within the bounds of their traditional role take actions that ultimately propose the transformation of the patriarchal society of Victorian England.

Chapter 2

Victimized Women: "My pain was needed for the fulfilment"

In chapter 1 I explored the mechanism by which the condition-of-England novel ensured that women would play a leading part in the fictional reformation of English society. My description of the industrial terrain in which heroines find themselves is incomplete, however, without a consideration of victims—those particular individuals who suffer directly from the disjointed condition of England. Chapter 1 has shown that these novelists generally represent industrial suffering in terms of its danger to the home. But the more specific issue of how novels represent particular suffering individuals raises different questions. Who counts as a victim? What value do the particularities of victims' stories have to the narrative? In this chapter I will argue that we need to pay special attention to the use of female victims in the condition-of-England novel if we are to understand the sources of the visionary element in heroines' solutions. For heroines will ultimately propose changes in society that go beyond simply offering to mediate labor disputes; their radicalism is of a piece with what Nina Auerbach has called the "dream of transfiguration"[1] that female victimization evokes in Victorian literature. The presentation of women as especially representative of industrial suffering provides the novels with access to this cultural myth and legitimates the transformative quality of their social solutions.

But before I reach that point I will briefly trace the collateral circumstances that help determine the novels' focus on female victims. A novel that indicts suffering requires victims as dramatic examples of that suffering. Yet the particular pressures on this genre created difficulties for the selection and delineation of such individuals. Although the industrial debate often made vivid use of the figure of the factory girl, the appearance of substantial male victims in these books (Stephen Blackpool, John Barton, Nicholas Higgins, Michael Armstrong, Alton Locke, James Wilson) suggests a different dynamic in the condition-of-England novel. Since the middle-class fears of working-class violence that helped generate this fiction centered on the threat posed by workingmen, there seems to be an effort to include this population in the novels' miniaturized worlds. Indeed, Catherine Barnes Stevenson has pointed out that *North and South,* contrary to the reality of Preston, depicts workers as almost exclusively male.[2] At the same time, the fictional presentation of male victims carried with it certain problems. Foremost among them was that, in describing oppressed workingmen, novels came uncomfortably close to the violence middle-class society feared. We must recall here that the novels had rejected the social paternalist ethos that contained such violence by figuring workers as merely children in need of parental care.

A few contemporary reviews of these novels reveal anxiety about their potential effects. Interestingly enough, this becomes an issue only for books that put a premium on male victimhood. The most striking example comes from a review of *Michael Armstrong* in *The Athenaeum.* Significantly, only the first six numbers had appeared at the time of this piece—and, of course, the first half of the novel focuses on Michael's travails with the sadistic Sir Matthew Dowling. After quoting a long passage, in which Sir Matthew terrorizes Michael while complaining about the willful slowness of factory operatives, the critic fulminates against its possible effects:

> Can [Trollope] be ignorant of the consequences such statements must produce, when disseminated among an ignorant and excited population, to which her shilling numbers are but too accessible? Or is she writing in a careless indifference to the mischief she is doing, and the dangers she is provoking?[3]

Trollope's work is particularly dangerous because it is available so cheaply, but even the more expensively formatted *Mary Barton* gives rise to similar worries. One reviewer suggests that Gaskell's inadequate renunciation of John Barton's Chartism conveys an inappropriately radical meaning: "The authoress professes to have nothing to do with political economy or the theories of trade, . . . but she allows the discontented to murmur in prolonged strains without an attempt to chasten the heart or to correct the understanding."[4] Another, who focuses particular attention on John Barton's part of the novel, observes more openly that such a novel constitutes a species of "Agitation."[5] *Alton Locke* excited the passionate condemnation of the *Quarterly Review*; in a long essay on a variety of "revolutionary literature," mostly from France, J. W. Croker reserves particular scorn for Christian Socialism. After quoting Alton's assertion that society's denial of rights makes working-class revolution comprehensible, Croker adds his own comment: "We beg our readers to observe here the *un-English* menace of the 'barricade,' which reveals at once the source of these doctrines and the end to which they point."[6] I hasten to add that the great majority of critics did not find condition-of-England novels inflammatory. Nevertheless, I have quoted the preceding reviews because I believe they give us insight into the cultural tightrope condition-of-England novels had to tread in order to conform to standards of literary propriety. To represent social distress, particularly male distress, was to address a subject surrounded by intense passions—potentially even to stimulate working-class rage.

An examination of male victims in the condition-of-England novel shows that the representation of men as victims inevitably raises the specter of violence, even in novels that did not catch the eye of the wary reviewer. Frances Trollope herself recognizes this danger in her preface to *Michael Armstrong*, which describes her original plan of a sequel in which the adult Michael would become politically active in the working-class movement. She has abandoned this scheme, she says, in reaction to the violence of workingmen. Although not all the men are guilty of lawlessness, "the sufferers [have been] too closely associated in the public eye with those who have been guilty of all she most deprecates, to permit her continuing the work as she intended" (iv).[7] We will discover elsewhere that there is indeed no such thing as a safe male victim. However important they are to the narrative, victimized men are problematic: they require some counterpoise to offset any propensity to violence. There are two chief means of managing the potential for violence the genre possesses. In one pattern a male and female victim are paired in a way that elevates the woman's representative function. In another, analogies are established between industrial suffering and other forms of (female) suffering to provide a more distanced expression of industrial anxieties. The upshot of these strategies is an emphasis on women as victims that opens up particular imaginative possibilities.

Stephen Blackpool of *Hard Times* provides an excellent example of a male victim of central importance to the narrative. He is quite evidently the representative workingman of the tale—the worker through whom we get insight into the contemporary condition of the working class. Eight chapters center on his thoughts and experiences, and he becomes involved (with Bounderby) in some of the most explicit discussions of social injustice. His relationship to his wife and his rejection by both employer and fellow workers firmly establish his victimhood. His dramatic death after falling down a mine shaft provides an indictment of industrial carelessness. And yet he is not precisely a type of what F. R. Leavis calls "the good, victimized working-man, whose perfect patience under infliction we are expected to find supremely edifying."[8] Stephen's patience is not perfect enough to dispel the specter of male violence. He is to begin with a suspect victim because he presents an implicit threat to the social and moral fabric of English life. However understandable his dismay at the return of his wife, the vehemence with which he expresses his feelings becomes disturbing, particularly given the novel's high valuation of domesticity. Stephen's desire to dispose of his alcoholic spouse finds surprisingly blunt expression in his discussion with Bounderby: "I ha' coom to ask yo, Sir, how I am to be ridded o' this woman. . . . I mun be ridden o' her" (56). His violent language here suggests a suppressed murderousness that soon makes a more open appearance. He delays going home from work in spite of his wife's evident need for care, and (as Anne Smith observes) "thinks dangerously of the arbitrariness of death, that good women die while his wife still lives."[9] That night Stephen dreams of suffering public execution—apparently for violating one of the Ten Commandments ("Thou shalt not kill"?) so that he might marry the woman he loves. He awakens from his guilty dreams only to find himself powerless to raise a hand to stop his wife from drinking poison.

At this point the male victim quite literally requires the assistance of a female counterpart. It is only Rachael's intervention that prevents the evening from culminating in his commission of murder by inaction. Rachael does not hesitate to behave in accordance with accepted social and moral behavior by preventing the woman's death, even though it is in her interest as much as Stephen's to see Mrs. Blackpool removed from the scene. Stephen characterizes Rachael's action as superhumanly angelic; nevertheless, the sympathy Dickens would have us feel for his workingman does not banish the cloud of suspicion under which Stephen hereafter lives. He does vow, with a wholesome horror of his own thoughts, to think only of Rachael in times of trouble. But he has irrevocably shown his capacity for seeking physically violent solutions to his discontent. And Bounderby's contemptibly reductive assessment contains for once an iota of truth: Stephen's desire for change has, as Bounderby observes, "traces of the turtle soup, and venison, and gold spoon" (58), if we understand that phrase to mean an inclination to rebel violently against the conditions of his life. Stephen begins to seem more like an open revolutionary than a symbolic victim; or perhaps it is simply that he has internalized industrialism's violence, just as he has internalized the factory machinery that always seems to have "worked and stopped in his own head" (49).

Stephen's propensity for violence most obviously requires Rachael's efforts to reestablish the proper status of industrial victims. However, she also provides a useful counterpoise to his other obvious weaknesses. In the process she becomes an important embodiment of industrial victimization who remains uncompromised by overt acts of disobedience to social laws. Dickens puts Stephen Blackpool in an awkward situation: positioned at the center of a political controversy, Stephen is nonetheless consistently denied any semblance of political comprehension. By draining his worker of political intelligence, Dickens avoids one (but as we have seen not all) opportunity for violent self-assertion. Stephen's attempts at understanding the social situation that has entrapped him lead monotonously to a conclusion that everything is "awlus a muddle" (51). Yet Dickens draws the targets of his social criticism (marriage laws, patriarchal industrialism) so boldly that it seems impossible that anyone should fail to recognize them. Stephen's obtuseness, which superficially seems so winning a proof of his harmlessness, comes to seem irritatingly simpleminded when he fails to draw the inevitable conclusions from his experiences of injustice. Even on his deathbed, after receiving the mental illumination he says the stars have provided, he is still unable to sort out his experiences of life in Coketown—"Fro' first to last, a muddle!" (206)—and wishes rather naively that Bounderby had taken the time to know him. Dickens typically has Stephen approach an issue of concern and then quickly back away with a shake of his muddled head, as when he talks to Bounderby about the reasons for worker discontent.

> Look round town—so rich as 'tis—and see the numbers o' people as has been broughten into bein heer, fur to weave, an' to card, an' to piece out a livin', aw the same one way, somehows, 'twixt their cradles and their graves. Look how we live, an' wheer we live, an' in what numbers, an' by what chances, and wi' what sameness; and look how the mills is awlus a goin, and how they never works us no nigher to onny dis'ant object—ceptin awlus, Death. Look how you considers of us, and writes of us, and talks of us, . . . and how yo are awlus right, and how we are awlus wrong, and never had'n no reason in us sin ever we were born. . . . Who can look on 't, Sir, and fairly tell a man 'tis not a muddle? (114)

The last remark clearly underestimates human intelligence; Smith rightly observes that, "as he describes it, it appears to be no muddle at all."[10] In these lines Stephen has so forcefully delineated Dickens's own case against the mechanization of human lives and the tyranny of the industrialist that his final withdrawal from judgment and his inability to suggest a remedy seem at the least disingenuous. This unconvincing perch between the adoption of an overt political stance and the simple oxlike endurance of suffering undercuts his claim to representativeness as a victim. After somewhat the same fashion, Stephen's passive refusal to cooperate with the United Aggregate Tribunal falls uncomfortably between the stools of political action and inaction and makes him a singularity rejected by both employers and men. Dickens expects Stephen to be at once the analyst and the emblem of industrial suffering: both the interpreter and the immanence around which interpretation can coalesce. He comes to seem anomalous rather than archetypal, because he gets caught between the contradictory aims his author sets out for him.

Rachael provides an antidote to Stephen in her disconnection from both violence and those specifics of industrial exploitation that in Stephen's case seem to demand his analysis. While we are given many particulars about Blackpool, down to the exact day of his wedding (55), we never even learn Rachael's last name. Her introduction into the narrative is piecemeal: she exists first as a shawl in the distance and then as a collection of physical attributes.

> [R]aising her hood a little, [she] showed a quiet oval face, dark and rather delicate, irradiated by a pair of very gentle eyes, and further set off by the perfect order of her shining black hair. . . .
> "Ah, lad! 'Tis thou?" When she had said this, with a smile which would have been quite expressed, though nothing of her had been seen but her pleasant eyes, she replaced her hood again, and they went on together. (50)

Like Stephen, we are vouchsafed only parts of her, but these are, like her all-expressive eyes, profound and evocative parts. When he muses on her suffering, Stephen creates a poignant tableau in which Rachael is a striking though distanced portrait of victimization.

> He thought of Rachael, how young when they were first brought together in these circumstances, how mature now, how soon to grow old. He thought of the number of girls and women she had seen marry, how many homes with children in them she had seen grow up around her, how she had contentedly pursued her own lone quiet path—for him—and how he had sometimes seen a shade of melancholy on her blessed face, that smote him with remorse and despair. He set the picture of her up, beside the infamous image of last night [his wife]. (62–63)

Rachael, who never offers us any lengthy analysis of the industrial situation, is able to remain above the muddled waters of industrial argument. Her detachment frees her from the need for overt interpretation of the contemporary situation without divorcing her from it. While Stephen must tread an impossibly fine line in order to remain both haplessly victimized and reasonably intelligent, Rachael floats beyond such considerations. Because she is not susceptible to the same sort of analytical, logical quibbles as Stephen, she becomes a victim with a kind of symbolic force he lacks.

The examples of Tom and Louisa Gradgrind provide further evidence of the dangers of male victims and the particularly forceful role victimized women, in contrast, can play. Although Tom, as much as

Louisa, has been shaped by his father's philosophy, his actions throughout the novel undermine his status as one of the "victims bound hand to foot" sacrificed to the "grim Idol" Reason (151). For once again the male victim acquires the ugly characteristics of the system that oppresses him. Despite the minute specification of her life (so detrimental to effectiveness in Stephen's case), Louisa retains her initial status as victim. This distinction between girl and boy is clearest in an early conversation between Tom and Louisa. While the latter sits to one side of the fireplace and broods over her fate in near silence, her brother sprawls squarely in front of the flames and speaks at length of his nascent aggression:

> As to me, . . . I am a Donkey, that's what I am. I am as obstinate as one, I am more stupid than one, I get as much pleasure as one, and I should like to kick like one. (39)

> I wish I could collect all the Facts we hear so much about, . . . and all the Figures, and all the people who found them out: and I wish I could put a thousand barrels of gunpowder under them, and blow them all up together! (40)

A volatile substance that could be sparked into combustion at any moment, Tom is more obviously actor than acted upon. Immediately following this outburst of violent fantasy he begins the course of action that loses him all residual force as a victim—the oppression of Louisa. Tom aligns himself with industrialism, not only in his employment with Bounderby but also in his exploitation of his sister. By giving him a role in the world of business, Tom's masculinity ensures his corruption by patriarchal values.

Louisa, because of her sex, cannot be contaminated by industrialism in the same way. She observes that "the little I am fit for" (77) within a society dominated by men is to play the role of martyr for Tom. While he reaps the benefits of industrialism at the same time that he is victimized by it, Louisa obtains no personal reward from her actions. She can serve as a much stronger instance of victimhood than Tom because her suffering is the direct result of forces outside herself: she is a type of the utilitarian child who can ultimately embody, as she lies in "an insensible heap, at [Gradgrind's] feet," "the triumph of his system" (167)—all the pain inflicted by his twisted philosophy. So, Tom's repeated assertion (hypocritical though it seems) that his sister has the better lot because "a girl comes out of it better than a boy does" (40) contains a certain amount of truth; women characters cannot lose their symbolic significance through conversion to the vices of industrialism. In these two victims, rooted as they are in the class responsible for industrialism, representative victimhood necessarily becomes a function of one's freedom from complicity in oppression—an indicator of ideological purity.

Helen Fleetwood also reveals male victims' limitations, which it foregrounds with a sprinkling of violence. Most obviously there is Tom South, who not only lives off the industrial earnings of his own children but also belongs to a mysterious secret organization of threatening cast. He has joined up with those ever-popular figures of middle-class myth, outside agitators: Hudson describes them as "men who long to overturn all right government . . . and [have] endeavoured to make our grievances a pretext for engaging in rebellious schemes" (609). But a variant of this violence infects even the godly men of the Green family. Angered by the treatment Helen receives, Richard grows wrathful and at one point nearly attacks the leering Charles Wright (599). Such understandable retributive action finds outlet in a man of whom we know nothing: an unnamed father who assaults the overseer guilty of beating his child (567). Unlike men, women in this novel are not tempted to the brink of violence by the abuse of the mills.

Despite the familiarity of the pattern, *Helen Fleetwood* seems to represent a different case from *Hard Times*; it pairs its heroine Helen with the unthreatening male victim James Green. James undoubtedly does his share of suffering: never very strong to begin with, in the town of M. he steadily declines under the onslaught of consumption. He remains godly and becomes important to his family as "the chief bond of union among them" (546); his goodness seems to increase as his sickness progresses, until he is giving instruction in Christian resignation to his brother Richard, older by four years. If he grows intensely irate at hearing of Helen's being beaten, he does not consider physical assault as a recourse. Nevertheless, as an industrial victim James has certain drawbacks. Unlike the other children in his household, he is too ill to undertake mill work. He retains his purity but without ever having it tested; he is not subjected to the horrors that to some extent contaminate all workers. Mary Green becomes ill-natured and tough and Willy Green almost alcoholic under the pressures of their jobs. As James exclaims to Richard, Helen manages to rise above the others: "[I]f it was not for Helen I should say that the mills are made of pitch—that nobody could touch them and not be defiled; but you never saw such a creature as Helen" (600). And even she is affected by her job so far as to assume an unchristian air of self-righteous haughtiness toward Phoebe Wright (546). James's superlative goodness does not convincingly exalt him because it is so closely related to his freedom from work and his illness: he "alone retained the [moral] characteristics that had but a while ago distinguished them all; but his bodily health declined with a rapidity that startled [his grandmother]" (545). Widow Green may demur when James suggests that "it is not so much the Spirit of God as the sickness I feel, that makes me care so little about idle play, and love the Bible as I do" (559); nevertheless, even she exclaims to herself, "[H]ow merciful is the affliction that keeps thee alike from the snares of the wicked and the rod of the cruel!" (568). In one interesting scene James and Willy lie side by side in sleep. The former presents the perfect calmness of the ideal sickly Evangelical child, while the latter furrows his brow and clenches his fist (552). It resembles nothing so much as a before-and-after picture. James belongs to a lovely spiritual world, but it is not the same world as the rest of his family. He seems as misplaced as Tonna's own Evangelical bromides for industrial distress.[11]

Unlike James, Helen does work in a factory, and there she meets with the most grinding physical and spiritual horrors industrialism has to offer. "[Y]ou never saw such trials as Helen has had to go through," says James to Richard (600). Unlike Dickens, Tonna does not inevitably assign some taint of industrialism to all her male characters. Yet she also places more emphasis than Dickens does on the ill effects of the workplace, so that the factory becomes as important an arena of oppression as *Hard Times*'s schoolroom. If *Helen Fleetwood* were simply a novel about poverty, or about sickness, then James Green would be adequate as a representative victim. But, because the novel is concerned with industrial life and its spiritual consequences, he lacks the specific victimization Helen receives in her capacity as factory worker. In the novel's scheme she becomes a far more impressive and *effective* victim, for her victimization involves the whole community and has a wide significance for that group. While James does die a splendid death, the only beneficiaries of it are his immediate family and Mr. Barlow. In contrast, Helen is a public victim, and her death has communal significance:

> Helen did not die in the mill: but her last seizure took place there, and so alarmed her companions as to give a great effect to the few words she was enabled to speak to them before being carried home. (642)

Helen is the novel's archetype of innocently suffering victimhood, and her full significance proves, as I will show in the next chapter, to lie in a realm considerably beyond James's reach—Tonna's envisioned solution of the condition-of-England question. Although James is a significant object of pity, the novel requires a victim such as Helen to experience the direct assault of the forces that cause England's problems. Again we see the necessity of female victimhood to an unthreatening representation of industrial suffering.

Frances Trollope's prefatory remarks to *Michael Armstrong* demonstrate considerable uneasiness about the inflammatory potential of victimhood. In her own novel she addresses this issue by using Fanny Fletcher as a supplement and even a substitute for Michael. By the time Michael reaches Deep Valley Mill, he has already endured considerable suffering with commendably passive tears. But Deep Valley, the ne plus ultra of industrialism, challenges his pacific nature in new ways. In an interesting passage Trollope suggests that the sight of boys at a pig trough on his first morning would naturally give rise to thoughts of "vengeance":

> Michael Armstrong was a child of deep feeling; and it was, perhaps, lucky for him, that the burning sense of shame and degradation which pervaded every nerve of his little frame . . . come [sic] upon him while yet too young for any notion of resistance to suggest itself. (184)[12]

Indeed, Michael is on the verge of becoming capable of serious aggression. When the narrative returns to him (after supposing him dead for four chapters) he quickly grows a little older (fourteen) and more dangerous. After watching a Deep Valley overseer mistreat a young worker, Michael thinks, "with a sort of trembling exultation, that if he *had* seized the craven overlooker . . . he might have held him with a grasp that would have stopped his breath for ever! . . . It was a horrid and a murderous thought!" (285).

So, it is appropriate that Fanny Fletcher enters the novel immediately after Michael witnesses the scene at the pig trough—just as he is beginning to experience those scenes that drive him to the edge of violence. She replaces Michael as the most pitiful example of industrial suffering, just as she will soon replace him as the object of Mary Brotherton's benevolence. Fanny has some of the advantages of Rachael in *Hard Times:* her own virtuous resignation counteracts the rebellious tendencies Michael may harbor. The novel makes a point of the pathos of her appearance, while Michael's appearance at roughly the same period is not described.

> [T]hough pale and lamentably thin, [she] had not yet lost thereby the sweet expression of her delicate features, neither had the soul within yielded to the paralyzing influence of the hopeless, helpless, unvarying misery by which she was surrounded. Her soft gray eyes still retained their eloquent power of speaking. (257)

Whereas Fanny proves to be an exceptional exemplar of the suffering of child workers, Michael ultimately proves to be merely an exception. Of course, his experiences with Sir Matthew Dowling were never exactly ordinary, but they were representative of the torture the upper classes inflicted on the lower. But, just as *Hard Times* insisted upon the uniqueness of Stephen Blackpool's relation to his fellow workers, the end of *Michael Armstrong* makes a point of underlining Michael's atypicality. Martha Dowling remarks upon one of the unusual circumstances of his life, and Mary Brotherton replies rhetorically: "[I]s not every event connected with a hero of romance . . . singular? And whom did Fate and Fortune ever fix upon more unmistakably to fill that distinguished position in society, than Michael Armstrong?" (377). By the book's close Michael's importance to his novel lies in this tired convention of heroism: more active and mobile than Fanny, he nevertheless becomes trapped in romantic cliché in a way she does not. Her difficulties, less singular than his, become more emblematic of the suffering that is Trollope's central concern.

Alton Locke provides an interesting variant on this pattern that suggests the incompatibility of outright violence and female victims in the condition-of-England novel. Kingsley does not bring in a female victim to offset his hero's violence, but he does interweave suffering men and women in the set piece of the riot scene. When Alton Locke visits the countryside as a Chartist delegate he encounters an assembly of workers in more desperate straits than those of *Hard Times, Helen Fleetwood,* or *Michael Armstrong.* The initial speakers at the rally are men who discuss prices and wages and the possibility of sending a round-robin to the local squires. Alton observes that all their "advice seemed . . . sadly unpractical. . . . [The onlookers] were getting every moment more fierce and desperate at the contemplation of their own helplessness" (263–64). Once again men fail to represent other victims adequately because they become enmeshed in the machinery of industrialism—here, in its bureaucracy.

For a more forceful and accurate representation of distress the novel needs to turn to one of those women who, we have already been told, look "even more pinched and wan than the men" (259). A single female speaker at the gathering delivers an impassioned narrative of her own sufferings that vividly captures the mood of the crowd. She looks the part of a tortured spirit with "her scanty and patched garments fluttering in the bitter breeze, . . . [her] face sharpened with want, and eyes fierce with misery" (264). Yet even here, in a scene that makes violent impulses normative within a group, the iconographically powerful female victim does not express explicit aggression. Her ringing denunciation of the system closes suggestively with "Oh! If I was a man, I know what I'd do, I do!" (265), but she never gets the chance to advocate violence because a friend pulls her off the speaker's stone. It is left for Alton himself to incite the crowd to riot. Here Kingsley has not used a female victim to defuse the incendiary potential of the male victim. He has, however, used a woman to exemplify (and even articulate) social injustice most effectively while associating violence exclusively with men. His use of female and male victims in balance also reveals the usefulness of their complementarity.

Elizabeth Gaskell is familiar enough with the usefulness of offsetting male violence with female suffering to create a moment of schematic opposition between the two in *North and South.* Bessy Higgins describes the working-class people who came to see her father during the strike in dualistic terms:

> Some spoke o' deadly hatred, and made my blood run cold wi'
> the terrible things they said o' th' masters,—but more, being
> women, kept plaining, plaining (wi' the tears running down
> their cheeks, and never wiped away, nor heeded), of the price
> o' meat, and how their childer could na sleep at nights for th'
> hunger. (202)

Yet Gaskell chooses a different means of defusing male violence in
Mary Barton: she employs analogy to establish connections between
the suffering of workers and the suffering of working-class women.

For Gaskell in *Mary Barton,* as for Disraeli in *Sybil* and Dickens
in *Hard Times,* analogy provides a means of describing the condition
of the working class without tapping the seething violence their audience feared. If the yoking of male with female victims I have discussed provides a strong counterforce to violence, analogies offer
translations of the suffering that produces violence—other frames for
the understanding of industrial pain. The shifting of ground that
analogy involves produces its own difficulties for these novels. As
Karen Sánchez-Eppler has pointed out in the context of American
feminist abolitionism's conflation of women and slaves, one term can
all too readily efface rather than illuminate the other.[13] Yet, if something is lost with analogy, something is also gained. We have seen
how difficult it was for social novelists in the mid-Victorian critical
climate to represent workers without seeming to threaten society.
To say that analogies obscure the reality of the working class is to
lose sight of the fact that there is no simple reality to which language
(then or now) could have unproblematic access nor any way of writing that could transcend cultural constraints. Operating within Victorian norms, analogy offers the condition-of-England novel a different
register of expression, not merely a means of evasion. And, as it
turns out, in neutralizing violence by drawing analogies to women,
novelists are avoiding one form of subversion only to embrace another.

Mary Barton establishes two important analogies. Mary's aunt
Esther does not work in the mills, but her suffering bears affinities
to what the hands endure. Like theirs, her mismanagement of money
in good times leaves her no hedge in bad times, and like them she
must endure squalor and the loss of her child to illness. She has fallen
victim not to the mill owners themselves but to another member of

their class—an officer who has seduced and subsequently abandoned her. The degradation that results from her failure to marry her seducer is a peculiarly female problem, but her suffering and its source resemble those of the industrially afflicted poor. Even more significantly, Mary's treatment by Harry Carson parallels the treatment mill hands receive from his family and their compeers. In different arenas, both young Carson and the mill owners are out to take as much advantage of the working class as they can. Mary's situation syllogistically underlines the analogy between Esther and Manchester workers when it provides an additional analogy between Mary and Esther: after all, Esther begs Jem Wilson to save her niece out of a conviction that Mary's fate could prove identical to her own.

These analogies temper the most violent single action in the entire condition-of-England genre: John Barton's murder of Harry Carson. Up to the assassination Barton has been a victim of unusual significance and force. Gaskell is quite explicit about her character's representativeness: her depiction of his conversion to Chartism after economic hardship and personal sorrow (60–61) almost precisely parallels her later overview of the reasons why many of the poor "spoke and acted with ferocious precipitation" (127). Yet with the murder Barton leaves the ordinary terrain of Manchester society. As Stephen Gill has observed, "When Barton becomes a murderer, . . . he becomes an outcast from all classes. His usefulness towards an analysis of the industrial scene is at an end."[14] He also becomes the realization of all middle-class fears of workingmen; clearly, his case calls for careful treatment to keep the novel from veering into dangerous territory. Modern critics have condemned the virtually exclusive interest in Mary that follows as a sign of Gaskell's own middle-class avoidance of the full reality of the working class under industrialism.[15] But the analogies Gaskell has established since the beginning of the book, as well as the characteristic feminocentrism I have previously traced, ensure that Mary's tale has an unavoidably political content. To follow Mary and her love story is to pursue by other means the investigation of industrialism. Because these analogies exist, it is possible for *Mary Barton* to escape the threat of large-scale social disorder that John Barton's actions have posed.

Sybil depends upon an analogy between the people's alienation from their human rights and the Gerard family's alienation from its hereditary privilege. In Disraeli's analysis these two categories are

UNIVERSITY OF HERTFORDSHIRE LRC

barely distinguishable. He construes the condition-of-England question as a matter of discovering legitimate leadership; Walter Gerard defines the people themselves as "a great family in this country, and rooted in it" (136), just like the aristocratic families of which Egremont has just been speaking. The Mowbray Castle riot at the novel's end expresses the working-class fury of the Hell-cats, but it also has an additional frame that analogy makes possible: its occasion for the recovery of papers proving Sybil's aristocratic lineage diminishes the mindlessness of the violence. *Sybil* also makes a connection across classes between Lady Marney's experience of her husband's tyranny (72) and his tenants' experience of his callousness. Here we have a different sort of analogy, one that *Hard Times* explores at greater length—a yoking of working-class suffering with the suffering of women under a patriarchal social order.

Louisa Gradgrind in *Hard Times* provides the clearest example of the contribution a middle-class woman's suffering can make to the delineation of the condition of England. The section of the narrative that Stephen Blackpool's situation dominates has its complement in the section that deals with Louisa's plight. The analogy that Dickens develops between workers and middle-class women at once acts as a further brake on the potential violence of the oppressed and strengthens the indictment of the masters. Gallagher has pointed out the parallel between Bounderby's advice to Stephen in chapter 11 and Gradgrind's to Louisa in chapter 15. "In each interview, the topic is marriage; in each the 'father' is called on to give advice to the 'child,' and in each the former fails to give the proper advice, leaving the latter with a diminished sense of life's possibilities."[16] Chapter 8 also explicitly establishes Louisa's victimization as a continuation of that of the working class. It opens with the admonition "Let us strike the key-note again, before pursuing the tune" (37) and then records an occasion on which Mr. Gradgrind rebuked his daughter for indulging in imaginative speculation (*wonder*ing). Immediately following this anecdote, Dickens uses the lengthy passage I quoted in chapter 1 to describe another sort of suppression: the stifling of all independent thought in the Coketown worker. Both cases strike the keynote of victimization by a single paternal and paternalistic source. Just as Stephen, when talking to Bounderby, "find[s] his natural refuge in Louisa's face" (113), workers and women both find that the other group reinforces their case.

Concern for the dangers and limitations of male victims has led the condition-of-England novel to accord female victims a particularly important role. I have already alluded to the fact that the conventions of industrial discourse also fostered an emphasis on the significance of women. Discussions of the pernicious effects of the Industrial Revolution centered on children and women. To some extent such attention reflected the important role both played in the work force, particularly in the cotton industry.[17] Yet the reformers' increasing preoccupation with women as victims served ideological ends as well. Female workers were perceived as particularly representative victims because of a supposed constitutional inferiority that made them more vulnerable.[18] What Sally Mitchell identifies as "the symbolic value of the [sexually] victimized woman" holds true as well for the economically oppressed woman: "Because women were naturally pure, passive and helpless, the figure of a victimized girl gave readers a quick and telling demonstration of the evil that made her a victim."[19] As Marianna Valverde has pointed out, a preoccupation with the dangers to domesticity of female employment could serve the masculinist bent of working-class and middle-class society.[20] The figure of the victimized woman was in one sense complicit with efforts to limit the power and respect granted women in English society.

Yet the particular representation of female victims in the condition-of-England novel often defeats stereotypes. Certainly, this fiction shares with other forms of industrial discourse a sense of horror at the consequences for the family of degrading women—this is part of what I have called the domestication of the industrial threat. Disraeli, for instance, characterizes his mine workers as horrifyingly unisex.

[They were] troops of youth, alas! of both sexes, though neither their raiment nor their language indicates the difference; all are clad in male attire; and oaths that man might shudder at, issue from lips born to breathe words of sweetness. Yet these are to be, some are, the mothers of England! But [how] can we wonder at the hideous coarseness of their language. . . . [when] an English girl, for twelve, sometimes for sixteen hours a day, hauls and hurries tubs of coals up subterranean roads. (140)

There is considerable fear that the Englishwomen who work in factories will end up like Sally, the crippled and insane old woman of
Michael Armstrong, who has been so ground down by work in Deep
Valley Mill that it is almost impossible to distinguish her sex (266).
These identifications of working women with degraded domesticity
do not, however, lead to generalizations about the incapacity of
women in general. Instead, they coexist comfortably with the feminist impulses that the victimization of women calls forth.

For the novels' reliance on women as representative suffering
workers evokes the suffering women endured in the patriarchal society of Victorian England. The supportive victimhood of Louisa in
Hard Times and Arabella, Lady Marney in *Sybil* has depended upon
an acknowledgment of women's entrapment in the roles of dutiful
daughter, marriageable woman, and wife. Novelists find a means of
supporting and broadening their arguments by employing the natural sympathy between workers and this other group of exploited
victims. Patricia Meyer Spacks has suggested that, in both *Mary Barton* and *North and South*, although "the nominal center of concern is
relations between master and man. . . . [h]idden analogies between
the plight of women and of workmen surge beneath the surface,
never quite explicit."[21] Yet I would disagree with those modern critics
who have seen industrial fiction as primarily of interest for what it
reveals about the woman writer's personal dilemmas.[22] Condition-of-
England novelists can bring to their analysis a related though largely
unacknowledged social problem without turning their initial concern
with class relationships into an empty pretense. What female victims
can do is open up the analysis both by buttressing examples of social
malfeasance and by providing access to an underlying myth of powerful womanhood.

I would like to approach the terms of this coexistence by calling
attention to one particular aspect of female victimhood: its frequent
association with extremes of innocence and passivity. On one level
such hapless suffering seems all too consistent with the limiting
stereotype of incapable womanhood. Yet the very extremity of their
purity and goodness allies women to the cultural myth Auerbach has
identified in the Victorian imagination. These excessively pure
women remind us that, as Auerbach puts it, "literary iconography
gave womanhood virtually exclusive access to spiritual depths and
heights."[23] Mrs. Armstrong in *Michael Armstrong* is one of these lamb-

like, nearly angelic victims. With her unselfish concern for her children, her poor but clean home, and her "mild countenance and gentle voice" (145), Michael's mother is almost ready for canonization. Her physical appearance makes her a universally legible industrial text: "[S]uch a history of patient suffering might be read in every line of her speaking countenance, that few ever looked upon her harshly" (39). Sarah Wright in *Helen Fleetwood* is a similar epitome of industrial suffering. Mutilated almost beyond human recognition and kept in spiritual ignorance, she is a sort of living sampler of what life in the city of M. can do. In conjunction with the female characters I have already described—women who complement male victims by being purer and uncompromised by suggestions of violence—such women as Mrs. Armstrong and Sarah form a class of angelic victims who attain great iconographic significance.

We can see the significant evocation of transcendent power most clearly by examining occasions on which a woman of angelic purity is paired with a woman whose victimization turns her demonic. Such comparisons suggest a shared, subversive source of personal power. The eponymous heroine of *Helen Fleetwood* demonstrates exceptional piety amid the corrupting influences of the mill. Her moral rectitude makes the incident in which an overseer strikes her one of the novel's greatest horrors. The Greens are beside themselves with dismay on this occasion because Helen is so profoundly undeserving of such treatment—"every bosom swelled with indignation hard to be repressed even by the pleadings of Christian forgiveness: all felt it would have been far easier to overlook such an outrage against their own persons than against their gentle Helen" (572).

Phoebe Wright, a cousin of the Green children, leads the persecution of Helen in the mill. Her venomous spite marks her as Helen's nemesis and demonic opposite. Although Widow Green believes that her worldly contempt for goodness proves her to be "born after the flesh" (554), Phoebe's ghastly appearance associates her with the less material realm of ghouls. Our first view of her is alarming:

> [She was] the spectre of a very pretty girl, whose naked arms resembled ivory wands rather than limbs of natural flesh and blood, while her hair, black as the raven's wing, . . . set off the deadly white of her complexion with such effect that she seemed like one in whose veins the current of life had already ceased to

circulate. . . . [W]hen [her eyes were] raised, the broad, unflinch-
ing stare of the girl was oppressive. Helen, who, sitting opposite,
had fixed a look of interest on her, encountered one of these
sudden gazes, and shrank before it, with an undefined sensation
of alarm. (519)

Interestingly, it is this passage that helps establish the odd affinity
Helen and Phoebe have for each other. Phoebe here begins a running
battle for preeminence in home and factory. While she wins this
round by making Helen break eye contact, later Helen will put on a
proudly self-righteous guise that compels Phoebe herself to look
away (546). Phoebe is altogether the opposite of the godly Helen.
Unlike her brother Charles and sister Sarah, Phoebe shows no signs
of tenderness of heart or susceptibility to religion: her hostility to the
heroic Christianity of her cousins' family is relentless. Phoebe is herself a victim of industrialism: "[T]he factory system, under which
Phoebe Wright had imbibed the peculiar wickedness that now per-
vaded her character, also fed the evil, guarded it, and armed it with
power to wound whatever excited its enmity" (554). But in the intensity of her malice she outstrips any of the men whom industrial
society has twisted, even the potentially violent but essentially sympathetic Tom South. Phoebe herself does not threaten insurrectionary
violence but stands outside the boundaries of political action; she is
a ghastly and frightening presence who cannot be contained within
either political categories or the Christianity of the Green family.

Mary Barton provides two angel-demon pairs. On the one hand
the saintly Margaret Jennings, with her occupationally induced blindness, is balanced by the vulgar-minded Sally Leadbitter. Margaret,
whose beautiful voice situates her among the angels (142 and elsewhere), counsels patience, while Sally advocates romantic precipi-
tancy. The two are respectively, as Rosemarie Bodenheimer observes,
"Mary's good and bad angels";[24] and, like the minor demon Sally is,
with "just talent enough to corrupt others" (132), she is easily driven
out of Mary's house by the entrance of good angel Margaret (135).
Still, behind Sally's humorous impudence lurks a serious attempt to
suborn the novel's heroine: Sally demonstrates the dangerous capacity for deceit and corruption that poverty can foster in young women.

But Margaret and Sally provide a muted expression of the theme
of angelic and demonic victims compared to the novel's other pair of

women. Although Alice Wilson is not a direct victim of industrialism, she does suffer under the same oppressive poverty that besets the working class of Manchester. Gaskell characterizes her as a meekly religious woman with great faith and a childlike simplicity. Alice's preparations for Mary's teatime visit evoke a typically condescending narratorial comment: "How busy Alice felt! it was not often she had any one to tea; and now her sense of the duties of a hostess were almost too much for her" (65). If, however, Alice is a somewhat silly saint for much of the book, once she falls victim to a stroke she exercises an enormous influence over her friends. It is more than just "the natural reverence to one 'stricken of God and afflicted'" (268) that brings Mary to visit Alice in the girl's own time of trouble; it is a confidence in the consoling and restorative power of Alice's regression to a spotless childhood and "the atmosphere of holy calm" (309) that surrounds her. Mary and the others who visit the stricken Alice gain more power from her victimized semiconscious state than they did when she was healthy; we see how strong an appeal the victimized, innocent woman has, not only to illustrate the distress caused by the industrial situation but also to act as a kind of totem of innocence in the midst of a violent and oppressive world.

The obverse of Alice Wilson's godly simplemindedness is the outcast agony of Mary's Aunt Esther. Alice influences Mary by the example of her piety, her exhortations to "Wait patiently on the Lord" (195), and the curious impact of her comatose presence during her final illness (309, 405). In contrast, Esther's influence is far less conventionally beneficent; her history provides what Kathleen Tillotson has called a "threatening parallel"[25] to her niece's unfolding story. Gaskell draws attention to the harmful effect of Esther's example: the older woman inculcates in the younger the desire to become a lady (44), and her influence over Mary's thought continues in absentia (62). It is as though she has communicated a long-incubating illness rather than an idea to Mary: "The old leaven, infused years ago by her aunt Esther, fermented in her little bosom" (121). This fallen woman is responsible for more than the social aspirations that lead Mary into dangerous territory: Esther's subsequent attempts to counteract her own early influence nearly get Jem Wilson convicted of murder. After the failure of even this well-intentioned effort, she understandably feels that "[t]he black curse of Heaven rested on all her doings, were they for good or for evil" (290–91). Her image of herself as an agent of the demonic and maledicted changes her attitudes toward her old home and her own niece. At the door of the Barton house, as she greets Mary, "[s]he had felt as if some holy spell would prevent her (even as the unholy Lady Geraldine was prevented, in the abode of Christabel) from crossing the threshold of that home of her early innocence; and she had meant to wait for an invitation" (293).

Yet, however uncanny a figure Esther may present, Gaskell does not let us forget that her condition has its roots in large-scale social injustice. Esther has suffered from a twofold deception: the beguilement of her officer lover and the cultural myth of class mobility. Gaskell calls her by the sympathetic nickname of Butterfly to underscore the beauty that Manchester life has crushed. Esther is a species of victim just like the rest of the Barton and Wilson families—a frightening yet complementary alternative to Alice's sanctity. Alice and Esther are connected through their mutual influence on Mary and their identity as single mothers (Esther had an illegitimate child, while Alice single-handedly raised her nephew Will); moreover, one of Alice's first acts in the narrative is to offer a toast to absent friends that reminds everyone unpleasantly of the vanished Esther (53). Angels and demons are merely different manifestations of a single phenomenon.

In Stephen Blackpool's wife the roles of victim and victimizer more explicitly converge. Broken by Bounderby's factory and ravaged by alcoholism, she nonetheless figures most prominently as her husband's eternal scourge. Her appearance is barely that of a person at all; she resembles instead a particularly sloppy monster:

> Such a woman! A disabled, drunken creature, barely able to preserve her sitting posture by steadying herself with one begrimed hand on the floor, while the other was so purposeless in trying to push away her tangled hair from her face, that it only blinded her the more with the dirt upon it. A creature so foul to look at, in her tatters, stains and splashes, but so much fouler than that in her moral infamy, that it was a shameful thing even to see her. (52)

Wracked by fits of alcoholic insanity, she hardly seems to have normal human understanding; Rachael remarks that Mrs. Blackpool does not recognize her, but "just drowsily mutters and stares" (65), as though she is in a different state of consciousness. Although she stands in sharp contrast to the luminously good Rachael, there are curious links between the two women. Both have an interest in Stephen, but Mrs. Blackpool has the greater power because her particular claim on him (marriage) precludes Rachael's full exercise of her own. Stephen expresses his own awareness of this close connection when he marvels at the unfairness of the balance of power: "Could it be, that the whole earthly course of one so gentle, good, and self-denying, was subjugate to such a wretch as that!" (63). Yet the wretch draws strength from the angel—not only when Rachael saves her from accidental poisoning but also when Rachael ministers to her long after Stephen's death.

Hard Times only makes explicit the connection between angel and demon that informs the other novels as well. In this symbiotic relationship between angel and demon we see a phenomenon somewhat like the one Sandra Gilbert and Susan Gubar identify, in the tradition of women's writing, as a projection onto "mad or monstrous women" of the "rebellious impulses" that pure heroines ought logically to feel.[26] As with the pattern Gilbert and Gubar describe, two characters operate conjointly to confront a single situation with a range of responses that official Victorian culture deemed incompatible. The affinity for rebellion I am describing here, however, does not arise so much from the writer's personal experience of victimization as from Victorian culture's propensity for seeing women as centers of oppositional force. Because they stand beyond the margins of ordinary human experience, both angels and demonic outcasts possess a similarly subversive power. What Auerbach observes about other Victorian cultural products holds true for condition-of-England novels as well: "It may not be surprising that female demons bear an eerie resemblance to their angelic counterparts."[27] When we look even more closely at the victimized women the condition-of-England novel is so careful to foreground, we find explicit signs of the visionary potential Auerbach attributes to them. It is through these visions that we find the victimized woman pointing the way to the more extensive visionary heroism of the female protagonist.

Bessy Higgins in *North and South* is one victim who, though pious and physically helpless, has a clear affinity for supernatural power. Her contemplative remark to herself after an early visit from Marga-

ret—"I wonder how she'll sin" (188)—proves oddly predictive when
Margaret lies to protect her brother. Bessy tells Margaret of her confidence in the life to come and her love for the Bible, but it seems that
the only book of the Bible she truly cares for is Revelation, with its
apocalyptic imagery and savage violence. She is insistent upon the
metaphysical grandeur that Revelation lends to her own suffering:
"[I]t seems as if my pain was needed for the fulfilment" of God's plan
(187). Margaret urges her to give up this fascination with preordained
doom and apotheosis, but Bessy demurs:

> [W]here would I hear such grand words of promise—hear tell o'
> anything so far different fro' this dreary world[?] . . . No, I cannot
> give up Revelations. It gives me more comfort than any other
> book i' the Bible. (187)

Bessy's apparently orthodox resignation to her own death hides a
nature inspired with the violence of her favorite reading material. She
has achieved her current state of mind, she says, not only because
of the hard life she has led but also because she "fretted again it"
(131); indeed, her rage against the suffering she has experienced is
never far from the surface. Without the support of her vision of
eternity, she explains to Margaret, she could not suppress (or, one
might say, sublimate) this anger.

> "And I think, if this should be th' end of all, and if all I've been
> born for is just to work my heart and my life away, and to sicken
> i' this dree place, wi' them mill-noises in my ears for ever, until
> I could scream out for them to stop, and let me have a little piece
> o' quiet—. . . I think if this life is th' end, and there's no God to
> wipe away all tears from all eyes—yo' wench, yo'!" said she,
> sitting up, and clutching violently, almost fiercely, at Margaret's
> hand, "I could go mad and kill yo', I could." She fell back com-
> pletely worn out with her passion. (145)

Her fury does not, however, work itself out in personal (or political) violence but instead transforms itself into dreams of transcendence. Gaskell provides little detail of these reveries, but it seems
clear that they enable her to surmount her own physical and economic limitations. She appears to be dreaming herself out of the

current industrial crisis: Nicholas is contemptuous of the impulse that creates "her dreams and her methodee fancies, and her visions of cities with goulden gates and precious stones" precisely because they keep her from being able to think of the immediate difficulties of the present; he believes that it is better to "set to work on what yo' see and know" (133). But Bessy's dreams have an interestingly ambiguous character. They can pacify her, yet, in the only one she specifically relates, they do so with images of Margaret and her capacity to lend her strength to others (200–201). Nevertheless, the dreams also have the power to disturb her. Near her death she tells of how they have begun to invade her waking consciousness with frightening visions: "I had a fearfu' night wi' dreams—or somewhat like dreams, for I were wide awake" (208). Bessy is a figure made at once touching by her suffering and fearsome by her special states of consciousness. She is victim as demon not only for the suggestion of violence in her nature but also for the supernatural tenor of her dreams. Auerbach reminds us that, in this "age possessed by faith but deprived of dogma, any incursion of the supernatural into the natural became ambiguously awful because unclassifiable."[28] In this light Nicholas Higgins's objection to Bessy's dreams seems to arise less from his pragmatism than from the inelasticity of his own mind; he cannot understand the transformation of reality that she imagines.

Bessy is not the only woman who, as victim, reveals visionary depths denied to her male companions. Louisa Gradgrind receives her revelations while she sits in her father's house watching the fire. To Harthouse, Tom describes this receptiveness as one of his sister's exceptional qualities: "[T]hough Loo is a girl, she's not a common sort of girl. She can shut herself up within herself, and think—as I have often known her sit and watch the fire—for an hour at a stretch" (103). While Louisa herself denies that she sees anything particular in it, she obviously uses the fire as a focus for her wonderings about herself and her brother (41). It holds no special meaning for Tom, who declares, "You seem to find more to look at in it than ever I could find" (40). Yet fire imagery is crucial to the novel: it metaphorically binds together all those suffering under industrialism and represents those human feelings and capacities that have been ruthlessly crushed by the modern age.[29] To take but one example, Louisa responds obliquely to her father's presentation of Bounderby's proposal by observing that the Coketown works that seem so languid by day nightly burst into flames (76); figuratively, she herself in time will do the same.

Louisa's ability to interpret the flames does not, however, simply point up her sensitivity and victimization; it indicates as well that there is something a little frightening about her. She is not a potential thief and pimp, like her brother, but she does have a kind of "un-wholesome fire" (170) within her that almost burns up filial devotion and the institution of marriage. Again we encounter a woman whose rebelliousness does not take an overtly political or physical form but who demonstrates her alienation from Victorian conventions in a threateningly radical way. Louisa's visions and her subterranean de-monism, not shared by any of the novel's men, are apparently sex specific: they represent, as Tom puts it, "[a]nother of the advan-tages . . . of being a girl" (41).

Mary Barton's Aunt Esther is a more immediately recognizable type than Louisa: the fallen woman who gains power from her out-cast status.[30] She is perhaps the most powerfully demonic of all the women in the condition-of-England novel. Like the Ancient Mariner to whom Gaskell compares her, Esther has a fearsome power over Jem that compels him to listen to her story and heed her advice against his will (208–16). Mary, too, feels the power of her presence just as the older woman is about to appear at her door—it is "as if something spiritual were near" (286)—but, interestingly, Esther for-feits that power (and Mary's sympathy) when she makes her appear-ance in the guise of a respectable woman rather than a prostitute (293). Her actual, degraded status gives her extensive access to the supernatural, and a plethora of dreams arises from "the witches' cauldron of her imagination" (292). These dreams, which she can avoid only by the health-destroying expedient of alcohol, depict peo-ple to whom she feels some sort of responsibility: her mother, her dead child, and Mary. While just what these figures demand from her remains unclear, they seem to accuse her with their unremitting gaze (213) and with a reminder that she must not think of rejoining the world of respectability (292). Although Esther apparently looks upon her visions as punishment for her offenses against propriety, they signify her access to potentially creative powers. The figure of her dead child that reminds her that the past can never be undone may also be suggesting the folly of Esther's longing to reenter the narrow conventions of an oppressive society. For victimization has led Esther and the genre beyond the orderly world of domesticity to a realm in which radical, dramatic transfiguration is imaginatively possible. The millenarian spirit of the condition-of-England novel first becomes evident with the transgression of commonsensical boundaries the victimized woman provides. Without accounting for this spirit the radicalism of fictional solutions cannot be understood.

The importance of female victimhood, then, lies not only in its function within the scheme of the novels' depiction of industrialism but also in its anticipation of woman's transformative capacities as heroine. These victimized women help release the imaginative power contemporary mythology accorded to women, power that accrued to them partly as a function of women's exclusion from mainstream political and economic power. So, the portrayal of victimized women provides not only a tellingly pitiful depiction of industrial suffering but also a reinscription of the oppressed status that already gives women an iconographic evocativeness beyond politics and reason. Novels that have made a point of describing the failure of conventional masculine power must establish the distinctive nature of their own authority. By identifying an almost supernatural power in women that is well beyond the limits of patriarchy, victims pave the way for queens. And it is in this sense that Bessy Higgins's remarks are most accurately understood when she declares, "[M]y pain was needed for the fulfilment."

Chapter 3

Active Measures and the Future Dream: The Solutions Women Offer

The condition-of-England novel has paved the way for activist heroines in several ways. Feminocentrism, with its location of the public world within the private, has given women the capacity for meaningful intervention. A focus on female victimhood has evoked the Victorian myth that ascribed uncanny, subversive powers to womanhood. The heroines of this genre fulfill their promise by taking preeminent roles in combating the industrial problem the novels have defined. I will begin by considering in turn each heroine's work of reform. They do not all follow identical courses of action: some, like Gaskell's Mary Barton and Trollope's Mary Brotherton, take an aggressive public stand; others, like Dickens's Sissy Jupe and Disraeli's Sybil, operate more indirectly and influentially. Yet all these characters prove instrumental in the battle against a disjointed social order.

Once I have described the actions these heroines take, I will go on to assess first the success of each intervention and then the larger implications of the solutions women offer. To take arms against a problem is not necessarily to succeed in eradicating it. Although every heroine makes some progress in changing the injustice chiefly at issue in her book, these women are not uniformly able to transform the conditions of industrial life. But each example of heroic assertion does succeed in making some significant impact, not least of all by demonstrating the efficacy of nonpatriarchal modes of social organization and interaction. The social innovations that the heroines propose and enact contain a significance beyond their localized deployment. By modeling alternatives to capitalism and to patriarchy, these

75

novels suggest that the true reform of industrial England will occur only when the organization of society is utterly transformed.

This radical undercurrent in the condition-of-England novel is visionary rather than pragmatic. It may be this very quality, a seeming impracticality of approach, that has led to the critical deprecation of the genre. Indeed, these authors do not provide a how-to text for budding feminist revolutionaries; there is no blueprint for the transformation of English class relations. But these novels do offer a kind of inspiration in showing how far the contemporary imagination could go in dreaming of a different way of life. However apparently unattainable they may be, ambitious dreams are the foundation of any plan of improving the world. Sybil Gerard suggests, in evaluating Stephen Morley, that the practical reformer must of necessity be at base a dreamer:

> "But then Stephen does not want to recall the past," said Sybil with a kind of sigh; "he wishes to create the future."
> "The past is a dream," said Gerard.
> "And what is the future?" inquired Sybil. (169)

The condition-of-England heroines offer a dream for the future that remains an inspiration rather than an inspired prediction. Because of the class tensions and emerging gender ideology of their particular historical moment, Victorian novelists could subconsciously point the way toward a kind of feminist utopia; Victorian society, however, lacked the transformative capacity to put this dream into practice.

Like Gaskell's Mary Barton, confronted with "the necessity for exertion on her part" (301) that the current crisis demands, the condition-of-England heroine does not step forward with trivial or reflexively conventional solutions. The answers she provides come from a deep contemplation of herself and a reliance on her own social analysis. Some of the novels underline the seriousness of their heroines' responses by providing them with a time of meditative retreat. While all those around Trollope's Mary Brotherton assure her that there is no fundamental flaw in the industrial system, she withdraws into herself and finds differently:

> "There must be something wrong," argued the young girl, as day by day she paced her gravel walks in solitary meditation;

"there must be something deeply, radically wrong in a system that leads to such results. . . . I will find out why this is so, or be worried to death by Sir Matthew Dowling and his fellow great ones in the attempt." (98)

Gaskell's Margaret Hale, too, comes to intellectual maturity by calling upon her own resources, conducting a sort of spiritual retreat on the beaches of Cromer and learning that it is time she "took her life into her own hands," because she "must one day answer for her own life, and what she had done with it" (508). Lady Eleanor of *Alton Locke* undergoes a year-long apprenticeship in working-class life, staying with the needlewomen of London, before she establishes her own community of women (352). The deeply considered solutions all the heroines come to espouse invariably give them a powerful role in reform, whether they are fighting in the trenches or supervising the battle.

The eponymous heroine of *Mary Barton* springs into action the moment the appropriate pretext arises. Although, as Tillotson observes, her "emergence as active and heroic heroine" does not truly occur until after the murder of Harry Carson,[1] she is then only drawing upon personal resources she has always had. She has always been strong-willed and "fond of power" (52), and her mother's death has fostered her innate independence: Mary becomes her father's housekeeper and gains "more of her own way than is common in any rank with girls of her age" (58–59). One result of this upbringing is that her individuality and personal strength are not ground down by conventional notions of proper feminine behavior:

Three years of independence of action (since her mother's death such a time had now elapsed) had little inclined her to submit to rules as to hours and associates, to regulate her dress by a mistress's ideas of propriety, to lose the dear feminine privileges of gossiping with a merry neighbour, and working night and day to help one who was sorrowful. (62)

Gaskell's partly censorious attitude to Mary's high-spiritedness springs not from disapprobation of her heroine's energies but rather from a realization that they are misdirected. She is "ambitious" (121), but for such false honors as elevation to the upper class through marriage, and anxious about "making an impression" with her beauty (67).

But, once she learns the truth about the murder of Harry Carson, she gets the opportunity she needs to use her strength of will more appropriately—in the public arena. Gaskell notes that this newfound knowledge of the situation is precious to Mary because it convinces her that "Jem's innocence might be proved, without involving any suspicion of [her father]" (311). However, her joy seems to have a particular basis in the outlet provided for her individual energies: her "spring of comfort" is "the necessity for exertion *on her part* which this discovery enforced" (301; emphasis mine). While she involves others in her scheme to exonerate Jem, she refuses to give them anything truly important to do because "[s]he could not bear the idea of deputing to any one the active measures necessary" (340). The narrator indicates that she is averse even to involving the accused in his own defense.

> And even if she could have gone to him, I believe she would not. She longed to do all herself; to be his liberator, his deliverer; to win him life . . . by her own exertions. (312)

It is left to Sally Leadbitter to draw the obvious conclusion that, by the second half of the novel, Mary has become too high-minded to admit—that she has found a means of self-realization in public action. As Sally admiringly observes, "You've set up heroine on your own account, Mary Barton" (426).

Mary does become crucially important in the resolution of the social crisis depicted in *Mary Barton*, as Coral Lansbury has recognized.

> It is Mary who redeems both Jem and her father, by saving one from the gallows and the other from committing a double crime, of murder and allowing an innocent man to hang. This redemptive power is not the passive grace exerted by the angel in the house. . . . Mary confronts society at every turn and eventually overcomes it.[2]

Her special knowledge determines that "[e]very thing rest[s] on her" (304): she gains a power over life and death, as she realizes when she comes to the "conviction of how much rested upon her unassisted and friendless self, alone with her terrible knowledge, in the hard, cold, populous world" (303). But her mission to save Jem requires help from others, and her courage in the face of all difficulties enables her to enlist the aid of both Job Legh and total strangers in Liverpool. The most dramatic action, however, is left to her. She personally rides out in the rowboat to catch Will Wilson's ship, and when she reaches it she gestures almost as though she had a magical power over it: she "stood up, steadying herself by the mast, and stretched out her arms, imploring the flying vessel to stay its course by that mute action, while the tears streamed down her cheeks" (357). Her appearance as she testifies at Jem's trial confirms the uncanny effect her elevation to heroic status has had: her by now more than "mere flesh and blood beauty" makes an impression on the listeners "that would keep its hold on the memory for many after years" (389). Her greatest triumph at the trial is to keep her resolution not to go mad, for she knows that from her madness may emerge the truth of her father's guilt. She lets down her guard only after Will arrives to provide Jem with an alibi; until then she unflinchingly shoulders all the burden and responsibility that have come along with her frightful knowledge. The novel's central crisis has called out the heroine's latent power and elevated her to a commanding height so that she can effect its resolution.

Mary Brotherton of Trollope's *Michael Armstrong*, like Mary Barton, finds in the problems of those around her an outlet for her abundant energies. Although the heiress has grown up accustomed to doing as she likes, her nature is tenacious as well as willful. Nurse Tremlett remarks, "I . . . know you too well to fancy that if you have set your mind upon [something], you will give it up" (114). Once Mary decides to investigate English industrialism, she is admirably persistent. She accurately predicts to Mrs. Tremlett:

> [I]f, through all the years we have passed together, I have shown such a determined spirit for no reason in the world but only to get my own wanton silly will, do me the justice to anticipate that I shall not be less obstinate in this one thing, that I believe to be right. (114)

Even the inspiration for her quest is a by-product of her self-will. Mary stumbles upon Sir Matthew cuffing and cursing Michael Arm-

strong when, out of boredom, she leaves a musical performance at
Dowling Lodge. This first encounter with an industrialist's injustice
occurs precisely because "the heiress, . . . instead of having been in-
structed to endure annoyances patiently, had been rather taught
never to endure them at all" (109). Her upbringing has nurtured an
independence that enables Mary to see clearly and to take action: she
is able "obstinately [to] persevere in judging for myself" only because, as she says to Sir Matthew, "I am a spoiled child" (126).

Once the spoiled child is turned loose on the industrial scene she
is a formidable agent of change. As she penetrates deeper into the
contemporary morass, she attains greater power. Mrs. Tremlett tries
without success to lead Mary away from the deathbed of a poor
working woman with a large family:

> [The nurse] looked anxiously into the face of her charge. It was
> deadly pale, and wore an expression of solemnity so new and
> strange, that the good woman threw her arms around her in an
> agony of fond anxiety, exclaiming, " . . . Mary, Mary, come away!
> you can do no good. This scene is not a fit one for you to wit-
> ness."
>
> "You mistake me, nurse. It is fit for me. It is necessary for
> me." (134)

Mary's economic and personal power makes her growing interest in
the condition of the poor threatening even to such an entrenched
capitalist as Sir Matthew. He recognizes her unusual abilities: as he
notes to his overseer Parsons, "[N]ot the old one himself could stop
Mary Brotherton if she got a whim in her head. . . . [I]f such a girl as
that . . . once gets it into her head to go about among the factory
people, she'll kick up more dust than we shall find it easy to lay
again" (140). Just as the knowledge of Jem's innocence energized
Mary Barton, the knowledge of industrial exploitation calls out Mary
Brotherton's inherent potency. She takes action by penetrating the
forbidding isolation of Deep Valley Mill. She embarks upon her journey in defiance of convention and in spite of the quiet disapproval
of the reforming clergyman Mr. Bell; through her, as Kestner remarks, "Trollope repudiates the female role expectation established
even by benevolent male authority figures like Bell."[3] Mary gains
entry to the mill through a deception to which Nurse Tremlett ini-

tially objects as improper—a pretense that the two women are looking for Mary's brother (247). But in a pinch Mary can overcome convention, and even conventional morality; she buys her way in to see the children, and when she hears that Michael is dead she recovers her poise quickly enough to save Fanny Fletcher instead.

The incident at Deep Valley Mill marks the zenith of Mary's heroism and the dramatic high point of the novel. In the face of an intimidating overseer and an implicit threat to bar her exit from the mill, Mary manages her money and her manner with sufficient skill to ensure the safety of herself and her two companions. Although the narrative subsequently returns to the plight of Michael Armstrong and the death of Sir Matthew Dowling, nothing challenges Mary's role as the author of good in the novel. The benefits she bestows upon Edward Armstrong and Fanny, and later Michael himself, reconfirm her status as powerful heroine. Michael recognizes who deserves credit for transforming the lives of those dearest to him: "It is Miss Brotherton, . . . it is she who has done all this, and may God bless her for it! But yet, truly, it still seems a mystery" (325). Even Michael's later realization that his oppression provided the original impetus for her actions does not dispel the air of mystery that clings about Mary's good deeds. We will find that many condition-of-England heroines share this aura of uncanniness that comes from the sudden use of those subversive powers in womanhood that the spectacle of female victimhood evoked.

While both Marys make a sharp (if not wholly unprecedented) break with their previous activities when they step into the public arena, Margaret Hale in *North and South* moves much more smoothly toward her assertion of social power. Throughout the novel those who encounter her emphasize her capacity for governance and self-government by characterizing her with queenly epithets. Doctor Donaldson, who tells her about her mother's physical condition, has a typical reaction:

> What a queen she is! With her head thrown back at first, to force me into speaking the truth; and then bent so eagerly forwards to listen. . . . [I]t's astonishing how much those thoroughbred creatures can do and suffer. That girl's game to the backbone. Another, who had gone that deadly colour, could never have come round without either fainting or hysterics. But she

wouldn't do either—not she! And the very force of her will
brought her round. (174–75)

Others see in her the same qualities, although their feelings are expressed with somewhat less enthusiasm: in Mrs. Thornton's eyes
Margaret has "the noiseless grace of an offended princess" (394) and
in the police inspector's estimation a "regal composure" (345); at his
first meeting with her Thornton feels that she has acted "as if she had
been a queen, and I her humble, unwashed vassal" (117). Even those
who are reluctant to give way to her feel the subjugating power of
her personality.

She lives up to her description in her behavior toward others.
As we saw earlier, Margaret gains sovereignty over her parents'
household when they prove weak and feels perfectly competent to
intervene in Thornton's relations with his striking workers. Her
authority extends to the Higgins family as well: Bessy sees her as a
nearly mythological figure who has arisen out of her dreams, while
the more pragmatic Nicholas yields to her "silent yet commanding"
presence and power by deciding to follow her home rather than go
out to drink (282). Her hold over Thornton, at once sexual and ideological, is the power "to melt away every resolution, all power of
self-control, as if it were wax before a fire" (251). Even when her
brother Frederick appears there is no resurgence of patriarchal
power; he cannot undercut Margaret's authority, either to do such
mundane tasks as arrange her mother's funeral or to perjure herself
to ensure his safety. Whether she is agreeing to tell Mrs. Boucher of
her husband's death or "battl[ing] it out" with Edith's passionate little
son (495), Margaret has the courage and the power to take the appropriate action.

But, like Mary Brotherton, Margaret Hale begins her most significant action only after she withdraws into herself and gathers her
forces. When, her mother dead, her father travels to Oxford for the
visit that will see his final days, Margaret feels liberated and ready
for serious reflection:

It was astonishing, almost stunning, to feel herself so much at
liberty; no one depending on her for cheering care. . . . For
months past all her own personal cares and troubles had had to
be stuffed away into a dark cupboard; but now she had leisure

to take them out . . . and seek the true method of subduing them into the elements of peace. . . . Now, once for all she would consider them, and appoint to each its right work in her life. (425)

Later, after her father has died and she has gone to stay with Edith, she sleeps in what was her childhood day nursery and considers how she has not lived up to her youthful ideal of having "as brave and noble a life as any heroine she ever read or heard of in romance" (502). This time alone and her subsequent period of seaside rest "enabl[e] Margaret to put events in their right places, as to origin and significance, both as regarded her past life and her future" (506). She does indeed take "her life into her own hands" (508); she takes action that will raise her to the supremely heroic level she always imagined for herself.

One of her goals is to atone for the lie she has told about Frederick's role in the death of Leonards. In her solitary meditations Margaret returns repeatedly to her sin and blames herself for this "wrong, disobedient, faithless" deed (485). But her self-recrimination is dominated by shame that Thornton should know of her perjury.

If she had but dared to bravely tell the truth . . . how light of heart she would now have felt! Not humbled before God, as having failed in trust towards Him; not degraded and abased in Mr. Thornton's sight. She caught herself up at this with a miserable tremor; here was she classing his low opinion of her alongside with the displeasure of God. (358)

Margaret is at least as concerned with Thornton's opinion of her as she is with God's; his knowledge entails a shift in the balance of power between them that makes her uncomfortable. She hates contempt, but especially from "Mr. Thornton, above all people, on whom she had looked down from her imaginary heights till now! She suddenly found herself at his feet, and was strangely distressed at her fall" (356). Where once she challenged him in courage and political insight, and mastered him with her chilling manners and demure beauty, she now finds herself a supplicant for his approval. "She wondered if she should have minded detection half so much from anyone else" (377), perhaps because he has been her most powerful vassal and her closest tie to the industrial situation.

Her final actions at once bring her decisively into the public sphere and consolidate her power in the private sphere. Given Margaret's concern that Thornton have a "true understanding of what she had done" (505), we might expect a pivotal scene in which she outlines the reasons for her lie. This, however, does not occur; Margaret never justifies herself to Thornton, who receives only partial enlightenment about the incident from Nicholas Higgins. Instead, the turning point of their relationship comes when Thornton reveals the extent of her ideological influence upon him. At a London dinner party Margaret overhears his explanation of his experiments in labor relations. He has finally realized the importance of "cultivating some intercourse with the hands beyond the mere 'cash nexus'" (525) and has begun to lower the barriers between himself and his workers. Thornton has made precisely those reforms that Margaret advocated during their acquaintance at Milton. Once she realizes that her power over him remains strong, Margaret takes steps to cement their relationship. Although she is already his landlord, she has a proposal drawn up that will lend him money sufficient to run his mill according to his own (her own) principles. Thornton gladly accepts this proposal, in which he recognizes another (of marriage) that he is also eager to accept. For the last time in *North and South* we see the convergence of private and public affairs.[4]

The means Margaret Hale uses to deal with the condition-of-England crisis involve the selection and use of a suitable instrument of action. Her growing knowledge of the industrial situation includes an ever-increasing appreciation for the capabilities of the Milton manufacturers. An early recognition of their potential comes as she surveys the guests at the Thorntons' dinner party:

> She liked the exultation in the sense of power which these Milton men had. It might be rather rampant in its display, and savour of boasting; but still they seemed to defy the old limits of possibility, in a kind of fine intoxication, caused by the recollection of what had been achieved, and what yet should be. (217)

By the time Mr. Bell comes to visit the Hales, Margaret is so far a defender of the modern age as to warrant his accusation that "[s]he's a democrat, a red republican, a member of the Peace Society, a socialist" because, as she puts it, "I'm standing up for the progress of commerce" (409). After she revisits her old home at Helstone and observes the "change everywhere; slight, yet pervading all" (481), she is ready to embrace industrialism as the only force able to deal with the inevitability of change in the world. Her involvement in Thornton's business affairs shows her determination to turn technology to her own ends and to harness the same sort of mind as that responsible for the steam hammer (which Thornton characterizes in awestruck terms as "this imagination of power, this practical realization of a gigantic thought" [122]). She has chosen to effect change in the system by becoming the controlling ideological and economic power behind a mill and a man and by using both as her tools.

While the heroines of *North and South, Mary Barton,* and *Michael Armstrong* move overtly into the public sphere when they take action against condition-of-England ills, other heroines operate more surreptitiously. Sissy Jupe of Dickens's *Hard Times,* unlike Margaret Hale or Mary Barton, does not self-consciously undertake a quest for the source of the contemporary crisis. Instead, Louisa Gradgrind is the woman who comes to an intellectual understanding of Coketown and passionately denounces industrialism's deadening influence. Sissy Jupe has only an instinctual appreciation of such matters. In opposition to the brutal logic of utilitarianism, Sissy asserts her own values with a humility that downplays their philosophical viability and cloaks her rejection of patriarchal thought.

> "Then Mr. M'Choakumchild said he would try me once more. And he said, Here are the stutterings—"
>
> "Statistics," said Louisa.
>
> "Yes, Miss Louisa . . . —of accidents upon the sea. And I find . . . that in a given time a hundred thousand persons went to sea on long voyages, and only five hundred of them were drowned or burnt to death. What is the percentage? And I said, Miss;" here Sissy fairly sobbed as confessing with extreme contrition to her greatest error; "I said it was nothing."
>
> "Nothing, Sissy?"
>
> "Nothing, Miss—to the relations and friends of the people who were killed. I shall never learn," said Sissy. (44)

Sissy's behavior, rather than any explicit statement of her point of view, proves the validity of her opposition to industrialism. Even near the beginning of her stay in Coketown, Gradgrind becomes "possessed by an idea that there was something in this girl which could hardly be set forth in a tabular form" (71). Eventually everyone in the family perceives Sissy's significance, from Mrs. Gradgrind, in whom the presence of Sissy inspires the belief in "something—not an Ology at all—that [her husband] has missed" (153), to little Jane Gradgrind. By the end of the novel Sissy has become its most active force. She has insinuated herself into the Gradgrind home and made herself an indispensable influence for good. It is she alone who has the foresight to send Tom away before he can be apprehended by the authorities, thus accomplishing what Gradgrind claims "[t]en thousand pounds could not effect" (210).

But, most important, she saves Louisa from the disaster to which utilitarianism has led her. Louisa's implicit acquiescence in industrialism through her acceptance of Bounderby's hand has involved a tragic alienation from Sissy.

> When Mr. Gradgrind had presented Mrs. Bounderby, Sissy had suddenly turned her head, and looked, in wonder, in pity, in sorrow, in doubt, in a multitude of emotions, towards Louisa. Louisa had known it, and seen it, without looking at her. From that moment she was impassive, proud and cold—held Sissy at a distance—changed to her altogether. (79)

This separation from Sissy represents Louisa's abdication of her own female powers of regeneration—a resigning of herself to patriarchal oppression. Her rejection of Sissy mirrors the process by which, as she exclaims to her father, she has "almost repulsed and crushed my better angel into a demon" (166). Louisa's ultimate appeal to Gradgrind is that he, having "brought me to this" should "Save me by some other means!" (167). But the person who transforms her is not her contrite but now ineffectual father but, rather, Sissy alone. Convalescing from her emotional upheaval, Louisa tells Sissy that she could not possibly "want a guide to peace, contentment, honour, all the good of which I am quite devoid, more abjectly than I do." And Sissy becomes that guide: she shines "like a beautiful light upon the darkness of the other," and Louisa falls to her knees and looks up "almost with veneration" (172).

Sissy effectively manages the threat to Louisa's well-being from without as well as from within. James Harthouse, with his experience in the public worlds of the army and diplomatic corps, and his "low estimate of everything" (166), seems unlikely to be subdued by a quiet stroller's girl. But Sissy is able to extend her power into the world in which Harthouse is so comfortable. When she comes to Harthouse to convince him to leave town she does not rely on social convention or traditional authorities—she has "no advice or encouragement beyond my own hope" (175). Her own authority and strength, however, are more than sufficient to master Harthouse. Like "a clear sky" or any other powerful imponderable, she is impervious to ridicule, his chief weapon (178); she overpowers him with her astonishing self-assurance, her "simple confidence in his being bound to do what she required" (177). Such an unquestioning belief in her own capacities recalls other condition-of-England heroines: Mary Barton impresses those around her with her unswerving intention to exculpate Jem, while Margaret Hale bends Higgins to her will with a voice in which "there was no fear or doubt . . . either of him or of his compliance" (282). Like them, Sissy has the fearless ingenuousness of one with almost unlimited power. But, unlike them, she has not dramatically seized control: through a pattern of influential behavior she has quietly built herself up into a bulwark of impressive strength. The authority she has heretofore exercised covertly and insinuatingly in the Gradgrind household is transferred easily to the world outside the home, so that Harthouse is forced to admit himself "vanquished at all points" (178–79).

With Helen Fleetwood, as well as with Sissy Jupe, we encounter a sort of covert control that only gradually manifests itself as power. A common element in these two novels is the heroines' class identity. The selection of a working-class protagonist by a middle-class author seems to entail an especially careful treatment of female self-assertion. Working-class heroines, by virtue of their class and gender, are doubly transgressive. Disraeli minimizes any difficulties by identifying his heroine as an anomalous proletarian—a convent-educated crypto-aristocrat. Gaskell's Mary Barton has no such cover; however, we will see that, perhaps not coincidentally, Mary proves to be the least successful condition-of-England protagonist. But Dickens and Tonna provide an especially heavy initial cloak of insignificance for

their heroines that makes their entry into the narrative apparently
inconsequential. Only gradually, with a movement that seems natural rather than aggressive, do these women come to the fore.

The young orphan Helen Fleetwood, like Sissy Jupe, is admitted
into the heart of an unrelated family. In common with the other
heroines, once she comes in contact with the contemporary social
crisis she begins to draw upon previously hidden strengths of character. When we first see her she appears a pleasant but unremarkable
young woman: "a girl of delicate mind, such as is often found in our
sequestered villages. . . . There was nothing in her character unusually elevated above the class to which she belonged" (517). But the
Green family's migration to the city of M. reveals more of the real
Helen. From the first she has "obtained," to an almost prophetic
extent, "a view of their probable trials" (527) in the mill town: unlike
her foster grandmother, "she had a presentiment of evil, as it
seemed. In reality it was only the effect of her natural sagacity drawing plain conclusions from obvious premises" (522). Increasingly, she
is willing to use her perspicacity to help the rest of the family:

> The truth is, dear Granny, I have always thought more than I
> spoke; but now I see you are likely to have many difficulties and
> few helps, I desire to be, after my poor fashion, more useful to
> you. (521)

Helen's new strengths surprise and almost abash her nominal protec-
tor, Widow Green, who both depends upon her ward "for solace and
for aid" and realizes that according to convention Helen "needed for
herself the guardianship that others must seek at her hands" (526).
However, the widow learns soon enough that, rather than being
weakly in need of a champion, Helen has more assertiveness than is
consistent with Christian behavior. When she treats Phoebe Wright
with supreme haughtiness, her foster grandmother is "startled at
discovering in the girl's character strong traits of high spirit and en-
thusiastic feeling, where all had appeared so quiet, so humble, almost
too timid and shrinking for the necessary conflicts of life" (549). The
situation in M. brings to light not only the great resilience and maturity of Helen's character but also a strain of almost subversive self-will
that frightens Widow Green.

Helen begins to assert her power in the mill town, in both her

quiet domestic actions and her bolder public stance. Because of
Tonna's Evangelical background, the self-assertive actions that ex-
press Helen's inherent power take a soteriological form—Helen is
not setting up heroine on her own account, but on Christ's. Yet
Helen's authority is not exclusively attributable to an obedient discipleship. Widow Green's early perception becomes increasingly valid:
Helen Fleetwood is in many ways the head of the Green household.
As Richard eventually discovers from his brother James, Helen is
their main economic prop: they could not "get enough to live on, if
Helen and her earnings were both away" (601). Helen also gains a
less tangible power over the family by keeping the truth of her on-
the-job persecution from Widow Green. Such secrecy, and not only
on Helen's part, pervades the novel; it is an ambiguous activity, at
once a commendable attempt to spare the feelings of others and an
impious denial of family bonds. Shortly after their arrival in M.,
Helen decides to hide her suffering from her guardian: "[S]he resolved, [instead] of adding her calamities to the general stock, to take
a double share of those which oppressed her benefactress" (539).
This appears to be an unselfish gesture, but it is also an attempt to
put herself in a position of superior knowledge and compassion—a
form of self-aggrandizement. Indeed, this secrecy leads Helen into
the display of pride to Phoebe Wright that so startles Mrs. Green.
When Helen realizes she has "added to [the widow's] troubles by
trying to avoid it," she agrees to "tell [her] all" (548), but she subsequently conceals an overlooker's physical abuse as well as her frequent fainting fits in the mill. Although the woman to whom she
owes respect and obedience has forbidden it, Helen continues in her
deception. The novel's official explanation for this is that she "always
thinks more of others than herself" (599); a plausible alternative explanation is that this heroine, so conscious of her own strength, desires to control others by bearing their burdens.

Helen also takes notable action outside the home—action that is
inseparable from the affliction she undergoes at work. Unlike other
condition-of-England heroines, she unites the characters of protagonist and chief victim. In chapter 2 I touched upon the force of Helen's
victimhood. From the beginning of her factory work, Helen experiences the greatest suffering of all the Greens; at the mill she finds
"herself at once marked out for the contempt and dislike of the people around her" (538). The example of other working-class heroines

suggests that some experience of victimization is indispensable for a figure positioned at the site of industrial oppression; Mary Barton and Sissy Jupe spring to mind. Yet *Helen Fleetwood* represents a unique articulation of this paradigm. For Tonna's Evangelical Christianity demands that those who would have spiritual power must endure persecution: as James says, "before we reign with Christ we must suffer with him" (583). By a twist of this logic Helen's suffering brings her temporal power; her action outside the home is possible because of her torments. As an example to others, Helen enacts a strongly pedagogical role. Widow Green is shocked to learn from Mr. Malony that Helen has been struck by an overseer, but the girl's deprecation of the incident makes the widow control her anger, realizing "the immediate importance of such a practical lesson of Christianity as Helen was giving" to the Malonys (571). Those around her come to recognize that her life is a lesson; she attains a symbolic dimension in their eyes. James observes to Richard: "[Y]ou never saw such a creature as Helen. She seems to me . . . to be sent just to show us that there is no situation where the grace of God is not sufficient for his children, if they do but seek it always" (600).

Helen is a teacher by word as well as by example. Her attempts to instruct her fellow factory workers meet with mixed results, but ultimately she sees that her work has not been in vain: "[O]ccasionally, when emboldened to speak to some of her more immediate associates in labour, she had marked the operations of the hands suspended, and the eye turned with inquiry, not unmixed with anxiety, to her face" (629). Her greatest success occurs when socialism, to Tonna's mind the most unspeakable evil on earth, makes an assault on the mill workers. Here a particularly urgent situation brings out Helen's latent talent for organization and political infighting.

> She . . . succeeded in partially putting down this outrage on behalf of herself, and a few companions who were not totally lost; she compelled them to join her in a solemn declaration that they would lay a public complaint before the Messrs. Z. by means of the newspaper, if any more was said in their hearing on the subject: and the aggressors seeing them in earnest, and conscious that the mill-owners must in that case take it up, thought it prudent to desist. (628)

Like other heroines who work at cross-purposes to such progressive movements as Chartism and unionism, Helen cuts a strongly conservative figure here. As always, it is not in the explicit politics of these narratives (which in this case are almost rabidly reactionary) that their radicalism lies. Beneath the surface of *Helen Fleetwood* we will find, astonishingly enough, a species of the very socialism that sets Tonna to raving.

Helen is the great active and positive force in the novel, easily outstripping South and his shady schemes and even those well-intentioned Christians who look to Lord Ashley for help. Hudson, one of these well-intentioned men, recognizes Helen's unique status: "If ever there was a persecuted Christian enabled by well-doing to put to silence the ignorance of the foolish, and to shame them of the contrary part, she is such a one" (608). Her sense of having souls to save keeps her from retiring from the factory in her final illness (634). Although she does not actually die in the mill, she uses her incipient death as a weapon against Godlessness: "[H]er last seizure took place there, and so alarmed her companions as to give a great effect to the few words she was enabled to speak to them" (642). Like Sissy Jupe, Helen has moved gradually from prominence in the home to eminence in the outside world.

Whereas the other condition-of-England heroines step personally into the public sphere to take action against industrialism, Lady Eleanor Ellerton of *Alton Locke* and Sybil Gerard of *Sybil* stand one step removed from the fray. Their intervention, like that of other heroines, is crucial to the resolution of the condition-of-England crisis, but they make their contributions by purposefully manipulating the chief male characters. Their crucial actions are even more cloaked than Sissy Jupe's or Helen Fleetwood's; nevertheless, they, rather than the men they employ, are the real saviors of a diseased English society. Lady Eleanor does not confine herself to covert activity on behalf of reform. Her first attempts to resolve the class tensions of the age come on the Ellerton estate, where she becomes "utterly devoted, body and soul, to the welfare of the dwellers on her husband's land" (235). Although she later judges her efforts a failure, the experiment reveals her potential for exercising power: she was "a philanthropist, a philosopher, a feudal queen, amid the blessings and the praise of dependent hundreds" (374). Once she redefines her commitment to the poor, she begins to live among them as the leader and benefactress of a kind of commune. She considers this new occupation to be more consistent with Christian ideals than the old one, but it also involves a greater assertion of her unassisted abilities. Where she was once "a help-meet . . . for her husband" (235), constrained by her conventionally subordinate role of wife, she is now an independent woman following a less traditional path. She has, as she says, "broken the yoke of custom and opinion" (375). Her unconventionality marks her as one of those condition-of-England heroines who rise to meet the exigencies of English social life.

Lady Eleanor plays her most significant part, however, in her relationship with the hero. She is not only his benefactress in a variety of situations but, ultimately, the ruling force in his life. The actions she takes to save him fit her for a role Alton has tried repeatedly and until now unsuccessfully to cast—that of the hero of English society. For *Alton Locke* is the story of a man in search of a true idol. Although the background to the novel he narrates is an industrial society in crisis, Alton himself is singularly unfit for the role of savior. While Sandy Mackaye's phrenological analysis indicates the young poet's strengths in imagination and perception, it also (accurately) reveals a personality in which "[f]irmness [is] sma'—love of approbation unco big" (33). Easily led astray by others, Alton is usually in a "distracted, rudderless state" (28) when he is not under the immediate influence of some strong leader. After his early alienation from his mother, he finds it difficult to define for himself a single set of values. Initially he comes under the tutelage of Mackaye; when temporarily separated from him, however, Alton turns avidly to Crossthwaite and Chartism. He falls for the eloquent rhetoric of the Emerson-like Windrush; he yields to the yellow journalism of O'Flynn.

But his greatest susceptibility is to the influence of women. The narrative persistently suggests that Locke has a regressive need for a mother figure: a woman who will unite eroticism and maternity. Latent even in his relationship with Sandy Mackaye is such a longing for reunion with the mother, for at the old man's death Alton "seemed to trace in [Sandy's features] the strangest likeness to my mother's" (320). His infatuation with Lillian inspires him with an adoration that has more than a tinge of oedipal desire: "No child ever nestled upon its mother's shoulder with feelings more celestially pure than those with which I counted over night and day each separate lineament of that exceeding loveliness" (75). This confusion looms larger in his feverish dreams near the end of the book, in which he pictures himself "a child, upon a woman's bosom. Was she my mother, or Eleanor, or Lillian?" (343). When he awakes he discovers that the answer, figuratively speaking, is Eleanor: she has been caring for him, and he watches her "with a sort of sleepy, passive wonder, like a new-born babe" (351). Alton has achieved the state of total dependency he desired, in which a strong mother figure makes all decisions for him.

Alton's need for a controlling woman, which becomes the novel's need through his first-person narration, is at first met by Lillian Winnstay. Entranced by her outward graces, Alton makes her his "living outward idol" (80). Yet she does not prove to be the "goddess" (160) who can help him to solve the problems he finds around him. In her presence he cannot bring himself to describe the true condition of the working class, because "the sight of Lillian made me a coward" (153). But the clearest indication that Lillian is a false idol comes when Alton's publisher suggests that Locke delete some potentially controversial political passages from his book of verse. Even though these sections constitute "the very pith and marrow of the poems," he agrees; the "popularity, money, patronage. . . . [that will result] involved seeing more of Lillian" (182). And so he becomes "a flunkey and a dastard" (183), blinded by his worship of a false idol.

The true idol he eventually finds does not demand such a sacrifice of truth and talent. Eleanor instead denounces his self-censorship as "Weak!" (183). Her effect on him is to strengthen rather than to corrupt. Although he recognizes her sovereignty late in the novel, she has exercised an influence for good in his life for a long time. Even during the period of his early hostility to her, he echoes her uplifting conversation in an argument with his cousin George (222). She attempts to dissuade him from joining the ill-fated 10 April Chartist rally, and only his thoughts of Lillian prevent her from conquering him then and there (323). She provides him with tangible assistance as well: it is she who pays his debt to George and, presumably, she who provides the money for his legal defense. Even in the depths of his unjust resentment of her he is compelled to recognize the striking power of her personality:

> She was beautiful, but with the face and figure rather of a Juno
> than a Venus—dark, imperious, restless—the lips almost too
> firmly set, the brow almost too massive and projecting—a queen,
> rather to be feared than loved—but a queen still. (147–48)

The genuineness of this strength, which Alton at one point explicitly
juxtaposes with the superficiality of Lillian's appeal (216), eventually
wins out in the battle for control of Alton and of English society.

Once Alton finally recognizes her sovereignty she begins to exert
the full force of her ideas upon him. The ideology that Eleanor espouses is Christian Socialism, but Alton evidently conceives of it as
a cult of personality. He becomes convinced of its truth because of
Eleanor's manner while describing it:

> The sense of her intense belief, shining out in every lineament
> of her face, carried conviction to my heart more than ten thou-
> sand arguments could do. It must be true!—Was not the power
> of it around her like a glory? (355–56)

His newfound faith in God looks more like faith in Eleanor; he has
simply transferred the belief he had in Lillian: "[H]er I loved, and
love no longer; but you, you, I worship, and for ever!" (358). Although Eleanor disparages this idolatry, she also uses it to control
Locke's actions: when he begs not to be sent so far away from her,
she prevails by insisting, "[Y]ou are my servant now, by the laws of
chivalry, and you must fulfil my quest" (384). Despite its apparent
impiety, Alton's idolatry is appropriate, for Eleanor is the force that
shapes his resolution of his inner conflict. Her virtue is not that she
makes him abandon all idols but, rather, that she is at last his true
idol. While others have sought to use his talents against the best
interests of himself and his class, Eleanor adjures him to recover his
health by going abroad: there he can use his gifts to write a book that
will inspire all with an understanding of the plight of the poor. As
Alton recognizes, she has almost recreated him: "Me, at least, you
have saved, have taught, have trained!" (384). She gains total control
over Alton's life and uses him to achieve her goal of improving the
condition of England. Though cloaked by the language of Christianity, her action is both an example of female self-assertion and a confrontation of the contemporary crisis.

Even more than Eleanor, Disraeli's Sybil Gerard takes control of the condition-of-England crisis by taking control of important people. Sybil shares the uncanny, exalted status of the other condition-of-England heroines; Thom Braun has recognized that "her nature is rather inhuman, even spectral."[5] The narrative describes her as something between a monarch and a saint. Not only does she possess a voice "of almost supernatural sweetness" (66) and an "almost sacred repose of . . . mien and manner" (194); she seems to Egremont (who at the time does not recognize her) to have about her head "a kind of halo" (232). But she possesses a certain power as well as a passive sanctity. It is not a meaningless sentimentality that makes the village children call out "the queen, the queen" at Sybil's approach (183). Her natural capacities become evident through her courageous journey into the worst slums of London to save her father and in her effortless leadership during the climactic riot at Mowbray Castle: "Sybil . . . had collected around her a knot of stout followers, who, whatever may have been their original motive, were now resolved to do her bidding" (409).

Nevertheless, the most obvious outlet for her abilities comes in her relationship to Charles Egremont. Disraeli's melodramatic prose makes it difficult to take the true measure of this relationship. It is much easier to dismiss Egremont's protestations of rapture over Sybil than to take them seriously. His proposal is typical:

> [Y]our picture consecrates my hearth, and your approval has been the spur of my career. . . . I cannot offer you wealth, splendour, or power; but I can offer you the devotion of an entranced being, aspirations that you shall guide, an ambition that you shall govern. (278)

But careful examination reveals that these apparently overblown assertions are actually accurate assessments of the situation in *Sybil*. She *is* the force that propels Egremont into the role of social reformer: it is she, along with Morley, who lends him books to aid his understanding of his country; she who charms him into convictions like her own (both 194); she, rather than her father, whom he quotes when he dares to question his brother's account of workers' lives (151). Her power over him is not really that of an inspiringly beautiful object but, rather, of a frustrated politician seeking to carry out her own designs through his agency. Her conversation with her father indicates that the change she desires can come about only through the offices of a powerful man who is like the old kings of England. She exclaims, "Ah! why have we not such a man [as King Harold] now . . . to protect the people! Were I a prince I know no career that I should deem so great" (168–69). Even though such an occupation is nominally closed to her, she achieves her goal by using Egremont as a surrogate. There is a natural affinity between them because they share a subordinate status in society, she because of her femininity, he because being a younger son in a noble family is "as bad as being a woman" (136). Of course Charles Egremont, M.P., is not quite so badly off as all that, but this affinity helps establish his appropriateness as Sybil's representative.

For Sybil eventually learns that to improve their lot she must make use of the existing power structures to which Egremont has access. The disorderliness of Chartism shows her that "the People" cannot succeed on their own.

> She [had] thought that the People . . . had but to express their pure and noble convictions by the delegates of their choice, and that an antique and decrepit authority must bow before the irresistible influence of their moral power. These delegates . . . [turned out to be weak and selfish], while the decrepit authority that she had been taught existed only by the sufferance of the millions, was compact and organised, with every element of physical power at its command. (290)

Her mind turns to Parliament, and she wonders whether it could foster the kind of reform she deems necessary—"Could the voice of solace sound from such a quarter?" (291). In reading the newspaper she finds such a voice in Egremont, who has been delivering wise speeches before the House of Commons; almost magically, the M.P. appears in person to dispel her lingering doubts that his class can be effectual. Her acceptance of his aid and (eventually) his hand appears to make her dependent, but it is an open question who has mastered whom. When he rescues her from prison after her father's arrest, her reflections on his prompt intervention are suggestive of her own power rather than his: "Had she breathed on some talisman, and called up some obedient genie to her aid, the spirit could not have been more loyal, nor the completion of her behest more ample and precise" (334). One can as easily say that she exercises an uncanny control over him as that he is her rescuing white knight.

We learn as well that Egremont is not the first man Sybil has used to further her political ends. Stephen Morley seems clearly to have been an earlier disciple who proved unworthy. In his confession of love he explains the motivations that have guided his public actions for years past.

> "And love of you, Sybil," he continued, in a tone of impassioned pathos, "has been to me for years the hoarded treasure of my life. . . . [F]or this I have served your father like a slave, and embarked in a cause with which I have little sympathy. . . . It is your image that has stimulated my ambition, developed my powers, sustained me in the hour of humiliation." (303)

But Morley proves to have insufficient personal and political force to serve Sybil's ends. Gerard blames him for being impractical in his ideas of social improvement: "He is a visionary, indulging in impossible dreams, and if possible, little desirable" (297). And Sybil herself disapproves of his too-prosaic goals, insufficiently influenced by spiritual considerations; "Stephen Morley does not believe in angels" (173), she sighs. He is at fault both for dreaming too much and for being insufficiently radical in his dreams. Moreover, his cynicism makes his devotion to Sybil suspect: lacking the total commitment of a true convert, he has ulterior motives in serving her purpose. She recognizes his inadequacies as a follower when he presses his suit on her in "the hour of exigency" (304) preceding Gerard's arrest; he not only directs his energies away from the subject foremost in her mind but also attempts to subdue her by taking advantage of her father's plight. Like Margaret Hale in *North and South*, she experiences a discomfiting shock when a man she had ruled takes control of her. His behavior exiles Stephen from Sybil's affections but does not quite dispel the lingering influence she exercises over him, for he gives his life in the riot at Mowbray Castle to obtain the proof of Sybil's ownership of the estate. Since Stephen has no further means of advancing Sybil's interests, he dies, her name on his lips (415).

There are two others whose talents are somehow subject to Sybil's control, although neither is so ardent a slave as Stephen Morley or Egremont. Baptist Hatton is sufficiently inspired by his meeting with her to plot to reestablish her on the lands that are rightfully hers, and he continues to provide his indispensable assistance even after his hopes of marrying her are at an end. Walter Gerard himself seems to be under the subtle influence of his daughter, whether he is articulating the ideas that are her deep convictions (194) or growing increasingly wrongheaded as he spends less time in the holy presence of his daughter and more in the company of other Chartist delegates. Although she never acknowledges her own power, wherever she goes Sybil bends the wills of others to her own.

Egremont's description of Sybil's effect on his public life must, then, be taken seriously. Not long after their first meeting, "her supremacy over his spirit [is] revealed to him." Prevented by the presence of others from declaring to her "his entire subjection" (198), he returns to London a changed man. His colleagues recognize that he "is as much altered as any fellow of our time" (204), because "he has got crotchets about the people" (205). When Sybil learns his true identity and scorns his offer of continued friendship, Egremont gains a heightened awareness of her importance to him, and not just as a desired wife: she is identified with the "principle of order" that emerges out of the "anarchy and returning chaos" of his grief (246).

He prefaces his proposal of marriage with an explanation of why the People will never rule themselves and how the "new generation of the aristocracy" can (276). Like Margaret Hale's business proposal at the end of *North and South,* which Thornton understands to be a marriage proposal as well, Egremont's words serve a dual purpose. They constitute an offer of both matrimonial and political partnership. Given the status Egremont has already attained in Parliament, his offering of "aspirations that you shall guide, an ambition that you shall govern" is not a trivial gesture. Her ultimate acceptance of him is based as much on the realization of how significant her power will be as on her affection for him. Sybil's sudden elevation to the nobility and precipitous recovery of her family fortune do seem wildly inappropriate to a woman obsessed with her solidarity with the People. But, in light of her growing recognition of the dynamics of her society, her apparent abandonment of the lower class takes on a different appearance. Far from being a betrayal of her working-class upbringing (and another of Disraeli's quaint romantic notions), Sybil's social mobility entails a realistic acknowledgment on her part that the upper class is where the power is. If she hopes realistically to effect change in English society, she cannot afford the luxury of residing in a vine-covered cottage far from Parliament, the only possible source of reform. Like the other condition-of-England heroines, she has found her own route to public power, her own means of action in a society in crisis.

Each heroine of the condition-of-England novel encounters a situation that requires her to act; each rises to the occasion by using the means at her disposal. Her ultimate success as an agent of social change is perhaps less readily apparent. As I have indicated in my introduction, critical opinion is almost universally hostile to the solutions of these novels. I would suggest, however, that most of these solutions are quite successful in meeting the industrial crisis *as presented in the book.* For these women can be judged only with reference to their own enclosed fictional worlds, not by the standards established by contemporary politicians or social scientists. All heroines achieve a certain success as the principal agents of plot resolution, and in all but a few cases they achieve an even greater triumph by resolving the condition-of-England crisis. Their resolutions carry enormous symbolic weight as the ultimate expression of what Bodenheimer usefully calls "the politics of story"—part of which is the way "plots define and delimit imagined possibilities for social thought, action, and change."[6] Condition-of-England novels can imagine quite visionary forms of social reconfiguration: their conclusions embody nonpatriarchal social values that implicitly offer a radical critique of English life. In their confrontation of social crisis with new solutions, these women inscribe feminism and a prophecy of apocalyptic change: assertive women lead the way toward a complete transformation of the way society is organized.

One development common to Gaskell's *Mary Barton* and Trollope's *Michael Armstrong* influences our initial appraisal of the success of each heroine. Both books end with the principal characters in exile: Mary Barton and the Wilsons in Canada and Mary Brotherton and her associates on the Continent. Mary Barton's exile seems particularly indicative of a failure to change the shape of English society: Raymond Williams would appear justified in observing that "there could be no more devastating conclusion,"[7] both as condemnation of society and proof of industrialism's survival. Mary has taken action to resolve the primary dramatic tension of the novel (Jem's unjust arraignment) and managed to save her lover; nevertheless, her inability to change the society around her makes her the least successful of the condition-of-England heroines. While Jem has been released by the jury in Liverpool, enough of his coworkers disbelieve in his innocence to force his resignation. The end of the novel sees improvement in the Manchester worker's lot (460), but this is owing to Mr. Carson's humanization by his son's death and his confrontation with the dying John Barton. Mary plays a role in making this transformation possible: by preventing Jem's execution, she enables Carson to meet the true murderer and gain insight into the workers' plight. So, although Mary and Jem are compelled to retreat from Manchester, it is not before the former has effected some amelioration of the current situation. She does not transform her world, but her indirect agency in changing Carson makes her a partial success.

Exile takes on a different meaning in *Michael Armstrong*. Mary Brotherton and company do not leave England under duress but voluntarily. In the terms of the novel their action is more of an assertion than a retreat, for English industrial society is incapable of redemption. Mary asks the benevolent clergyman Mr. Bell to propose a means (other than the stalled Ten Hours Bill) of abolishing the industrial tyranny under which the poor suffer, but he considers the case hopeless: "Nothing effectual [can be done], my dear young lady. . . . [The system's] power is stupendous, awful, terrible!" (208). The insinuative strategies that work so well for Sissy Jupe in *Hard Times* cannot work in this thoroughly corrupt society. The failure of Martha Dowling's pious efforts to save Sir Matthew conclusively demonstrates the folly of working within this industrial system. Martha determines never to stand "in rebellion to my father" (228), but her quiet remonstrances neither change Sir Matthew's public actions nor effect a deathbed conversion. The imperviousness of this manufacturer to the private manipulation often so effective in the condition-of-England novel indicates that men like Sir Matthew Dowling cannot be reformed but only overthrown.

The conclusion to the novel provides its social crisis with a resolution for which Mary Brotherton is only partially responsible. Unlike some of the other heroines, she is not instrumental in the destruction of the industrialist's power. The fall of Sir Matthew represents the inexorable collapse of industrial society from within; the bankruptcy that punishes and subdues him is the inevitable end product of his overreaching greed. The miniaturized version of English society over which this industrialist has held sway is a shambles. After presiding at the death of Sir Matthew, Michael Armstrong can escape the ruins of Dowling's world only by joining the alternative society that Mary Brotherton has set up on the Continent. This novel's disenchantment with English industrial society is so complete that the only use to which the heroine's nearly magical powers can be put is first to extricate individuals from the factory system and then to create a totally new society elsewhere. In a sense this is a survivalist novel in which a few lucky or wise people manage to escape a man-made holocaust and rebuild the world. By fleeing the industrial scene, both *Michael Armstrong* and *Mary Barton* demonstrate their pessimism about existing society but also their optimism about human potential. Theirs is not a regressive escape from the issues that they have addressed but an assertion of the need to start from scratch in building a humane world.

Other novels provide less ambiguous resolutions of the problems of English society. Heroines effect at least part of the necessary solution to crisis in *Helen Fleetwood, Hard Times,* and *North and South.* Helen Fleetwood is not responsible for the transformation of the factory system because Tonna is less concerned with industrial oppression per se than with its consequence—the disintegration of Christian spirituality. Helen is successful in removing this danger by transforming human souls: her activities at home and in the workplace address the problem most at issue for the author. Helen plays a central role in Sarah Wright's conversion, provides examples of Christian behavior to Mr. Malony and others, and eventually softens some of the other factory workers (who "appear to seek the pious instruction that she is so anxious to give" [634]). Her exemplary death is only the last ministration in a beatifically potent life. This novel by no means offers a thoroughly triumphant close. As in *Michael Armstrong,* much of the world of *Helen Fleetwood* lies in ruins at novel's end: the Green family is dispersed, James is dead, and Widow Green is in the poorhouse. Yet Helen has succeeded in creating spiritual victory out of poisonous circumstances and in pointing toward a different way of life for those around her.

Likewise, Sissy Jupe and Margaret Hale solve those problems that their authors have identified with the condition-of-England

question. By her insinuative methods Sissy undermines the utilitarianism that has caused Louisa and Tom, as well as the Coketown
workers, so much pain. She also resolves the central tension of the
novel, Louisa's troubled relationships with the men who embody the
oppressive authority of society. Because Sissy succeeds both in confronting the most glaring failures of industrial society and in offering
a remedy, within the terms of the novel she has heroically prevailed.[8]
Margaret Hale, more than any other condition-of-England heroine,
takes a conspicuous place in the world of public affairs. But even
before she becomes a landlord and industrial investor she has
achieved a substantial amelioration of the novel's factory problems.
At her urging Nicholas Higgins goes to Thornton to seek work. The
relationship of mutual respect that ensues forms the cornerstone of
Thornton's subsequent experiments in employee affairs. Margaret
ratifies Thornton's adoption of her own system when she agrees to
finance his mill with her newly inherited capital; she ensures that the
condition of workers in Milton will be improved. She has resolved
the major industrial issue of *North and South*, the relation of manufacturer to laborer, by insinuating her ideas into Thornton's consciousness and by using her economic power. In any terms, she has succeeded in solving the contemporary industrial crisis as it exists in
Milton.

The heroines of Kingsley's *Alton Locke* and Disraeli's *Sybil* succeed because they have an amazing ability to make the condition-of-
England crisis disappear. Both heroines address those facets of the
current crisis to which the narrative gives greatest prominence:
Eleanor redirects Alton's radical energies, while Sybil agrees to join
forces with Egremont against social injustice. Since *Alton Locke* has
been almost exclusively concerned with the title character's shifting
ideologies, Eleanor's presentation of Christian Socialism to him resolves the crucial issue of what philosophy a workingman should
embrace. If, as Brantlinger says, "Alton is able to do almost nothing
right until . . . his conversion by Eleanor Staunton to Christian Socialism ends his 'damnéd vacillating state,' "[9] Locke can do nothing
wrong thereafter. Not merely because he is near death, his problems
are over: this workingman, and by implication other workingmen,
will resolve their conflicts by accepting Eleanor's newly minted variety of Christianity. The ultimate solution to the problems that beset
the world of *Sybil* comes in the scene of the riot at Mowbray Castle.

In the novel's moment of greatest social crisis, Bishop Hatton's tatter-demalion army erupts with a long-simmering class rage. Yet, inter-estingly enough, what closes this scene (and the book on mob vio-lence) is the romantic reunion of Egremont and Sybil. By exchanging melodramatic assurances of devotion with Egremont, Sybil accepts his discipleship; instantly, the threat to England evaporates. As we have found before, private and public actions are coterminous: a solution in the private sphere has public implications. It has taken Sybil a long time to accept a role in the ruling hierarchy of England, but once she does so the country's problems vanish. *Sybil's* plan of social reform is fanciful rather than grittily realistic, but within the terms of the novel it is a successful one.

These success stories have implications that reach past the reso-lution of the condition-of-England crisis. Beyond the achievement of their immediate goals heroines offer a visionary feminist model of far-reaching change. By putting female protagonists in positions of significant authority, these novels have called into question the con-ventional assumption that women had no role to play in public life. When tested, these women show surprising resources that suggest the desirability of more widespread female leadership. Such feminist impulses can only be articulated within a rationalizing framework of concern for the family, but their presence is unmistakable. Margaret Hale constitutes a particularly compelling advertisement for women's equality; Mary Barton, as Coral Lansbury has observed, exudes a progressive self-sufficiency as "a woman deriving strength and dig-nity from the ability to earn her own living."[10] We have seen that the other heroines also evince a similarly assertive, independent streak. Such capabilities seem to stem from both the domestic authority of women and the same suppressed cultural awareness of women's subjugation that produced the power of female victimhood.[11] These heroic powers point toward an ineluctably feminist conclusion: women have immense resources that are underutilized by a patriar-chal society; women's emancipation would be a boon to Victorian society.

But these novels go beyond making a case for something fairly close to modern liberal feminism. They implicitly advocate a more radical unleashing: the establishment of a society led by women. In chapter 1 we saw that a precondition for women's heroism was the discrediting of paternalism and other forms of conventional authority. Similarly, before coming to the conclusion that female rule is necessary, two of the novels must discount the possibility of any viable alternative—any oppositional male-dominated government. Richard Green in *Helen Fleetwood* is a largely sympathetic figure who for the most part escapes the taint of patriarchy. He has praiseworthy ambitions, but, unlike Helen, he is unable to achieve his goals. As a boy, he vows to establish a benevolent masculine protectorate over the rest of his family:

> I will be like Strut [a rooster] when I am a man. I will take care of my granny as he does of his, and of the rest as he does of the chickens. To be sure I have no mother, as Strut has; but then I have you, Helen, and I will take care of you, and give you a big share out of all I can earn. (581)

But this barnyard model of human society does not prove adequate in dealing with the industrial town. While Richard remains personally comfortable in the countryside, his family suffers severely in the city. When he becomes aware of the full extent of their burden, he makes more vows to shelter them from harm. "[A]lmost unconsciously, [he] assumed the headship of the family, feeling his respectability bound up in them, no less than his happiness, and resolved to place them in a different position, both with regard to the world and to each other" (601–2). Richard's concern here seems to be as much for his "respectability" and his masculine pride as for others' suffering: elsewhere we learn that he feels indignant "[t]hat any female belonging to his household should become mixed up in such a mass of human degradation as he had just seen assembled" and that he wonders unworthily if Helen encourages the impudence of the male workers (599). More important, despite his brave words, he fails to save his family from distress: in his impotence he cannot prevent the death of Helen or save his grandmother from the poorhouse and Mary from a menial apprenticeship. He truly helps only Willy, the other surviving male of the family. Richard's ineffectual masculine authority degenerates into suspicion and empty gestures. In the inadequacy of his response to industrial oppression Richard is reminiscent of the male victims we saw in chapter 2. While the town of M. brings out new strengths in Helen, it only brings out in Richard, as he says, "such wicked, rebellious, impatient, angry passions in my heart, that I hardly believe myself so good as a heathen" (626). Never-theless, Richard does not remain identified with this heathen anger. The image of him that lingers derives from his spectatorship at the trial of Mary's overseer—he is preeminently a man who stands by while Helen witnesses.

If Richard Green's masculine authority proves ephemeral, Frederick Hale's in *North and South* is actively misguided. Although Frederick is not fighting precisely the same enemy as his sister Mar-garet, he nevertheless offers a model of how not to attack injustice. Serving under a willful, tyrannical captain, Frederick becomes the leader of a mutiny against him. To a certain extent he is upholding ideals that Margaret herself values; she observes of his case that "[l]oyalty and obedience to wisdom and justice are fine; but it is still finer to defy arbitrary power, unjustly and cruelly used" (154). But Frederick's defiance of his captain involves a good deal of Richard Green's strutting and posturing; it is only one step removed from the swaggering immaturity of Frederick's first days as a midshipman, when he was always "cutting open all the newspapers with [his dirk] as if it were a paper-knife" (151). His actions as a mutineer involve removing the captain and other officers from command and setting them adrift in a small boat. This eliminates the immediate threat of the captain's tyranny, but it does nothing lasting to ensure that he does not take power again; its only substantial result is the execution of those common sailors who are caught. This episode brings into question Frederick's good judgment and qualifications for leadership, which come to provide an implicit contrast to Margaret's. Margaret does nothing so dramatic and violent as Frederick, yet her leadership in the condition-of-England crisis leads to permanent reform without violence. Clearly, the female principles of governance that she repre-sents win out in this comparison. Again the condition-of-England novel raises the specter of male violence: the leadership of men in the current industrial difficulties would presumably lead (as the riot at the mill would have led without Margaret's intervention) to death and additional tyranny rather than progress.

In place of a reformed society headed by men, the condition-of-England novel points toward a world guided by women. My discus-sion of female protagonists has called attention to the often queenly character of women such as Margaret Hale. *Sybil* and *Alton Locke* follow this figure through to its logical end. Curiously enough, the two novels that most fully represent men as agents of change are most insistent on the spiritual significance of female leadership. Jane Tompkins has traced a similar elevation of women in sentimental American fiction. The elevation of domesticity in a work such as *Uncle Tom's Cabin* leads to the vision of a "new matriarchy . . . [that] constitutes the most politically subversive dimension of Stowe's novel. . . . Centering on the home . . . is the prerequisite of world conquest."[12] Kingsley and Disraeli also imply the need for a reorganization of society that will permit the exercise of women's almost mystical power. Egremont's declarations of fealty to Sybil mark her as the object of his devotion, but there are suggestions that worship of woman should become a general principle. Sybil is, of course, a good Catholic, but surely it is no coincidence that her religion takes the form of Mariolatry.

> "I know how deeply you feel upon this subject [the People]," said Egremont, turning to Sybil.
> "Indeed, it is the only subject that ever engages my thought," she replied, "except one."
> "And that one?"
> "Is to see the people once more kneel before our blessed Lady," replied Sybil. (173)

Presumably "the Convent and the Cottage" (177), the two ideas that alone have touched her imagination, are connected: the convent has taught her the power of a society that looks to a supernatural woman for guidance and aid. The exaltation of Sybil to high rank at the end of the book signifies not only her future participation in the solution of the condition-of-England crisis but also her enshrinement as resident goddess of the struggle.

Although *Alton Locke* makes a point of its hero's lack of philosophical firmness, it also endorses his propensity to venerate women. Locke's despicable cousin George provides a sharp contrast to Alton as an example of how women ought not to be treated. As the representative of all that is self-serving and callous in the contemporary social system, George is guilty of taking an ideologically unsound attitude toward women. After first meeting Lillian he rhapsodizes leeringly:

"What a lovely girl she is! . . . By Jove, what a face! what hands! what feet! what a figure—in spite of crinolines and all abominations! And didn't she know it? And didn't she know that you knew it too?" And he ran on, descanting coarsely on beauties which I dared not even have profaned by naming. (74)

To George a woman is not an object of worship but a set of body parts served up for his personal delectation; his vulgar undervaluation of womanhood later leads him to describe Lillian, by now his fiancée, as nothing better than "one little bit of real property which I have no intention of sharing with my neighbours" (326). The dismemberment and possession of women mistakenly denies their role as saviors and identifies them as consumer goods.

Kingsley endorses the notion of woman as ruler by his characterization of Eleanor as not only Alton's final teacher but also a being with unusual powers in her own right. She has a gift for prophecy, which allies her to those victimized women who had apparent access to supernatural powers: not only does Lillian jokingly speak of her "prophetic glances into the future" (176), but Dean Winnstay more seriously remarks that she "prophes[ies] confidently" (171). Alton describes her as "a Juno" (147); her function in the novel is indeed that of a queen goddess. The female rule that Eleanor personifies is central to Kingsley's vision of a reformed society: Eleanor's allegiance to Christianity, like her devotion to her conveniently deceased husband, is a respectable cover for what are her own assertions of power over others. Alton finally finds salvation for himself, and potentially for his society as well, when he turns to Eleanor, who takes on a curiously pagan role—that of a strong, omniscient, nearly divine leader.

Disraeli's and Kingsley's canonization of their heroines provides the most explicit instance of placing women in positions of authority and changing the rules of English life. Yet all of these novels implicitly offer a similarly radical recommendation for social reform: a vision of a woman-led society without conventional class lines, in which cooperation rather than competition prevails. The elements of this dream are not wholly unexampled in nineteenth-century English culture. They are reminiscent in some ways of the Owenist socialism that had flourished in the decades prior to the genre's emergence.

Owenism, despite its rejection of orthodox religion and the conventional family, also embraced egalitarian, noncompetitive principles; it even provided, as Barbara Taylor has shown, opportunities for feminist self-assertion.[13] Still, while the condition-of-England novel may draw upon ideas available in its cultural context, its solutions mark a sharp break from convention. Since its vision is so profoundly different from the contemporary order of society, its implementation would entail extraordinary change. To express its aspirations this genre turns to millenarian imagery—what Taylor calls "the only language of social optimism possessed by most men and women."[14] Through its employment of this apocalyptic language we will see the condition-of-England novel at its most radically visionary.[15]

Lady Eleanor Ellerton suggests to Alton Locke that masters and workers should cooperate rather than fight in words that discreetly echo the apostle Paul's analogy of the members of the church to the parts of the body: "[I]t is only by the co-operation of all the members of a body, that any one member can fulfil its calling in health and freedom" (379). Margaret Hale expresses similar sentiments to Thornton, although she couches them in the language of economic efficiency as well as religious duty: because employees and employers are "mutually dependent" (169) and because the former are morally responsible for their workers, both sides should stop "running each other down" (165). In this instance cooperation does not represent an excuse for maintaining the status quo, as critics have charged, but an alternative to Thornton's laissez-faire individualism: Margaret's advice comes in the context of a head-on confrontation with Thornton and his entrenched ways of doing business.

Where Sissy Jupe unobtrusively rules, cooperation is particularly valuable because it exemplifies a mutual concern lacking in Coketown society. Sissy's responses to M'Choakumchild's questioning indicate her resistance to any system in which the comfort of one group sanctions the sufferings of another—in which the "five-and-twenty [out of one million] . . . starved to death in the streets" (44) are systematically excluded by statistical trivialization. By her actions Sissy advocates the interdependency that comes to characterize the improved Gradgrind family. Her ideology stands in contrast to the standard ideology of industrialism that Bounderby espouses. His myth of belligerent self-help—that he has "nobody to thank for my being here, but myself" (12)—offers no scope for human relationships beyond the savagery of competition and exploitation. His final humiliation, the revelation of his mother's active role in his economic rise, is not just proof of his hypocrisy but also a demonstration of the fallaciousness of his social views (and, by implication, the correctness of Sissy's).

The heroines of the condition-of-England novel work for a transformation of industrialism that will leave no place for Bounderby's values. This transformation of labor relations augurs an additional change for which the heroines of these novels work: an alteration in the way all society is organized. A crucial part of this change is the virtual abolition of class boundaries. *Helen Fleetwood* enunciates this aim most explicitly. Helen quickly discourages Katy Malony from considering herself to be subordinate to Mary Green because of the nature of their factory jobs. Widow Green greets the girl:

> "So, you are Mary's little friend, Katy Malony."
> "I'm Miss Mary's scavenger, ma'am."
> "And Mary is your piecener," added Helen, who saw the old lady look grave at this distinction of ranks. (562)

The widow herself outlines the objections to rank more emphatically when Katy subsequently refers to her as a "lady": "[T]here are no ladies or gentlemen here. We are poor people all, and so we must regard each other. Happy are we, if we be among the poor of this world, rich in faith, whom God has chosen to be heirs of his kingdom!" (569). The point here is not simply that class distinctions are inappropriate between different levels of poverty but that the very notion of a class-ordered society is inimical to Christian living. In the society that the Green family and Helen Fleetwood envision there are no such artificial constructs.

The egalitarianism of *Helen Fleetwood* might be explained away as merely a side effect of Tonna's Christianity if other novels did not present the same sentiment in more secular contexts. As a member of a privileged class, Margaret Hale is in a good position to make small but significant gestures to undermine the class structure. Although common notions of propriety dictate that she not attend her mother's funeral, she insists on following the example of the lower class: "Women of our class don't go, because they have no power over their emotions, and yet are ashamed of showing them. Poor women go, and don't care if they are seen overwhelmed with grief"

(336). After her initial assumption of class superiority to the Higginses, she comes to treat them so much like equals that Dixon complains:

> Why master and you must always be asking the lower classes up-stairs, since we came to Milton, I cannot understand. Folk at Helstone were never brought higher than the kitchen; and I've let one or two of them know before now that they might think it an honour to be even there. (380)

In the face of a new and demanding situation, Margaret helps break down class barriers in her search for a new set of social rules. Other heroines do even more to escape the confines of class: both Kingsley's Eleanor and Trollope's Mary Brotherton create their own little (nearly) egalitarian communities. The former leaves her life of privilege to share the burden of subsistence living in a house with "the fallen and the lost ones" (352). While in her married life she emphasized class distinctions by her attitude to those "dependent hundreds" on her husband's estate (374), she now humbly takes her place among the greatest social outcasts of all. Mary Brotherton is even more overt in her establishment of a new, classless society. She moves to the Continent with Fanny Fletcher and Edward Armstrong (later joined by Michael and Martha Dowling) and creates a life for them in which all, despite their differing social origins, are equally privileged. It is not just, as Kestner observes, that the projected marriage of Edward and Mary, like the marriage of Sybil and Egremont in *Sybil*, "[s]ymbolically indicat[es] the interdependence of the social classes";[16] it suggests as well the meaninglessness of class distinctions. This new society is not entirely egalitarian, for Mary Brotherton continues to control the purse strings.[17] These novels require the continuing influence of a woman's guiding power to keep the community faithful to its highest ideals; however, they dispense with English society's conventional conceptions of class.

The ending of Trollope's novel suggests the ultimate implication of this genre's vision of social revolution: not a literal revolt but an inexorable apocalypse to come. Michael Armstrong, in joining Mary Brotherton's circle, abandons an industrial England in the last stages of decay: Dowling, the exponent of modern economic force, collapses financially and dies, bankrupt and despised. A type of apocalypse takes place in *Hard Times* within Louisa Gradgrind, but there is a covert threat that all of Coketown may eventually be involved. In drawing an analogy to her own state, Louisa reveals the violent potential of the city's factories: "There seems to be nothing there but languid and monotonous smoke. Yet when the night comes, Fire bursts out, father!" (76).

Such hints take on greater significance when we consider the obvious pattern of apocalyptic imagery in some other condition-of-England novels. Patrick Brantlinger is the first to have noticed this figure in *Sybil, Alton Locke,* and *Helen Fleetwood.* The same mythopoeic impulse that enshrines Sybil Gerard also provides a fierily mythic solution to contemporary problems. Brantlinger observes sardonically, but with justice:

> [Disraeli's] portrait of social England reveals so many complexities and shatters so many clichés—not least of which is the two nations idea—that finally the only logical program appears to be the one described by the heroine: "'It sometimes seems to me,' said Sybil despondingly, 'that nothing short of the descent of angels can save the people of this kingdom'."[18]

Such dramatic heavenly intervention does not explicitly occur within the bounds of the novel; as in *Hard Times,* the novel provides a less supernatural conclusion. Nevertheless, the identification elsewhere of Sybil with queens and angels suggests an affinity between her ultimate ascent to power and this angelic descent. In contrast, Alton Locke actually experiences a personal apocalypse of sorts. Having become disillusioned with a variety of stale doctrines, he comes face to face with Christian Socialism's vivid truth through a series of explosive dreams that signal his entrance into a new life. If Alton Locke, the representative of the English worker, must go through such a trial to reach the spiritual truths that alone can solve the social crisis, we may presumably conclude that society at large must experience a similar shattering process. Again the principle of miniaturization makes an appearance, this time to enforce a prediction of apocalyptic change.

Of all the novelists Tonna most enthusiastically manifests a chiliastic sensibility.[19] Although the solutions she allows her heroine Helen to offer involve spiritual transformation, her prediction of the

ultimate fate of industrial society involves a more comprehensive
Judgment Day:

> Oh, it is an awful thought that so many believing, confiding
> prayers of the poor destitute are recorded in the book of His
> remembrance. . . . Very terrible will be the day of public inquisi-
> tion and divine retribution. God keeps silence now. . . . [But] he
> hath appointed a day for the open vindication alike of his justice
> and his faithfulness. (517)

Brantlinger comments with reference to this passage that, although
she would not have acknowledged it, Tonna has a great deal in common with those who advocated industrial sabotage and revolution:
"[S]he approaches [Richard Oastler and J. R. Stephens] in her own
statements, and her revolution will come as surely as that which cast
down the Bastille."[20]

Such is the visionary imagination of condition-of-England writers: Christian rhetoric or domestic clichés imperfectly conceal their
desired goal of the utter transformation of English society. The violence and radicalism of their prophecy proceed logically from the
placement of women at the center of social change. This radical ascription of power inevitably leads to radical consequences: the expectation of a benevolent Socialist monarchy that will reorganize or, in
some cases, destroy industrialism. The word that best describes these
visions of the future is utopian; they share the impulses of their
literary descendants, the creators of feminist utopias. Carol Pearson
has described a genre that includes Charlotte Perkins Gilman's *Her-
land* (1915) and a number of later works in terms that are by now
very familiar:

> Feminist utopias do away with the division between the inhu-
> mane marketplace and the humane hearth. This is not accom-
> plished by moving both men and women out into a brutal public
> world. Instead, the entire society is patterned after the principles
> which (ideally) govern the home.[21]

Condition-of-England novels, it is clear, cannot be simply understood
as documents of bourgeois complacency; if anything, they are mani-
festoes of a Victorian visionary sensibility.

The condition-of-England novel achieves the insinuation of a radical message into an apparently conservative art form. Because society is in a state of crisis and because traditional authorities have failed, this fiction can make a crucial leap—the ascription of power to female protagonists. Once women are given the chance to lead, they call upon the special powers contemporary mythology granted them to make uncanny transformations of English life. Yet the assertions of self these heroines make are always safely cloaked: they never acknowledge their own radicalism and certainly not their own feminism. In spite of the active measures for change they take, they remain respectable Victorian women. Their future dream is largely undiscussed: it sits glimmering on the margins of the novel, in the adjectives and epithets, and very occasionally in the incidents, the novelists employ. But this dream of a society without competition and class distinctions is very real in these seven novels. Its absence will be keenly felt as we turn to novels in which the subversive and reconstructive powers of women fail to come into play.

Chapter 4

The Tamed Captives of *Shirley*

The industrial climax of *Shirley* finds the novel's two heroines, like Margaret Hale in *North and South*, on the scene when masters and workers clash. Caroline and Shirley have ventured out of the parsonage at night in the hope of warning Robert Moore of the approaching band of armed workers, but once they come within sight of his mill they realize that they are too late. They can do nothing but stay on the hill overlooking the action. Both wish to play a role in events: Caroline avows "my will—my longing to serve [Robert],"[1] while Shirley "would have given a farm of her best land for a chance of rendering good service" (388). But this chance is denied them, and they remain passive spectators. Although Shirley is proud to have confounded male expectations by witnessing the battle, she and Caroline have made no substantial feminist point. They have proved no more useful in a crisis than if they had actually been what the gentlemen think they are—"asleep in our beds, unconscious" (377).

Where Margaret Hale intervened between master and man to avert bloodshed, Shirley can only watch from afar as men are killed or wounded. She is fated to muse impotently on the shattered windows and crimson-stained gravel of the mill yard and say, "This is what I wished to prevent" (389). For this novel represents a distinct departure from the familiar condition-of-England narrative: it depicts the failure of female power. Both Shirley and Caroline have attempted to comprehend and alter the structure of industrial capitalism, but their efforts have not prevented violence. Moreover, as we shall see, their efforts will not prevent patriarchal retrenchment and the solidification of oppressive power. Unlike the heroines of the other novels, the women of *Shirley* do not take control of the contemporary situation.

And yet this novel exhibits a more explicit feminist impulse than any other work in the genre. Caroline laments the plight of unmarried women in English society and lays blame at the door of those men who deny them useful employment. Shirley plays a traditionally masculine role in business dealings with her tenant Robert Moore and in her presentation of herself in society. Indeed, together the two heroines at times act out a Socratic dialogue on women's rights:

> [Shirley:] "Can labour alone make a human being happy?"
> [Caroline:] "No; but it can give varieties of pain, and prevent us from breaking our hearts with a single tyrant master-torture."
> (257)

Shirley goes so far as to invoke those myths of womanhood that secretly empower the heroines of other condition-of-England novels. But neither mermaids nor the primordial Eve who was the mother-creator of Titans can give Shirley much help when she is trying to exercise power in her own world: both she and Caroline end the novel as submissive, almost invisible wives to unimpeachable patriarchs.

Why is it that such assertive feminism does not find expression in the solution of industrial problems? Why is it that women remain powerless to change their own lives, despite Brontë's clear analysis of their problems? I will be exploring the nature of and the reasons for the failure of female power in *Shirley* by examining the novel in the light of condition-of-England structures I have already delineated. We will see that Charlotte Brontë cannot envision the practical application of her feminist mythology because she does not credit women with significant power in *any* sphere of English life and because she does not detect exploitable instability in patriarchal society. The result of her clear-sighted appraisal of women's oppression as well as their potential is an inevitable, tragic destruction of female rebelliousness when her heroines fall under the spell of masculine society.[2]

In more than one sense *Shirley* is a condition-of-England novel with a difference. Although it was written in 1848–49, at the same time as the others in the genre, it deals with events of a considerably earlier era: the Luddite disturbances of 1811–12. Nevertheless, critics have found little difficulty in affirming its relevance to the concerns of her own day; Terry Eagleton goes so far as to say that "Chartism is the unspoken subject of *Shirley*."[3] Like the other condition-of-England novels, it depicts an English society in crisis: in the very first scene Malone must leave his meal to protect Robert Moore from Luddite attackers, and the rest of the novel exhibits a continuing concern with industrial unrest. Brontë's analysis of this crisis locates the problem in the relations between classes, but unlike the other novelists she expands the crisis to include relations between men and women. Yet *Shirley*'s most significant divergence from the generic norm lies in its assessment of visionary solutions. Whereas other condition-of-England novels wholeheartedly advocate radical change, Brontë's novel reveals the desperate need for such change only to back away, ultimately, from calling for it.[4] Its rejection of the visionary element, together with its other singularities, places *Shirley* on the margins of the genre. To study the novel is to discover the narrowness of the limits within which the condition-of-England novel could successfully operate.

Shirley, like the other condition-of-England novels, is a feminocentric work. Brontë's novel, however, does not establish all of the elements common to the others' feminocentrism. Women are certainly the bearers of the novel's social conscience: it is Caroline who critiques Robert's relationship to his workers and she who concludes after bitter personal experience that "there is something wrong somewhere" in society (441). Shirley is even more outspoken in her analysis of contemporary unrest. She locates the chief problem of industrialism in the attitudes of the ruling classes. "I cannot get out of my head a certain idea that we manufacturers . . . are sometimes a little—a *very little* selfish and short-sighted in our views, . . . rather heartless in our pursuit of gain" (369–70). But she does not merely analyze the situation with ironic understatement. Her own distress at the suffering of the Briarfield poor leads her to establish a special fund for them under the direction of Miss Ainley. As she says, "I cannot forget, either day or night, that these embittered feelings of the poor against the rich have been generated in suffering" (301). The only other person in the parish capable of fully comprehending the situation is Yorke, whose bigoted misunderstanding of the upper classes makes him fall short as a social conscience for the novel. Caroline and Shirley stand alone in their objective understanding of the plight of the poor.

But this is where the full feminocentrism of the novel ends. For

Shirley presents a world in which reality and the industrial threat are only partially domesticized. The other novels depict the public sphere in the context of the domestic sphere. Brontë's novel, however, opens with the presentation of a level of English social reality to which the heroines have no direct access: the masculine world of the curates. The three young ministers sit greedily devouring their dinner as Donne's landlady, Mrs. Gale, waits upon them; it is a scene in which a woman is servant rather than master in her own house. It is as well a scene that provides early proof of Brontë's reluctant commitment to antiromantic values. For the curates who dominate the early pages are part of the triumphant world of Monday morning that spreads a bitter banquet for the novel's heroines. Significantly, this mealtime scene concludes with Helstone's recruitment of Malone as Robert's assistant in the defense of the mill. Though thuggish and underbred, Malone is a necessary prop for the patriarchy of which he is a part: unlike John Thornton of *North and South*, Robert Moore cannot protect his property with the "two women left about the place" (18) at Hollow's Mill. These women, presumably Hortense and her servant, are extraneous to the business at hand. Caroline, whose consciousness is to dominate the first two volumes of the novel, will not appear until chapter 5. By the time she makes her entrance, the omniscient narrator has delineated the industrial problem and even depicted the morning routine at Robert's mill. Although Caroline and Robert talk about labor relations at Hollow's Cottage, industrial reality is not fully domesticized; we know more about the current crisis from direct observation than from what we learn through Caroline's experience.

Moreover, women are not completely in control of the domestic sphere, diminished though it is in importance as an arena of discussion. Caroline is a mere cipher in Helstone's household: she is "very docile, but not communicative" (112), and her uncle pays little attention to either her thoughts or movements. Although more of a dominant figure in her own home, Shirley too has limited power in this sphere. She is notoriously unable to control the dishonesty of her servants. Though she is "fearless, physically," she admits:

> I am a poltroon on certain points—I feel it. There is a base alloy of moral cowardice in my composition. I blushed and hung my head before Mrs. Gill, when she ought to have been faltering

confessions to me. I found it impossible to get up the spirit even to hint, much less to prove, to her that she was a cheat. (298)

This scene provides an amusing contrast to the bold figure Shirley customarily cuts, but it also affects our perception of her power. Similarly, the gloomily impressive Mrs. Yorke appears a diminished figure within her own family unit. Her usual response to her son Matthew's explosive temper is "a fit of hysterics" followed by a retreat to her bed (655). Helene Moglen sums up her character nicely— "Powerless in a larger world, she behaves in a way which renders her powerless in her home as well."[5] She is only superficially a matriarch: "It was strange, that with all her strictness, with all her 'strong-mindedness,' she could gain no command over [her children]: a look from their father had more influence with them than a lecture from her" (458). Mrs. Yorke is the reverse of Sissy Jupe in *Hard Times*, who appears to be without power but actually manages the lives of those around her with quiet ease. But any condition-of-England heroine compares favorably with the women of *Shirley* when it comes to the exercise of domestic power. Helen Fleetwood, Mary Brotherton, Margaret Hale, Mary Barton, and Sybil Gerard have all firmly established their rule in the home as a necessary precondition to their invasion of the public sphere. The same cannot be said of any woman in Brontë's novel.

The final constituent of the typical feminocentric structure in other novels is also quite weak in *Shirley*. Just as reality is not as feminized, and women are given a less commanding role, the industrial threat is less domesticized here than in the genre's other novels. Brontë presents workers as the victims of industrial patriarchy, but she does not alert the reader to any imminent disintegration of poor families. Indeed, workers enter the scene so infrequently that there is scarcely a chance for them to embody any general principles. Eagleton and Pierce observe with justice that "[t]he sustained, ready sympathy for the lot of the poor and the involvement in the detail of their lives [present in other condition-of-England novels] is absent in *Shirley*."[6] There is a dearth of information about the working class in this novel: we catch only glimpses of a few evil organizers, the members of the faceless mob, and Michael Hartley. The only figure at all comparable to the workers of other novels is William Farren, who pleads with Robert Moore (unsuccessfully) for moderation. A "rea-

sonable man" (153) in the tradition of Stephen Blackpool, Farren airs
the grievances of his class before Shirley and Caroline. The appeal of
worker to heroine is typical, but the novel's failure to pay much
further attention to him is not. For, although William has told Robert
of the danger industrialism poses to families, his own home life enters the novel only briefly. His wife and children exist as only the
most rudimentary outlines of characters. We do not get a feeling for
the personal consequences a financial failure would have for his family, as we do for instance even for the Bouchers in *North and South*.
Moreover, the Farrens' discovery of employment outside the factory
system confuses the economic issue: William obtains a job as a gar-
dener, while his wife opens a small shop. They are the only representatives of the industrial poor, and yet they manage to escape industrialism without leaving English society. Other novels do not similarly
water down the industrial issue by describing a heterogeneous local
economy. Because Farren easily finds an economic niche for his family, the dangers he describes lose much of their potential impact; his
discussion with the heroines cannot demand from them the sort of
immediate personal response characteristic of other novels. Industrialism has not really compromised the domestic sphere, over which
in any case women have little power. There is no special reason for
them to act.

The slight attention paid to Farren's family is itself indicative of
a different alignment of the usual condition-of-England forces. Not
only is Mrs. Farren barely visible and largely irrelevant, but she is
not joined in suffering by other poor women. Whereas other novels
have important female victims (such as Bessy Higgins, Fanny
Fletcher, and Rachael) who arouse the sympathy of the more pros-
perous heroines, *Shirley* consigns both victimhood and heroism to
the upper classes. At her first appearance Caroline Helstone does
not seem to be a victim but, rather, a heroine after the pattern of
Margaret Hale in *North and South*. In the course of her visit to Hollow's Cottage she criticizes Robert Moore's labor policy and attempts to offer remedies for his current troubles by using Shake-
speare's Coriolanus as a negative example. At this point her
interplay with Robert is similar to Margaret's with Thornton, even
down to Caroline's wonderment that Moore cannot extend his personal benevolence to the public sphere. But Caroline's genteel at-

tempts at industrial intervention go nowhere, and the subsequent events of the evening transform her from a possible agent of change to a victim of patriarchy.

It is hardly surprising that Caroline's efforts do not lead to Robert's instant submission: even Margaret Hale's advice met with a hostile reception. But, unlike Margaret, Caroline is unable to elicit even angry words from Robert—he does not find her sufficiently threatening for that. He may call her "a little democrat" (105), but the adjective suggests that her ideas are adorably amusing rather than challenging. Instead of becoming angry, he interrupts her applied literary criticism to demand a poetry recital. Caroline's obedient performance is disturbing both for its content and the circumstances surrounding it. Beneath the seeming innocence of its subject matter, the alarmingly titled "La Jeune Captive" describes the impatience and frustration of a young woman anxious to escape from the beautiful but constrictive garden of adolescence. As a result of her cousin's coldness, Caroline will begin to experience a similar feeling of balked power in the next chapter. Unlike the girl in the poem, she will learn that the world of mature womanhood enforces its own debilitating limitations on female self-realization. Moreover, Robert's command that she speak in his native tongue serves to heighten his power over her. Assuming the role of pedagogue, he exhorts her to "have no English u's" (106); metamorphosing from social critic to little girl, she in turn asks, " 'Is that pretty well repeated?' . . . , smiling like any happy, docile child" (107). Everything about the situation enforces her powerlessness.

The differences between *Shirley*'s hero-heroine encounter and that of a more mainstream condition-of-England novel are striking. We see at precisely what points Brontë passes by opportunities to grant her heroine access to feminocentric energies. The aftermath of Caroline's visit demonstrates that Brontë's decisions here have far-ranging repercussions in the narrative. For this early failure of the condition-of-England pattern to establish itself is crucial to the novel's outcome.

Thornton's visits with Margaret Hale leave him enslaved by her beauty and intelligence. Robert's evening with Caroline leaves him interested but emotionally unattached. He says to himself after walking her home:

"This won't do! There's weakness—there's downright ruin in all this. However," he added, dropping his voice, "the phrenzy is quite temporary. I know it very well: I have had it before. It will be gone to-morrow." (108)

Tomorrow Robert can retreat to business affairs and escape his cousin's influence: "[H]e was wrapt from her by interests and responsibilities in which it was deemed such as she could have no part" (191). Because of her exclusion from the business world, Caroline cannot be privy to the greater part of Robert's concerns and experiences; she lacks the power necessary to master him.[7] Indeed, the opposite occurs: she becomes hopelessly entrapped by him. She is incapable of the detachment he maintains and inwardly acknowledges his influence over her:

Sometimes I am afraid to speak to him, lest I should be too frank, lest I should seem forward: for I have more than once regretted bitterly, overflowing, superfluous words, and feared I had said more than he expected me to say. (111–12)

The evening at Hollow's Cottage has been crucial in establishing the balance of power between Caroline and Robert. Like Moore's disgruntled workers, she is faced with the total ineffectuality of her efforts to change social inequities: while he can make decisions about his life and take action, the others can only passively react. Robert has the power to enforce his will; as he rudely says to a conciliatory Farren: "I will have my own way. . . . *I'll never give in*" (154).

Brontë follows this revelation of Caroline's powerlessness with an extensive description of the girl's suffering as a victim of patriarchal authority. Robert's rejection causes her great agony—the emotional equivalent of a scorpion's sting. But what links her to the working-class victims of other novels is the physical pain of her wasting sickness. Although Brontë assures us that "[p]eople never die of love or grief alone" (214), her heroine could easily be in the grip of the sort of fatal illness that afflicts such factory girls as Helen Fleetwood and Bessy Higgins. Her "bloom had vanished, flesh [had] wasted" (212); she has joined the ranks of the grieving who "are reduced to pallor, debility, and emaciation" (214). Caroline has never

worked in a mill, but she becomes nonetheless an example of industrial cruelty.

So, one heroine of this condition-of-England novel becomes its
foremost victim. While the suffering of Helen Fleetwood became in
itself a means to heroic power, Caroline's pain gives her a feeling of
diminishment. Instead of becoming an emblem of industrial agony,
she begins to engage her situation intellectually in hopes of finding
some escape from it. In this response she shows an affinity with
some other condition-of-England heroines. Just as Mary Brotherton
and Margaret Hale followed up glimpses of suffering with a more
thorough investigation of the industrial situation, Caroline moves
from the experience of her own victimization to an examination of the
position of women in English society. She is forced to confront the
frightening extent to which women's economic and social roles are
dependent upon masculine validation:

> Till lately I had reckoned securely on the duties and affections
> of wife and mother to occupy my existence. I considered, some-
> how, as a matter of course, that I was growing up to the ordinary
> destiny . . . ; but now, I perceive plainly, I may have been mis-
> taken. Probably I shall be an old maid. . . . What was I created
> for, I wonder? Where is my place in the world? (194)

Caroline's exploration of the paths open to women in the contemporary world puts her in contact with three sorts of women's lives—
those of married women, old maids, and Shirley. As we shall see, the
last of these provides a case of unique interest to the narrative. But
where wives and old maids are concerned Caroline, who expects to
find autonomy and fulfillment, encounters only more victimization
by male authority. Unlike other heroines who investigate the contemporary situation, she will not discover a route to effective self-assertion.

Caroline's thoughts inevitably wander to the institution that customarily grants women their status in her society—marriage. Her
fear, she tells Shirley, is that a wife may have no long-term power
over her husband and that, consequently, marriage provides no emotional nourishment for a woman. She wonders "whether it is necessary to be new and unfamiliar to [men], in order to seem agreeable

or estimable in their eyes; and whether it is impossible to their na-
tures to retain a constant interest and affection for those they see
every day" (241). The two exemplary marriages in Caroline's immediate family warrant this sort of cynicism. After Mrs. Pryor does her
best to dissuade Caroline from entering upon the powerless occupation of governess, she continues her warnings by remonstrating
against the profession of wife. Marriage, she asserts, is a "marsh"
with a temptingly green surface but a dreadful "slough underneath"
(427). Her own husband similarly had "a fair outside" that only thinly
veiled his almost demonic cruelty. Mrs. Pryor has suffered deeply
from the "anguish" and "terror" that resulted from completely trust-
ing a husband, for once she placed herself in his power there was
no recourse to the outside world, "no sympathy—no redemption—
no redress!" (489). Marriage is not a contract between equals but a
vehicle for the exploitation of women.

Even more alarming than Mrs. Pryor's tale of mistreatment is the
story of Mary Cave, for Mary suffered at the hands not of a madman
but of the eminently sane Reverend Helstone. Mary's marriage
united her with a man in whose favor the balance of power was
tipped from the beginning: while his "office probably invest[ed] him
with some of the illusion necessary to allure," her charms did not
similarly blind him.

> Mr. Helstone neither had, nor professed to have, Mr. Yorke's
> absorbing passion for her; he had none of the humble reverence
> which seemed to subdue most of her suitors; he saw her more
> as she really was than the rest did; he was, consequently, more
> master of her and himself. (61)

Within a short time after his marriage Helstone justified the deepest
fears of Shirley that a wife becomes "a burden and a bore" (242) to
her husband: "*His* wife, after a year or two, was of no great importance to him in any shape" (61–62). The rector's lack of sympathy
with Mary Cave reduces her from a quiet woman with some "capacity
for feeling and loving" (62) into a still monument of lifeless clay. Her
victimization takes the form of a neglect that is no less cruel for being
emotional. Her death represents the fate of women who seek to
conform to the demands of a corrupt institution. She is, Gilbert and
Gubar observe, "an emblem, a warning that the fate of women inhab-

iting a male-controlled society involves suicidal self-renunciation."[8]
Caroline, then, encounters two examples of the severe limitations
marriage imposes on a woman: both her aunt and her mother have
experienced the brutality of male authority within the domestic
sphere.

Since the Misses Mann and Ainley apparently exist apart from
the mainstream of domestic life, they at first seem to offer a way out
of the difficulties of marriage. Society despises them for their failure
to marry: Caroline's housemaid expresses what is perhaps a general
suspicion that their lives of celibacy are "selfish" (196) because they
do not obviously tend to others' needs. Robert Moore finds Miss
Mann sufficiently threatening to turn the rarely employed "lash of
[his] sarcasm" (198) on her. The freedom from family and home en-
joyed by the old maids does give them a potentially subversive autonomy.[9] Caroline finds this aspect of the old maids' lives inspiring and
thinks she has met role models—women who have defined their own
occupations. But her enchantment with them is short-lived, for
Brontë has not allowed her old maids to explore the radical possibilities of their role. Miss Ainley, the more dynamic of the two, does not
truly exercise power over her own destiny. Her deepest allegiance is
to conventional religion, and her misplaced loyalty makes her "blind
to ecclesiastical defects" even in the least worthy of the curates (302).
In spite of the independence celibacy grants her, she is slavishly loyal
to the masculine authority of the church. When Shirley wishes to
devise the best plan of local relief for the poor, she naturally turns to
Miss Ainley.

> She, who knew them all, had studied their wants, had again and
> again felt in what way they might best be succoured . . . was fully
> competent to the undertaking[;] . . . she showed them in her an-
> swers how much and what serviceable knowledge she had ac-
> quired of the condition of her fellow-creatures round her. (301–2)

But her subservience to the church makes her value her own estimable expertise less than half-informed ecclesiastical advice: she feels
"she must consult the clergy: yes, on that point, she was peremptory . . . —it would, she averred, be presumption in her to take a
single step unauthorized by them" (302).

Caroline is initially impressed by the admirable inner strength

of both old maids. Miss Ainley's selfless generosity to the poor is the
sort of useful action the younger woman is longing to perform. But
Caroline's work under Miss Ainley's direction does not satisfy her
desire for a meaningful occupation: it "[brings] her neither health of
body nor continued peace of mind" (206). The kind of work possible
for single women oppresses rather than frees. Even governessing, to
which she looks for fulfillment, offers no escape: as Mrs. Pryor tells
her, it is a "sedentary, solitary, constrained, joyless, toilsome" occupation that involves a "dreadful crushing of the animal spirits" (423).
The single woman who becomes a governess manifestly puts herself
in a class below that of her employers, who keep their distance from
her. The life of an unmarried woman in England involves at once the
exploitation of her energies and the suffocation of her feelings. Only
for a short time can the intelligent and percipient Caroline honestly
believe that

> her [own] love of nature, . . . her sense of beauty, . . . her more
> varied and fervent emotions, . . . her deeper power of
> thought, . . . her wider capacity to comprehend, [were nothing]
> compared to the practical excellence of this good woman [Miss
> Ainley]. (204–5)

She realizes that to embrace any conventional unmarried life is to
discard these valuable capabilities. The old maids quickly fade from
prominence in *Shirley* as Caroline finds that her earliest judgment of
their unselfishness was accurate: "Is there not a terrible hollowness,
mockery, want, craving, in that existence which is given away to
others, for want of something of your own to bestow it on?" (194). A
woman like Miss Ainley eventually stands revealed, like governesses, as masculine society's tool; she cares for the poor whom industrialists callously neglect, yet she receives "but little reward" from the
rich for her actions (204). Although the old maids do not belong to
the working classes, they provide examples of social injustice just as
surely as William Farren does.

The use of upper- and middle-class characters as victims is by
no means typical of the condition-of-England novel. In this respect
the only comparable work is *Hard Times,* in which Louisa Gradgrind's
victimization offers some of the book's most trenchant industrial criticism. But even in that book Louisa's role is partially balanced by the

presence of other female sufferers who are of the lower class: Rachael and Sissy Jupe. Brontë's presentation of female victims effects a significant change in the representation of society's structure. In the other novels class is the great barrier that divides English society: the successful resolution of the contemporary crisis involves women's reaching over it, often first toward their impoverished sisters. In *Shirley* there is a tripartite social structure: men, at the top of the pyramid of power, exercise their tyranny both over workingmen and over women, whose only representatives come from the upper classes. Brontë's critique has justly been called "a conception which attempts to foreground class and gender as problems of equal weight and complexity."[10]

This design closely links women and workers as the two victims of male malfeasance. As ever, there is a certain natural sympathy between the heroines and the oppressed workers, one that permits William Farren to converse freely and comfortably with Shirley and Caroline. Gilbert and Gubar seem justified in arguing that workers express women's anger—that both the rioters at Robert's mill and the prototypical vengeful laborers Caroline describes function as doubles for the heroines.[11] But the novel's association of the two groups extends beyond these instances. The two groups have almost precisely the same specific reasons for discontent. The workers chafe under the masters' authority because labor-saving machinery has denied them employment; the women suffer because patriarchal convention denies them "a profession—a trade" (256). Louisa Gradgrind of *Hard Times* also feels the heavy hand of the same patriarchy that oppresses workers. But Dickens does not explicitly invoke Louisa's femaleness to classify her sufferings—he does not discuss the larger pattern of women's suffering. Similarly, Gaskell does not point out the feminist implications of Esther's descent into prostitution in *Mary Barton*. We recall that Spacks has observed of such other condition-of-England novels that "[h]idden analogies between the plight of women and of workmen surge beneath the surface . . . ";[12] in *Shirley* these analogies lie on the surface. Whereas miniaturization in the other novels ensures that one downtrodden woman will implicitly evoke others, nothing could be more explicit than Caroline's bitterly ironic lament, "Old maids, like the houseless and unemployed poor, should not ask for a place and an occupation in the world: the demand disturbs the happy and rich" (441). Where critics have rarely noticed the other novels' linkage of spheres, many have remarked on the "analogous kind of enchainment,"[13] the "parallels,"[14] "[t]he analogies . . . potentially so revolutionary"[15] between the plights of workers and women. Brontë hammers home the point that industrial patriarchy exercises a widespread tyranny over English life. If, as Elaine Showalter suggests, "Protest fiction . . . translated the felt pain and oppression of women into the championship of mill-workers, child laborers, prostitutes, and slaves,"[16] then *Shirley* is a protest fiction that needs no interpreter.

The insistent presentation of women as victims directs our attention, and the novel's social analysis, toward a large-scale crisis in sexual roles in English society. Caroline ultimately makes her own assessment of what has gone wrong and how the situation can best be resolved.

> Existence never was originally meant to be that useless, blank, pale, slow-trailing thing it often becomes to many. . . .
> . . . I believe single women should have more to do—better chances of interesting and profitable occupation than they possess now. (441)

And, although she professes to be dealing with the unmarried, her plea for active involvement in society extends to married women as well. She takes as her example "Solomon's virtuous woman," who "was a manufacturer . . . an agriculturist. . . . a manager" at the same time that she was a rock in whom "the heart of her husband safely trusted" (442–43). Caroline calls for all women to be given "a field in which their faculties may be exercised and grow" (443). In the sense that extensive observation has led to a diagnosis of the problem facing society, Caroline's train of thought is reminiscent of the social analysis other condition-of-England heroines conduct. There is, however, a crucial difference: Brontë's heroine excludes the condition of workers from consideration when she makes her most wide-ranging assessment of English life. In *Shirley* the displacement of workers by women as victims of patriarchal society eventually makes women's condition the almost exclusive focus of the novel.

As this displacement makes feminist issues an explicit focus of the narrative's concern, it pushes labor relations out of the center of the picture. It seems that, once the Luddites and Farren have established the social frame, Caroline and later Shirley take over the novel with their own, personal concerns. The problems of industrialization do not disappear, but the vitality of the issue is sapped by the novel's preoccupation with what the heroines must endure. As the working class recedes, women do not really bask in their dominance of the narrative; rather, they lose a crucial base of their power. For, when the poor do not vividly exist as a problem that demands immediate attention, there is less impetus for English society to look for new answers from heroines rather than old answers from patriarchs. And when women come to the fore as a separate victimized class, their attempts at self-assertion begin to look like selfish special pleading rather than wise industrial counsel.

Like the other condition-of-England novels, *Shirley* presents a society with a problem in desperate need of management: the disgruntlement of workers and (particularly) women. But, unfortunately for the fate of subversive feminist power, the problem can be managed by men. Despite the seemingly insurrectionary passions its actions arouse, the patriarchy remains firmly in control. While John Thornton in *North and South* comes in contact with his workers only after the intervention of Margaret Hale, Robert Moore demonstrates an early acquaintance with his workers. Brontë depicts his direct supervision of his workers before either heroine has entered the narrative:

> Mr. Moore stood at the entrance to watch them pass: he counted them as they went by; to those who came rather late he said a word of reprimand. . . . Neither master nor overlooker [Joe Scott] spoke savagely . . . , though it appeared both were rigid, for they fined a delinquent who came considerably too late. (70)

Robert is also responsible for more extreme sanctions, as when he engineers the arrest of the agitator Moses Barraclough. Other novels of the genre present industrialists at the same work, but differences are more significant than similarities. When masters such as Sir Matthew Dowling of *Michael Armstrong* or the sweatshop owners of Kingsley's *Alton Locke* are shown conducting their business, the real focus for the scene is the victimization of the working class. But Robert's actions do not imply any abuse of his employees—Barraclough does not even work for Moore. After describing morning at the mill, Brontë specifically excludes Moore from the company of "[c]hild-torturers, slave masters and drivers" (71).[17] Neither is Thornton a member of this fraternity, but his most direct assertion of authority over his workers comes in the riot scene at his mill, in which only the assistance of Margaret prevents his assassination. Robert Moore is in no immediate danger of death when he deals with his workers: his authority triumphs. (Even the later attempt on his life is made not by dissident workers but by "Michael Hartley, the half-crazed weaver" [726].)

Moreover, Robert, unlike any other man in the condition-of-England novel, can effectively exercise benevolence without female help. Moore makes amends for his earlier haughtiness to William Farren by arranging the gardening job that leaves this once victimized worker "varry well off" (366). Robert by himself can take the reforming actions necessary to quiet the contemporary crisis. Like Thornton and Mr. Carson of Gaskell's *Mary Barton*, he comes to reassess his industrial policy. As he explains to Hiram Yorke:

> Something there is to look to, Yorke, beyond a man's personal interest: beyond the advancement of well-laid schemes; beyond even the discharge of dishonouring debts. To respect himself, a man must believe he renders justice to his fellow-men. Unless I am more considerate to ignorance, more forbearing to suffering than I have hitherto been, I shall scorn myself as grossly unjust. (616)

Like the other masters before him, he has recognized the necessity of extending the benevolence the heroine has discerned in him from the private to the public sphere. He ultimately determines to "take more workmen; give better wages; lay wiser and more liberal plans; do some good; be less selfish" (733). But the impetus for Moore's change of heart does not come from a woman's teaching. It is his visit to other parts of the country that has instilled this new resolve in him:

> While I was in Birmingham [and London], I looked a little into reality, considered closely, and at their source, the causes of the present troubles of this country. . . . I saw what taught my brain a new lesson, and filled my breast with fresh feelings. (616)

Significantly, he fails to mention Caroline's exhortations or her suggested literary model, *Coriolanus*. Patriarchy is sufficiently responsive to the industrial situation to make mid-course corrections. There is no room for women to insinuate themselves into economic relationships.

The way power is wielded has undergone no real reform. After all, the implementation of Robert's good intentions comes only once the Orders in Council have been repealed: his desire for good labor relations waits upon financial convenience. Roslyn Belkin argues that his language indicates continued hostility to true industrial reform.

> *"Now,"* he declares, "I can take more workmen. . . . " The word "now" poses an interesting question . . . about the controlling classes in British society: how would these men react in the event of another such crisis? Part of the answer may lie in William Farren's conclusion that " 'the people' will never have any true friends but theirsel'n."[18]

Another part of the answer may be that a patriarchal society limits the ways in which men can react to social crises. Faced by another upsurge of labor unrest, Moore would undoubtedly take the same actions: he insists even in his moment of confession to Yorke that he "should resist a riotous mob just as heretofore" (616). All that patriarchy can do is make a superficial response to an urgent problem. But this response is sufficient to deaden the widespread cries for industrial change in *Shirley*.

Robert derives considerable strength from the support of the Established Church. In the other condition-of-England novels the church is not a major player in the industrial action. When individual clergymen appear they are generally well-intentioned but powerless, like Reverend Bell in *Michael Armstrong* or the pastors of *Helen Fleetwood*. The only minister who sets himself against the interests of the working class is Alton Locke's cousin George, whose greed has clearly perverted his proper role. But in *Shirley* the clergy stands as a matter of course with industrialists rather than with their victims. Brontë realizes that the church has a vested interest in preserving the patriarchal social structure in which it flourishes: as Gilbert and Gubar observe, "[N]ot only is the church an arm of the state; both

church and state depend on exclusion and coercion which are economic, social, and sexual."[19] So, it is eminently logical for Reverend
Helstone to take up arms in defense of Robert Moore's mill; he explains, "I was there only to support the law, to play my part as a man
and a Briton; which characters I deem quite compatible with those of
the priest and Levite, in their highest sense" (411). In *Shirley* these
characters are not only compatible, but nearly identical. Although the
curates' offenses against human decency take place on a much
smaller scale than Robert's, they provide some of the most vivid
examples of men's abuse of power. The opening scene of the novel
shows how the three take advantage of their landladies by their "system of mutual invasion" (10) and by their rude personal conduct that
(in Malone's case) includes a "manner of command" (11). William
Farren remarks upon their haughty attitude to the lower classes:
"[T]hey talk to poor folk fair as if they thought they were beneath
them. They're allus magnifying their office" (364). The curates are
aware that, as clergymen, they are officers in the ruling class—the
second lieutenants of English society. The identification of church
with patriarchy gives them a prominent position among those who
take advantage of the less privileged.

But this relationship between the Church of England and England's leaders is a symbiotic one. While the clergy gains the privileges of membership in the ruling patriarchy, the patriarchy gains
an ideology that protects it from the potentially revolutionary power
of the disadvantaged. The piety of the family of Donne's landlady
protects the curates from her wrath: her husband "had been a church-
warden, and was indulgent to the clergy" (15). Piety protects industrialism as well as the church from the encroachment of women. Miss
Ainley's subservience to the clergy guarantees that the fulfillment of
Shirley's desire to help the poor will be achieved under the aegis of
the rectors' approval. Although Shirley obtains their unqualified as-
sent to Miss Ainley's plan through clever manipulation, Helstone
becomes aware that "female craft was at work, and that something
in petticoats was somehow trying underhand to acquire too much
influence" (305). With his arrogant behavior toward the assembled
women and his observation to Shirley that her "little female ma-
noeuvres don't blind me" (306), he takes pains to underline his own
final authority in the matter:

> He smiled a little grimly, and began to write [his authorization].
> He soon interrupted himself to ask questions, and consult his
> brethren, disdainfully lifting his glance over the curly heads of
> the two girls, and the demure caps of the elder ladies, to meet
> the winking glasses and gray pates of the priests. (306)

In this case the need for clerical consent has prevented women from
using the condition of the poor as an occasion for the full exercise of
their suppressed capabilities.

However, the church proves its ideological power over female
activity most clearly through more indirect means than overt clerical
coercion. Chapter 7 of volume 2 opens with Shirley's radical rejection
of patriarchal religious tradition.[20] Having decided not to take part
in the evening's church service, she proceeds to abjure the conventional Miltonic Eve in favor of a majestic titaness. But, subsequently,
as she and Caroline sit talking to William Farren about the industrial
situation (exercising a titaness-like freedom of thought), masculine
authority reenters the scene in the form of Joe Scott. Joe is clearly at
an intellectual disadvantage in the discussion that follows, yet he
presents the heroines with a religious injunction that gives them
considerable trouble:

> I've a great respect for the doctrines delivered in the second
> chapter of St. Paul's first Epistle to Timothy. . . .
>   Let the woman learn in silence, with all subjection. I suffer
> not a woman to teach, nor to usurp authority over the man; but
> to be in silence. For Adam was first formed, then Eve. (370)

Scott provides a reminder to the women that their religion, far from
allowing the majesty of an Eve, insists on the absolute primacy of all
Adams.

Both Shirley and Caroline attempt without success to defend
their own vision of woman's role against the onslaught of this conventional religious dogma. Caroline suggests that this passage is susceptible to an alternate reading more congenial to her feminist incli-
nations. As Joe accurately observes, however, "That willn't wash,
Miss" (371). For this doctrine, like the other manifestations of patriarchal power in the novel, is so tightly constructed that there are no

loopholes through which heroines can slip unnoticed. The only way
to deal with such an overtly misogynistic ideology is to reject it; as
we shall see, women toy with this option but ultimately cannot embrace it. In this particular case, the church's hold over Caroline and
Shirley negates the feminist potential of their earlier musings. Because the church exists here, as in no other condition-of-England
novel, as the proper source of all personal ideology, the heroines can
find no escape from Scott's appeal to this source. They have found
that the church, to which they must submit if they are to remain part
of their society, has conspired with patriarchy to constrict their roles
as women. Surely it is no coincidence that the next chapter of the
book finds them frozen between action and passive acquiescence at
the scene of the battle at the mill. Their surprising powerlessness is
the result of their encounter with the limits of female authority in a
society possessed of the patriarchal power to manage the industrial
situation and the ecclesiastical power to provide the justification for
masculine authority.

Confronted with a patriarchy of such strength, most of the women
of *Shirley* choose to remain subservient to men rather than try to
assume a leadership role themselves. The novel's older women never
even question their subservient position. Hortense Moore unthink-
ingly accepts her role as Robert's housekeeper and saves her energies
for battling the forces of English impropriety. The old maids cannot
exploit the radical possibilities of their celibacy. Even Mrs. Pryor,
who has been victimized by both her former employers and her de-
ranged husband, retains her allegiance to England's male-dominated
social order. Age and experience have given her a kind of regal stat-
ure, but her rule extends over only an insignificant kingdom—"of all
the high and rigid Tories, she is queen" (220). She is a parodic version
of the queenly women of other novels.

The heroines, in contrast, explore the possibilities of female rebellion. Early on, Caroline complains to Robert that the sort of occupation most congenial to her is off limits to those of her sex:

> I should like an occupation; and if I were a boy, it would not be
> so difficult to find one. . . .
>   I could be apprenticed to your trade—the cloth trade: I could
> learn it of you, as we are distant relations. I would do the count-

ing-house work, keep the books, and write the letters, while you
went to market. (81)

But employment in the public sphere is closed to Caroline, and she
is doomed to remain a frustrated accountant. Once Robert denies her
the occupation of wifehood, she looks for a way to get around the
conventional joblessness of womankind. However, her quiet attempts to escape her own oppression fail: she finds that the old maids
and governesses are even more in thrall to social authority than she.
It is at this point that her rebellious streak finds expression in her
friendship with Shirley.

Shirley enters the novel at a period of despair for Caroline,
whose ill health and faded looks have just begun to call attention to
themselves. Shirley, with her social and economic power, infuses
new life into Caroline's conception of English womanhood: Caroline
finds that her new friend possesses all the advantages she herself has
lacked. She is, as Bernadette Bertrandias has observed, Caroline's
double, who participates in public affairs as Caroline cannot.[21]
Shirley frequently asserts her power by aggressively adopting a masculine identity: "I am indeed no longer a girl, but quite a woman, and
something more. . . . They gave me a man's name; I hold a man's
position: it is enough to inspire me with a touch of manhood" (224).
She is certainly a woman unlike any Caroline has encountered before:
she runs an estate, she speaks to men with the boldness of an equal,
she discusses the management of the mill with Moore. Shirley appears to hold out more than one possibility to Caroline—that a
woman can find a satisfactory role for herself, one not based upon
self-abnegation, and that women have the potential not only to survive in society but also to rule over it. Shirley, after all, has sufficient
prestige in local society to claim fairly for herself the title of "the first
gentleman in Briarfield" (374).

But Shirley's greatest contribution to an ideology of powerful
womanhood comes in her elaboration of a feminist mythology. It is
Shirley who, unlike any other heroine in the condition-of-England
novel, expresses awareness of the subversive power women can
have. Her evocation of mermaids, those creatures who, according to
Auerbach, "typify the mysterious, broadly and evocatively demonic
powers of womanhood in general,"[22] reveals the supernatural might
latent in Caroline herself. For the mermaid whom she envisions as

having the power to lure men to their deaths has, she says to Caroline, "a face in the style of yours," although the eyes are different. The mermaid is a "monstrous likeness of ourselves" who will confront the women alone in the light of the matriarchal moon[23] and claim kinship with them. By presenting to a dubious Caroline—who cries, "[S]he is not like us" (276)—the possibility of a power beyond the ken of patriarchal society, Shirley is arguing for the same sort of hidden energy that transforms the societies of the other condition-of-England novels. For, like those manipulative heroines Sybil Gerard and Lady Eleanor in *Sybil* and *Alton Locke*, the mermaid is capable of exercising an irresistible power over the men who rule society.

Shirley provides not only proof of present power but also a mythological history of awe-inspiring female forebears. Shirley proposes an excursion to the forest of Nunnwood to visit ruins, and Caroline suggests significantly that the journey cannot appropriately be made in the company of men. As Linda C. Hunt notes, "'Nunnwood' and the nunnery at its heart . . . symbolize a mythic, matriarchal world" of female friendship,[24] but they also symbolize a potential source of ideological sustenance to women searching for a place in English society. Shirley's vision of the first woman provides the clearest indication of what could be recaptured by embracing a mythical past. Unlike Milton's history, Shirley's depicts an Adam of no perceptible force and an Eve with titanic powers.

> The first woman's breast that heaved with life on this world yielded the daring which could contend with Omnipotence: the strength which could bear a thousand years of bondage, . . . the unexhausted life and uncorrupted excellence, sisters to immortality, which, after milleniums of crimes, struggles, and woes, could conceive and bring forth a Messiah. (360)

Shirley's Eve has practically taken over the role of creator from the Jehovah to whom she speaks face to face. When Shirley declines to leave "my mother Eve" (361) and enter church, we see the practical implications of her mythology. She is rejecting the church's view of Eve (and hence all women) as incorrigibly irresponsible in favor of her own vision of a powerful, queenly Eve. Her embrace of matrilineal authority seems to enable her subsequent discussion of the industrial situation with William Farren. By harking back to female rather than male mythology, women can presumably fan the flames of their rebellion and seize the power that myth offers. And, by implication, they can wield this force to alter the unjust balance of power in English society.

But, just as Joe Scott's reassertion of the dicta of patriarchal religion stymies the women's free discussion of politics with a worker, social reality undermines Shirley's powerful myth. Her observation that "[t]hey gave me a man's name" is all too revealing: her wealth and power, as well as her name, are not self-created but derived from a patriarchal system of inheritance. Her adoption of a masculine identity is ultimately not liberating. The very necessity of becoming a sort of man in order to experience the full advantages of her position is more than a little disquieting: Gilbert and Gubar suggest that "independence is so closely associated with men that it confines Shirley to a kind of male mimicry."[25] The heroines of other novels did not have to deny their female identity to assert themselves, because femininity provided an adequate base of power. But this is not the case in *Shirley*. In any event, Shirley's masculine persona does not fool anyone into giving her the rights of men. She herself treats "Captain Keeldar" as a bit of a joke; in one of her "off-hand speeches" she declares:

> [I]f she had had the bliss to be really Shirley Keeldar, Esq., Lord of the Manor of Briarfield, there was not a single fair one in this and the two neighbouring parishes, whom she should have felt disposed to request to become Mrs. Keeldar, lady of the manor. (234)

When Mrs. Pryor takes this declaration seriously, only Shirley's strength of character prevents her from laughing at the other woman's gullibility. Mrs. Pryor's concern is misplaced; no one treats Shirley's assumption of masculinity with sufficient respect either to condemn her or to accord her the privileges of men. Even when Helstone entrusts his household to her as he would to "a gentleman" (374), he is more significantly excluding her from participation in the battle at the mill. Hiram Yorke's attitude to Shirley's boldness provides a still better example of patriarchy's response to her superficially subversive pose. Shirley rates him soundly for his classism and the insubstantiality of his philanthropy, but he does not take offense:

"From a man, Mr. Yorke would not have borne this language very patiently, nor would he have endured it from some women; but he accounted Shirley both honest and pretty, and her plain-spoken ire amused him" (415). Shirley's masculine identity is not threatening; initial appearances to the contrary, it signifies innocuous playfulness rather than a radical reorientation of social attitudes.

Shirley's feminist myths and her promises of female solidarity prove equally ephemeral. Hunt points out that the journey Caroline and Shirley plan to Nunnwood, symbol of a matriarchal past, "significantly never takes place."[26] For Shirley has evoked a feminist past that is glorious but imaginary. The real antecedent of these heroines, as Gilbert and Gubar observe, is the hopelessly reactionary Mrs. Pryor: "Formal and reticent, she is the prior woman, prior to Shirley as well as Caroline, because her experience, not the woman-Titan's, is typically female in the society these young women inhabit."[27] The visionary myth Shirley expresses so powerfully cannot be appropriated by women whose role models are subservient and passive rather than indomitably heroic. Similarly, the possibility of female solidarity raised by the heroines' friendship is not fulfilled, because roles typical of a male-dominated society come to dominate their friendship. Caroline and Shirley dream of a visit to Nunnwood that will exclude the disruptive presence of men, but even their friendship is contaminated by patriarchal values. Shirley cannot speak of her jealousy of Moore's effect on Caroline without using her male persona and images of typically male violence:

> I feel disposed to call him out, if I could only get a trustworthy second: I feel desperately irritated: I felt so last night, and have felt it all day.
>
> ... Upon my word, I could have found it in my heart to have dogged Moore yesterday evening with dire intent: I have pistols, and can use them. (294)

Here is the taint of the same aggressive hostility that has gotten Robert into such deep trouble with his workers; it is not the attitude likely to lead to significant change in the modus operandi of society.

But what finally unsolders the friendship of the two women is not their arrogation of male vices but, rather, their resumption of conventional sexual roles. Caroline's second psychosomatic illness dates from the moment in which she becomes fully aware that Shirley has a greater attractive pull on Robert than she herself does. She has spent the evening at Hollow's Cottage displaying all her alluring vitality for the benefit of both Robert and Louis Moore, but Shirley by the simple instrument of a bouquet of flowers makes a greater impression on the brothers. After this crucial scene (appropriately enough, the end of vol. 2) we do not see the two heroines together again. Brontë indicates that Shirley and Caroline continue to visit each other, but there is no scene of direct contact between the two. Their friendship and the feminist potential within it have been effectively dissolved.[28] Female solidarity has been broken because the two heroines have fallen into the conventional role of the husband-hunter who competes with other women for men. Like Shirley's unsuccessful toying with masculine identity, transcendent femininity has been sabotaged by the ineluctable influence of a highly efficient patriarchal society.

The third volume depicts the inevitable fate of women in patriarchal society, however intelligent and potentially rebellious they may be. Caroline retreats to the waiting arms of her mother and accepts her model of womanly behavior; Mrs. Pryor can now proudly claim of her daughter, "[T]he heart and the brain are *mine*: the germs are from *me*" (487). All question of Caroline's effecting change in the status of workers or the organization of society is over: her long search for a suitable occupation has come to an end.

Shirley, however, is still a figure of considerable energy. But the independence and economic power she retains will go the way of her visionary feminism. If her break with Caroline marks the end of her world of titanic feminism, the appearance of Louis Moore is the beginning of the end of her qualified independence. Her relationship with Louis has some promising characteristics. She has consulted her own judgment and affections in choosing him (Mr. Sympson terms such independence "indecorous!—unwomanly!" [533]). His economic position is considerably less secure than her own, so that the balance of power in the marriage should be decidedly in her favor. Moreover, Louis speaks of how she has made him "worship" her (597); hope briefly raises its head that Shirley, like Sybil Gerard, may find a subversive means of empowerment through him, despite her earlier failures.

But Louis is about to complete the transformation of Shirley from independent landlord to subservient wife. He takes control of her just as he, alone of *Shirley*'s characters, for a time takes charge of the novel through first-person narration. As he realizes that he has become subject to Shirley, he vows to alter the balance of power in the relationship:

> I will make privileges for myself: every feature of her face, her bright eyes, her lips, shall go through each change they know, for my pleasure: display each exquisite variety of glance and curve, to delight—thrill—perhaps, more hopelessly to enchain me. If I *must* be her slave, I will not lose my freedom for nothing. (599)

He plans to make her completely subject to his control: in a deft bit of foreshadowing, Brontë ends the chapter with him "pocket[ing] all the property" (599) that Shirley has absentmindedly left behind. Before long he will similarly appropriate her wealth and power.

Under the influence of Louis, Shirley once produced a different version of her myth of primordial womanhood. This devoir depicts a woman who has some of the might of the titaness Eve: she feels "something within her [that] stirred disquieted, and restlessly asserted a God-given strength" (550). This woman, however, cannot find satisfaction until she is claimed by a "Son of God" who becomes her "glorious Bridegroom" (552). With Shirley's rekindling of interest in the ideas of this old essay, her political consciousness takes several giant steps backward. Moglen aptly observes:

> This story belies the equality claimed by Shirley for the first mother and father. It offers, instead, in its vision of subsequent generations, a deeply personal mythology which justifies inequality and female dependence by reestablishing the patriarchal hierarchy.[29]

Yet this reactionary myth proves to be the dogma Shirley finally accepts. Brontë's description of her heroine's relationship with Louis is rife with metaphors of the breaking in of wild animals. At an earlier stage of their acquaintance Louis demonstrated his power over her by ordering her to recite a poem significantly entitled "Le Cheval

Dompté" (the tamed horse); now he continues the taming of his "Lioness" (689) until he has beaten her into sweetly dependent submission. Directly after her acceptance of his proposal, she indicates the extent of her enslavement in an astonishingly servile speech:

> "Mr. Moore," said she, looking up with a sweet, open, earnest countenance, "teach me and help me to be good. I do not ask you to take off my shoulders all the cares and duties of property; but I ask you to share the burden, and to show me how to sustain my part well." (712)

It is difficult to believe that this is the same woman who started a relief program for the poor, made politics her habitual study, and arranged a loan to Robert Moore. Despite her disclaimer above, she completes her submission to Louis by turning over full control of her estate to him: "[H]e was virtually master of Fieldhead, weeks before he became so nominally. . . . She abdicated without a word or a struggle" (730). Shirley, once the proud advocate of feminist power, has been conquered by her encounter with masculine authority. The words that come to mind here are those that Bertrandias applies to the entire third volume—"Dévalorisation, désacralisation."[30] It is a sad transformation that amounts almost to profanation.

Yet Brontë has demonstrated throughout *Shirley* that there is no other way for women to exist in English society. Even before the end of her search for an occupation, Caroline realizes that social change can occur only through the agency of men. Consequently, she addresses her inward meditations on the subject of work for women to the "Men of England" (443). The only possible alternative to subservience for women is emigration, the course chosen by Rose and Jessy Yorke. There are, of course, precedents for this move in other condition-of-England novels. But the situation of other emigrants is far more hopeful than that found in *Shirley*. America offers Alton Locke a chance of recuperation and eventual return to England; Canada offers Mary Barton a new social landscape in which she and Jem Wilson can build a better life; the Continent offers Mary Brotherton scope for the reconstruction of society. But the journey of the Yorke girls leads them into a barren, nameless exile: the vivacious Jessy will die in a foreign country after a life of "frequent sorrows," while Rose will become "a lonely emigrant in some region of the southern hemisphere" (167). They may have escaped the threat to their individuality, but they have left human society behind.

Despite the novel's grim conclusion that English society affords no possibility of female self-assertion, Shirley expresses lingering ambivalence at the dispersal of her power. Even after her demure acceptance of Louis's proposal, she strains against his yoke in trivial ways that are part of what Margaret Miller calls "[h]er disinclination to submit to her own suppression."[31]

> Louis had presaged difficulties, and he had found them: in fact, his mistress had shown herself exquisitely provoking; putting off her marriage day by day, week by week, month by month. . . .
> It had needed a sort of tempest-shock to bring her to the point. (729)

Brontë has proven that female power is illusory, but she is reluctant to relinquish it altogether. Even once her heroines have been forced to acknowledge the authority of patriarchal society, they persist in the small gestures of independence that are the novel's most pitiful actions. At best feminism in *Shirley* is a fragmentary affair, like the ruins of the ancient nunnery or the piece of old cross in Caroline's garden (731): the abilities women have can be expressed only in bits and pieces, not integrated into a real challenge to English society. Shirley's treatment of Louis's books, sadly, symbolizes the sole effect women can have on a male-dominated world:

> She had taken a crayon from the tutor's desk, and was drawing little leaves, fragments of pillars, broken crosses, on the margin of the book.
> [Louis:] " . . . my books would now, as erst, be unsafe with you. My newly-bound St. Pierre would soon be like my Racine: Miss Keeldar, her mark—traced on every page." (554)

Women are condemned to the margins of history; they are capable only of actions with slight effects, gestures that will amuse or annoy men but never threaten them.

Even this minimal empowerment of women vanishes in the novel's conclusion, which Brontë has sardonically entitled "The Winding-Up."[32] The events that constitute the novel's tying of loose ends provide a conventional happy ending of marriage and prosperity, yet in *Shirley* these familiar resolutions seem to mock the heroines' aspirations.[33] Nothing has been achieved in the course of the novel—except the exposure of the heroines' powerlessness. The problems of workers and women no longer seem so urgent, but only because patriarchy has asserted its authority and quieted dissent. Industrialists may have superficially altered their behavior, but they have left intact their economic philosophy. For the present the oppressed remain oppressed; the future looks even worse. Moore plans to uproot the forest of Nunnwood, the last vestige of feminarchic Nature, in order to expand his industrial holdings. Even though Caroline openly opposes this prospective violation by her husband-to-be, his "prophecies [are], partially, at least, fulfilled" (739)—the only visions in this novel that come true. Robert consigns both Caroline and Shirley to the role of Sunday school teachers; they are to become tools of the patriarchal religion they fought against for so long. They are, in fact, to lose their identities completely: our last view of them comes through the eyes of the narrator's aged housekeeper, who remembers them not as Shirley and Caroline but, instead, as "Mrs. Louis" and "Mrs. Robert." They have become appendages of their husbands. Only Shirley's "een that pierced a body through" (740) remain to haunt us.

The implications of 1811–12 for the condition of England in 1849 offer further grounds for despair. Brontë opens the novel with an indication of how the situation has worsened since Shirley's day: "Of late years, an abundant shower of curates has fallen upon the north of England" (7). Patriarchal religion in its least appealing form has spread over the landscape just like Robert's mills. Even the fragmented feminism of Caroline and Shirley's time has been extirpated by an ever more powerful industrialism. Martha, the old housekeeper, indicates that the now ravaged Hollow was once the home of fairishes, magical creatures of the same ilk as Shirley's demonic mermaids and godlike titanesses. Shirley, a "Peri" (597) with a hand as "fine as a fairy's" (227), is perhaps one of these beings. Although, as Martha informs the narrator, there have been no fairishes seen for fifty years, they have been heard within the last forty: their twilight is coincident with Shirley's final struggles for independence. Despite the failure of her vision, Shirley remains the closest thing to a condition-of-England heroine in the novel that bears her name. The whiff of rebellion she represents survives, in her piercing gaze, every effort to complete her disempowerment. So, the most damning indictment of contemporary British society that Brontë. through Martha, makes is that "there is no such ladies now-a-days" (740). Society has lost its last hope for the sort of transformation achieved by the women of other novels.

With the novel's final reminder that its events are historical rather than contemporary, we are in any case brought back to an aspect of the novel that virtually precludes radical social transformation. The novel, unlike the others in the genre, is set in the past. As Jacob Korg notes, even within the present time of the novel the past determines events:

> [N]early all the significant facts of the novel are already established when it opens. The two pairs of lovers are already in love. . . . The most exciting actions, like the battle at the mill or Shirley's clash with her uncle, do not develop the plot but simply reveal character or attitudes. Revelation rather than narration is, in fact, the method of *Shirley*.[34]

There is no question of any significant change in circumstances, either of the individual characters or their situations. Whereas the other condition-of-England novels end at the brink of a future that is indeterminate, *Shirley*'s future is the contemporary world of 1849. Brontë's readers know that the situation of workers and women remains unaltered in the modern age; they are aware that a feminist millenium has not arrived.

So, the ending of *Shirley* is preordained: it must be a hopeless one for its advocates of radical change. The limited access to traditionally female sources of power, the strength of the patriarchy, and the unavoidable pastness of the novel determine the outcome of women's struggle for power. The subversive powers of a Margaret Hale, a Sissy Jupe, or a Sybil Gerard are simply not available to Caroline Helstone and Shirley Keeldar. The myths they colorfully elaborate for themselves are not adequate substitutes for the genuine authority that runs beneath the surface of other women's lives. While *Shirley*'s explicitly feminist impulses may not doom its heroines to conventional fates, they do indicate an overcompensation for a weak position in society. Their attempts to empower themselves through this mythology ultimately fail because there is an insufficient social basis for their ambitions. When women are denied the cover of domesticity and the toehold of cracks in the patriarchal social structure, they cannot climb to the fortified summit of English society.

Chapter 5

"Of course, I don't give any orders": The Retreat to Passivity and the End of Female Empowerment

Shirley depicts a world in which oppressive male power structures are firmly in place and in which there is little opportunity for women to work for the transformation of society. The novel's pessimism, so distant from the outlook of the other fictions we have examined, is unfortunately not a temporary aberration but instead a harbinger of the decay of the condition-of-England genre. For Charlotte Brontë's despairing acknowledgment in 1849 that female empowerment was merely illusory anticipates the judgment of social novelists in the mid-1850s and 1860s. Authors such as Dickens and Gaskell, who had previously written condition-of-England fiction, could no longer envision revolutionary social change initiated by women. George Eliot, coming late to the topic of disturbed class relations, retrospectively assessed the 1830s as an age of masculine ascendancy.

Unlike Brontë, who protests the failure of feminist power as she charts it, novelists in the next two decades seem to countenance the suppression of women in a reinvigorated patriarchy. But, as we shall ultimately see, these later novels are not self-consciously reactionary battle cries but predictably straitened responses to a less volatile social situation. Writers no longer saw around them the preconditions for a condition-of-England analysis: a society in crisis, a breakdown in class relations, and a need for visionary solutions. Although novelists show an enduring interest in social problems and injustice, they no longer look to women for transformative solutions. It seems that the onset of an age of political stasis had removed the need for the imaginative ascription of power to women; fictional narratives cease

ɔre the revolutionary potential of domesticity and instead en-
n oppressive model of female behavior. The structure of relationships that underlay the condition-of-England novel's radicalism
is gone: both the role played by women in the public sphere and the
special status granted to the domestic sphere have nearly vanished.

For all its assertion of patriarchal conventions, this later generation of fiction exhibits a lingering affinity for the concerns of the
defunct condition-of-England genre. I have chosen to discuss in this
chapter three novels that exemplify both the residual influence of the
earlier genre and the sharp departure from its feminist analysis.[1]
George Eliot's *Felix Holt* (1866) is so explicitly interested in class consciousness and social unrest that critics such as Williams and Gallagher have put it in the same category as condition-of-England novels.[2] No one would call Elizabeth Gaskell's *Wives and Daughters* (1866)
an industrial novel, but it shares with Gaskell's *Mary Barton* and *North
and South* an interest in the problems social and technological change
brings.[3] Dickens's *Little Dorrit* (1857) returns to some of his preoccu-
pations in *Hard Times:* the economic exploitation of the poor, the
emotional role of the family, the effectiveness of individual action.
Above all, these three books explore issues of female participation in
society: they present women who, like condition-of-England heroines, search for an appropriate and effective expression of their inherent energies.

But, if the issues are familiar, the answers are not. We shall find
that these novels explore condition-of-England issues to conservative
rather than radical ends. Although, to varying degrees, these books
identify problems that afflict English society, they do not mark existing hierarchies of power for imminent change—if only because patriarchy exercises such a firm grip on its citizens that revolution is
unthinkable. The domestic sphere, once the source of power and
social cohesion, has lost both its sacredness and its links to the world
of public affairs. Women are thus deprived of their excuse for inter-
ference and their means of potency; they can acquire only limited,
almost negligible power in either sphere. Those female energies that
the condition-of-England genre collected and made purposeful are
misappropriated to trivial or (at best) subservient ends. Fiction has
lost its taste for revolution and its appreciation of the latent capacities
of women. The heroines of these works are reduced to helpless acquiescence in the conventional power structures that ensnare them. Like

Molly Gibson of *Wives and Daughters,* who matter-of-factly reveals her own domestic disempowerment to Cynthia Kirkpatrick, these women see their plight as inevitable—"[O]f course, I don't give any orders" (253). Sadly, the particular form of imaginative liberation represented by the condition-of-England genre does not become a permanent part of English literary expression.

Writers in the late 1850s and 1860s depict social conditions that are remarkable for their essential stability in the face of continuing reasons for discontent. The owners of capital in *Little Dorrit'*s class system are invariably unproductive and venal. Their foremost representative is Merdle, who to nobody's knowledge "had ever done any good to any one, alive or dead, or to any earthly thing" (464). Yet no widespread unrest has arisen in response to the exploitation of the poor by men such as Casby, or the parasitism on the body politic by the Barnacles: characters such as Arthur Clennam are largely resigned to a world in which "all the gains [accrue] to the gluttons, knaves, and impostors" (489). Although there is considerable provocation for the sort of class conflict described in *Hard Times,* there is no evidence of any perceived crisis, whether based in class differences or not.

Felix Holt presents a similar absence of crisis in different terms. Felix is a strong exponent of class consciousness, with his deliberate espousal of the life of a proletarian and his commitment to benevolent demagoguery. But his awareness exists in isolation from any significant occasion for its exercise: there is no specific crisis confronting the lower classes that urgently needs to be addressed. We do not see poverty or hardship or even noteworthy exploitation of poor by rich. The drunken riot that embroils Felix in legal difficulties is precipitated by Transome's electioneering procedures, which arise from nothing more profound than individual greed. Indeed, Felix's exhortations to class solidarity constitute merely a vehicle for Eliot's denial of the validity of interclass resentments. Whereas the condition-of-England novel depicted the tangible basis for the anger of the poor, *Felix Holt* presents an ungrounded peevishness that is itself the only problem. Holt tells a small group on nomination day that workers should, instead of childishly seeking the vote, seek to change their frame of mind: "The way to get rid of folly is to get rid of vain expectations, and of thoughts that don't agree with the nature of things" (400).

While *Little Dorrit* provides no one to interpret social inequities, *Felix Holt* provides no social inequities to be interpreted. In both cases, because the explosive material and the detonator are not simultaneously present, there cannot be a real threat to English society that calls for a revolutionary response.[4]

Revolution, in any event, is inconceivable in these novels. The power structures in place may be oppressive and unjust, but they are strong. Like the patriarchy of *Shirley*, these hierarchies have a capacity for occasional self-correction, but they more frequently confront difficulties with implacable obduracy. Much of the chastening that the unjust receive by the end of *Little Dorrit* has a largely impersonal character. Merdle's downfall does not occur through human agency but, rather, as a result of his having reached the limits of the thievery he can hide from the public. Similarly, Mrs. Clennam is not struck dumb and immobile by someone's retributive act: her affliction, like the collapse of her home that precipitates it, is the cumulative result of her own actions over the years. Even Casby's final humiliation by his employee Pancks is presented as a phenomenon of physics rather than a willed action: "The Dock of the Steam-Tug, Pancks, had a leaden roof, which, frying in the very hot sunshine, may have heated the vessel" (664); Pancks's explosion is the natural result of years of abuse. In *Michael Armstrong* the ultimate collapse of Sir Matthew Dowling's world provided a foretaste of social apocalypse—a sign that English society was so corrupt that it required complete reconstruction. A different principle seems to be at work in the just deserts of these later books: a mechanistic vision of society akin to the contemporary belief in evolutionary social change that Brantlinger has identified. With particular reference to a *Chambers's Journal* article of 1851, he observes:

> [S]ociety is to be its own reformer: it is a self-acting mechanism, beyond the influence of individuals . . . , and the spring that drives it is called "progress." So the idea of progress gradually emerges in liberal thinking as the antithesis of the idea of reform.[5]

The possibility of reconstructing English society (or even subjecting it to moderate reform) does not arise in *Little Dorrit*. In demonstrating that society has an inherent corrective impulse to weed out excesses of vice, Dickens implicitly suggests that radical change is not necessary to create a livable social environment.

Even where self-correction clearly fails to operate, the sheer inertia of the existing structure of society makes it unsusceptible to change. The abuses of the Circumlocution Office, for instance, are manifold and profound, but neither time nor the persistent badgering of Arthur Clennam alters this institution one iota. There is a sense of inevitability in these novels about most features of social construction. George Eliot's "Author's Introduction" to *Felix Holt* nominally establishes the temporal distance between her reader and the setting of the novel, but the chapter describes differences that are essentially cosmetic. In 1831, we learn, there were stagecoaches, an abundance of bucolic scenery, and an ill-lettered peasantry. The only observation that rises above this superficial level asserts the timelessness of certain social causalities:

> For there is seldom any wrong-doing which does not carry along with it some downfall of blindly-climbing hopes, some hard entail of suffering, . . . some tragic mark of kinship in one brief life to the far-stretching life that went before, and to the life that is to come after, such as has raised the pity and terror of men ever since they began to discern between will and destiny. (83)

On one level this passage testifies to the same sort of progressive mechanistic procedure that brought about the destruction of Merdle. Eliot, however, explicitly weaves consistency and even inevitability into her thematic concern with change. This seeming paradox is resolved in the novel's epilogue, in which the author wryly assesses Treby Magna's progress since 1833 in light of the events of the narrative.

> Whether the farmers are all public-spirited, the shopkeepers nobly independent, the Sproxton men entirely sober and judicious, the Dissenters quite without narrowness or asperity in religion and politics . . . —these things I have not heard, not having correspondence in those parts. Whether any presumption may be drawn from the fact that North Loamshire does not yet return a Radical candidate, I leave to the all-wise—I mean the newspapers. (605–6)

Purporting to deal with a time of transition in English history, *Felix Holt* suggests that substantive change in the social order is unlikely at best. Any attempt (presumably including that of the ostensibly flawless Felix) to reform the political or moral universe bespeaks naïveté or ulterior motives.

But the implications of Eliot's principles of unchangeability are far more serious than her lighthearted cynicism would suggest. Not only the mechanism that exacts retribution but also that which enforces masculine supremacy endures.[6] Mrs. Transome, who suggests by her appearance "an empress in her own right" (104), reigns for years as manager of her estate and husband. Yet all her competence and pride cannot give her independence in a patriarchal society; it is her son Harold, not she, who can fully participate in society as a landowner and political candidate. Her chance for self-fulfillment lies outside herself: "[S]uch hopes as she cherished in this fifty-sixth year of her life, must find their gratification in him—or nowhere" (89). Yet even that life at second hand is denied her, as Harold demonstrates that Radicals do not necessarily hold radical views on the role of women; he consigns her to the role of doting, self-effacing grandmother. As Deirdre David has observed, Eliot allows her to "possess only one negative form of power"—the power to destroy the political careers of the men around her.[7] Similarly, the progress envisioned by Felix Holt does not include a rethinking of the place of women in society. He rages against frivolous women who exercise what little power they can in manipulating men, but not on the grounds that they are wasting or perverting their own energies. He defines the problem they represent simply in terms of male experience: these women "hinder men's lives from having any nobleness in them" (209). In any social structure that *Felix Holt* can envision, women do not count as full human beings.[8] The central dilemma for its heroine, Esther Lyon, is not what she will make of her life so much as which man she will choose to marry. And the opportunity she has to attain through her own action the masculine ideal of womanly virtue is unusual; as she remarks to Felix, the usual female lot is total passivity: "A woman can hardly ever choose in [the] way [men can]; she is dependent on what happens to her" (367).

The social stasis Eliot underlines in her introduction and epilogue ensures that, despite the intelligence and ability of both Mrs.

Transome and Esther, no transformation of the role of women will be forthcoming. For change in the post-condition-of-England novel is largely illusory. The world of *Wives and Daughters*, too, is superficially in transition from the agrarian to the technological. But the patriarchal basis of society will not change: the torch will be passed from the old-fashioned squirearchy of Mr. Hamley and Lord Cumnor to the new hegemony of science represented by Roger and Lord Hollingford.[9] This new aristocracy will hold no new opportunities for women, who will continue to be forced to choose the role either of flirt or dutiful companion. In each of these novels society is stable, both in its present form and in any foreseeable future incarnation. There is no crisis to provide an excuse for women to take charge of public affairs and no weakness in the ongoing development of patriarchy to provide an opportunity for self-insinuation.

With the strengthening of the ruling hierarchy there is a concomitant weakening of the power of the domestic sphere. The world of private affairs is not as important when society is stable as it is when society is in tatters and looking for an alternative source of value. But the decline of domestic power is more than the result simply of de-emphasis: these novels actively work toward the disintegration of home and hearth. Authors present imperfect versions of domestic life more frequently than they embody the ideal in the experiences of their characters. Harold Transome envisions a soppily sentimental family life with his mother as a sweet "grandmamma on satin cushions" (95). The reality falls far short of both his vacuous ideal and the standards of domestic ideology: Mrs. Transome is readier to rule than to recline, and his beastly little son, Harry, shows a strong antipathy for her. *Wives and Daughters* presents a similar, though less harshly ironical, misapprehension of the benefits to be derived from domestic life. Mr. Gibson marries Hyacinth Kirkpatrick in the expectation that she will be an effective guardian of his daughter and provide stability to the household, but she proves to be a trial to both him and Molly and the cause of their alienation from each other. The condition-of-England heroine used her domestic authority to gain power in the public arena. In contrast, Hyacinth's eminence in the home does not serve subversive political ends: her activities serve to satisfy her personal vanity.[10] The earlier heroine's outward movement from her own home to society at large has been replaced

·d movement from domesticity to solipsism. The notion of ce and order within a feminocentric domestic sphere stands revealed as a fantasy.

But it is Dickens who calls this myth most into question with his often grotesque parodies of family life. Certainly *Hard Times,* with its joyless Gradgrind clan, has its share of unhappy domesticity; with the exception of Tom, however, the members of that family possess a latent affection for one another that Sissy Jupe's powerful influence animates. No such restoration is possible in the similarly repressed Clennam family of *Little Dorrit*—even the presence of Amy Dorrit does nothing to resolve the tension in the household. The heavy-handed symbolism of their house's precipitous and unexplained collapse dramatically demonstrates the unsalvageability of this family. Yet other late Dickens novels do even more to question the sanctity of the domestic sphere. *Our Mutual Friend* (1865) presents the ambiguous case of Jenny Wren and her miscreant father/"child": the relationship between the two is at least as much a disturbing inversion of the natural order as it is a sentimental paean to a girl's sense of family responsibility. Elsewhere invocations of the domestic unit are transparent ploys for concealing twisted relationships: Miss Havisham's adoption of Estella in *Great Expectations* (1861); Mrs. Joe's brutal foster motherhood of Pip in the same novel; Miss Wade's domination of Tattycoram in *Little Dorrit.* The existence of such destructive families of one sort or another calls into question the inherent sanctity of household life in the domestic sphere.

The theme of doubtful parentage that runs through many of these novels also helps effect the desacralization of domestic relations. If no others are forced to confront their spiritual parents in quite the same way as Pip in *Great Expectations,* many characters find their position in the private and public spheres shaken by the uncertainty of their lineage. The separation of such figures as Arthur Clennam, Miss Wade, and Tattycoram from their authentic relatives makes their integration into other domestic situations difficult; we see that family membership is often a problematic matter rather than a simple, universal experience. At the same time Esther Lyon becomes closely knit to a man she falsely believes to be her biological father, and Harold Transome effortlessly asserts rights he does not legitimately inherit; we see that people misinterpret as natural those attitudes that are in fact products of acculturation. The effect of such

challenges to its naturalness is that the family itself becomes a suspect, arbitrary creation of society rather than a fundamental source
of human values. The linkage of private with public sphere that
seemed so inevitable in the condition-of-England novel becomes un-
tenable when the private sphere is no longer the first term of human
life, the reality around which all else is defined. Whereas previously
actions in the domestic arena had repercussions for public life, now
Eliot can observe that "there is no private life which has not been
determined by a wider public life" (129)—but not, presumably, vice
versa.[11] The result of this reversal of influence is a diminishment of
female potential, for woman, the presiding genius of domesticity,
no longer has easy access to the mainsprings of English society.

But this homely spirit has in any case lost much of her power
within the now embattled domestic sphere. Most women are not as
silly as *Little Dorrit's* aging Flora Casby, who persists in moving and
talking "with a caricature of her girlish manner" (125) while she remains oblivious to her father's rapaciousness. Yet, as I have already
begun to point out, there is a general falling away of household
mastery from the halcyon days of Margaret Hale in *North and South*.
Molly Gibson, the heroine of *Wives and Daughters*, finds herself in a
home that is ill managed: her stepmother alienates the family's loyal
longtime servants and diminishes everyone's comfort. In this novel,
unlike *North and South*, the heroine does not have the option of seiz-
ing control. Molly must respond to mismanagement as Roger Hamley
and (most explicitly) Lady Harriet suggest: "The moral of all I have
been saying is, 'Be a good girl, and suffer yourself to be led, and
you'll find your new stepmother the sweetest creature imaginable'"
(195). Molly schools herself in self-suppression in the misguided notion that this will contribute to the smooth operation of the domestic
sphere. Such tolerance of the mishandling of the home would be
inconceivable in a novel that had a greater respect for the potential
power of domesticity; in the novels of the late 1850s and 1860s, however, it seems perfectly natural for a heroine to excuse herself from
responsibility for household failures as Molly does to Cynthia—"[O]f
course, I don't give any orders."

When women are put in positions of dominance within the home
the comprehensiveness of their mastery is still limited. Mrs. Hamley,
for instance, is "the ruling spirit of [her] house as long as she lived"
(285), but her physical frailty and early death limit her influence for

good. There is a curious impulse in all these novels to truncate female effectuality, even in the home. Mrs. Transome has an authority within her home and over her estate that is initially so strong that it threatens to give her the public powers of a squire: as she proudly tells her son, "I am used to be chief bailiff, and to sit in the saddle two or three hours every day." But Harold provides an immediate riposte that establishes her subservient role by denying her any true managerial responsibility—"Phew-ew! Jermyn manages the estate badly, then. That will not last under *my* reign" (95). For Eliot insists on limiting Mrs. Transome's rule by making her subordinate first to her lover and then to her son: her relish in "every little sign of power her lot had left her" (106) proves to be a pathetic attempt to fight against her essential powerlessness.

In the same novel Esther Lyon seems at first to have achieved, unlike Mrs. Transome, a sort of domestic authority that masculine power does not limit. She manages the household in some fashion through her mending and her supervision of tea, and she earns enough money in her own right to insist on wax candles, but her greatest mastery comes simply through her enshrinement as an object of reverence by Reverend Lyon.

> [He found] himself in timorous subjection to her wishes. . . .
> There will be queens in spite of Salic or other laws of later date
> than Adam and Eve; and here, in this small dingy house of the
> minister in Malthouse Yard, there was a light-footed, sweet-
> voiced Queen Esther. (160)

Language such as this evokes the powers of a Sybil or a Lady Eleanor and raises the possibility that Esther might have a similarly effective influence on the hero's struggles for social justice. But Felix Holt is no Egremont, and he is not capable of a modern brand of Mariolatry. His observation that Esther is beautiful is not a prelude to his own obeisance.

> He was looking up at her quite calmly, very much as a reverential
> Protestant might look at a picture of the Virgin, with a devout-
> ness suggested by the type rather than by the image. Esther's
> vanity was not in the least gratified: she felt that, somehow or
> other, Felix was going to reproach her.

"I wonder," he went on, still looking at her, " . . . [about] the force there would be in one beautiful woman . . . who made a man's passion for her rush in one current with all the great aims of his life." (364)

Felix's explicit raising of the issue of female influence comes only in the context of his calm denial of Esther's power. He conceives of a woman's possible role as a manifestly subservient one: she could not direct a man's energies or inspire him but only augment the power of his self-determined actions. Esther takes Felix's rebukes, here and elsewhere, to heart and changes her domestic behavior in accordance with his view of women's self-abnegating role. Instead of commanding her stepfather's admiration, she begins to take a subordinate position by attending to his wants and brushing his hair. Like the men in Mrs. Transome's life, Felix has eliminated Esther's chance of attaining an independent selfhood that would have the potential energy to reach from the private to the public sphere.

When women are cut off both from access to the public sphere and the full exercise of their powers within the sphere of family life, their domestic activities become limited in value and often even self-destructive. In *Little Dorrit* Amy Dorrit devotes her energies selflessly and fruitlessly to the care of her family. She assumes the role of a "little mother" to her brother, sister, and father, finding professions for the first two and tirelessly taking care of the third. Her benevolent ministrations ought to command our regard as the signs of a strong woman; they do indeed earn her the deep respect of other Marshalsea residents, who "stand out of the way to let her go by. . . . The men pull off their hats to her quite politely" (677). But it is difficult to see her activities as praiseworthy uses of domestic powers, for she accomplishes little of substance beyond her own mortification.[12] Edward's indolence makes her efforts on his behalf fruitless; Fanny's vanity makes her shove aside Amy's sound advice; her father's delusions of gentility make him turn a blind eye to her employment. They take her dedication for granted "as being vaguely what they had a right to expect, and nothing more" (78). Her servitude simply facilitates their selfishness and blindness by making it easier for them to overlook the oppressive realities of prison life.[13] If anyone benefits from her exertions, it is Amy herself. Her behavior feeds an almost masochistic desire for self-abnegation: "To pass in and out of the prison unnoticed, and elsewhere to be overlooked and forgotten, were, for herself, her chief desires" (242).[14]

Moreover, her domestic benevolence suffers from a severe geographical limitation. Inside the Marshalsea Prison she gains the respect of everyone except her family for her mostly ineffectual gestures; in the world at large she does not gain that general esteem, and she does not make even ineffectual gestures. Once away from the highly regulated, patriarchally ordered environment of the prison, she cannot even try to counteract her family's gradual degeneration, because she hardly feels herself to have an existence when there are "no cares of others to load herself with" (387). Only when back in prison again, newly imposed upon with the burdens of others, does she regain her capacity for activity. Her domestic goodness totally lacks the insinuative effectuality of Sissy Jupe's in *Hard Times*. Amy is caught in the snares of the society that made the prison necessary in the first place; she is, rather than a savior, a victim who is condemned to expend energy unavailingly in a narrow arena isolated from public life.

Amy's fate is hardly unique: it is the common lot of women in these post-condition-of-England novels to be confined to prison cells of one sort or another. There is no longer scope for female activities and domestic culture. Fanny Dorrit locks herself into a totally inappropriate marriage for the perverse pleasure she will derive from competing with Mrs. Merdle: because her options as a woman are so limited, such pointless mutual tormenting must become "the business of [her] life" (495). The circular quality of female activity, its tendency to feed upon itself, becomes clearest in the cases of Miss Wade of *Little Dorrit* and Miss Havisham of *Great Expectations*: neither can find any outlet for her energies save a perverse self-recreation through the education of a younger woman. The powers that women can seize in a world in which their role has been dramatically truncated are either trivial or self-consuming.

Cynthia Kirkpatrick in *Wives and Daughters* provides the most extended example of female energy put to trivial ends. She has an "unconscious power of fascination" that consists partly of an ability to change her form—"the most exquisite power of adaptation to varying people" (254). Her aptitude for gaining and wielding power over others is joined to a strongly proud and independent nature. Unlike her compliant stepsister Molly Gibson, Cynthia is unwilling to let others dictate her behavior: "[T]he very fact that she was expected by another to entertain . . . emotions would have been enough to prevent her expressing them" (498). She has "grown up outside the pale of duty and 'oughts'" (261) because of the early death of her father, and so she cannot be controlled by Hollingford's moral constraints. But, somewhat like Brontë's Shirley Keeldar, she is unable to use her gifts and her liberating social situation to attain any positive goal. Her chief accomplishment, repeated several times in the course of the novel, is to allure men and then reject them. Where a heroine such as Sybil could use the love of a promising M.P. to advance her humanitarian views, Cynthia can only toy with Roger Hamley, a member of the rising scientific elite. His status in the community feeds her vanity rather than her ambition.

> [While he was gone,] Cynthia missed her slave . . . [;] she had found it not unpleasant to have a man whom she thoroughly respected, and whom men in general respected, the subject of her eye, the glad ministrant to each scarce-spoken wish, a person in whose sight all her words were pearls or diamonds, all her actions heavenly graciousness. (398)

Despite her personal power, she is not a natural ruler but, rather, "one of those natural coquettes" (514).

Yet it is inevitable that Cynthia should misappropriate her talents in the novel's patriarchal society. The men of this world are in full possession of social authority, and there is no obvious opportunity or excuse for her to shake their grip. Indeed, even to maintain her independence Cynthia must devote considerable attention to eluding their attempts to define and judge her. Her hatred of Preston originates in his continual assertion of his rights over her as fiancé and financial benefactor: as she observes bitterly to Molly, "He made me feel as if I was in his power" (521). Cynthia's feeling of entrapment, as much as her repulsion from his vulgarity, precipitates the breakdown of their relationship. Similarly, her decision to dissolve her engagement to Roger arises out of the perception that she will no longer be able to control him. "I will not submit to his thinking less well of me than he has done" (600), she says, and observes that his enlightenment would involve her entrapment in the conventional morality she rejects: "I almost hate the idea of Roger judging me by his own standard, which wasn't made for me, and graciously forgiving me at last" (601). Paradoxically, the gestures that seem to mark her as a capricious, superficial girl offer the novel's closest approach to the radical dream of transcending the limitations her society puts on women.

The narrow range of action allotted them and the restrictions on their behavior even within that range amply account for the pettiness and destructiveness of these women. But these novels show something less than a broad sympathy for such would-be heroines. Mrs. Transome, for instance, is at once explained and judged early in *Felix Holt*.

> She had begun to live merely in small immediate cares and occupations, and, like all eager-minded women who advance in life without any activity of tenderness or any large sympathy, she had contracted small rigid habits of thinking and acting, she had her "ways" which must not be crossed, and had learned to fill up the great void of life with giving small orders to tenants [and exercising her will in other trivial ways]. (99)

Here Eliot makes an explicit connection between the frustration of ambition and the embrace of crotchety small-mindedness. Yet, as subsequent statements make even clearer, she blames Mrs. Transome for the fruitlessness of her life. For this and other novels denigrate the female impulse toward independence and advocate a strikingly reactionary posture: subservience to patriarchs and adoption of their ideologies as women's own. The answer that would have solved Mrs. Transome's problems long ago is not the opening up of society to her energies but her submission to the sort of duties laid down by Felix Holt.

The central heroines of these novels are not those who act upon a restless independence; they are the women who submit themselves to the moral guidance of a hero. Both Roger Hamley and Felix Holt present rules for living to young women with no clear sense of direction in their lives. Molly Gibson, unable to imagine how she will cope with her new stepmother, learns from Roger to suppress her personal feelings and "try to think more of others than of oneself" (152). She not only obeys this injunction in her immediate situation but also takes Roger as her philosophical guide; the love she comes to feel for him involves a surrender of her individual judgment to his. The question she asks herself in confusing situations throughout the book is not "What shall I do?" but "What would Roger say was right?" (210; see also 691). For Molly, unlike Cynthia, has fallen within the pale of "oughts" that help keep the existing patriarchal structure in place.

Felix Holt confronts Esther Lyon with a set of rules that constitutes a more fully articulated philosophy than Roger's. In his vision of the world, women have a limited role, one that is usually destructive: because men fall in love with them and strive to gratify them, "women [are] a curse; all life is stunted to suit their littleness" (212). If women only behaved with dutiful subservience to their men, the business of the world would be more readily accomplished. This misogyny, astonishingly enough, strikes a responsive chord in Esther that accompanies her growing love for its exponent:

> He was like no one else to her: he had seemed to bring at once a law, and the love that gave strength to obey the law. . . .
> . . . The first religious experience of her life—the first self-questioning, the first voluntary subjection, the first longing to acquire the strength of greater motives . . . had come to her through Felix Holt. (369)

Yet Eliot makes it surprisingly clear that this law is part of a desire to suppress women's expressions of individuality. Holt's first reaction to Esther is not a benign impulse to teach and uplift. "'A peacock!' thought Felix. 'I should like to come and scold her every day, and make her cry and cut her fine hair off'" (154). The hostility that accompanies his initial attraction to her foreshadows his subsequent actions: he will indeed deprive her of her feathers, the ladylike appurtenances that make up her self-determined ideal of behavior.

Nevertheless, through its insistence on the inevitability of female dependence the novel attempts to conceal the disturbingly oppressive aspects of Felix's ideology of female behavior. A woman has little control over her own fate, says Esther, because "[h]er lot is made for her by the love she accepts" (525). *Felix Holt* presents the other love Esther could accept, her only other choice in life, in a highly unfavorable light. Harold Transome offers her a life of luxury devoid of the thorns that a life spent in pious devotion to Felix will involve. But Harold is an even less attractive sort of tyrannical patriarch than

Felix. He has already pushed his mother as far into powerless obliv-
ion as he can; indeed, his attitude has "convinced [Esther] that
Harold had a padded yoke ready for the neck of every man, woman,
and child that depended on him" (538). His preferred model of
woman is dull witted and animalistic, completely without opinions;
it is no coincidence that his first wife was born a slave. With Harold,
Esther would have no possibility of any control over her family or
herself. In comparison the indirect, menial assistance she could afford Felix in his struggle for the workingman offers, if not a satisfying
career, at least a semblance of participation in social reform.

So, the patriarchal seduction of these two heroines is accomplished without much difficulty, and they must then confront the
strenuous task of self-suppression that has been enjoined upon them.
Esther shows her obedience to her new rule by performing small acts
of self-mortification in service to her father. But she also renounces
the Transome inheritance that could have made her one of the most
influential persons in the county; although Eliot presents this as an
active moral decision, it is, as Kestner observes, "not an assertive but
a submissive procedure."[15] Interestingly enough, Esther does not
separate her refusal of the property from her refusal of Harold: she
cannot seriously consider accepting only the former because the
novel does not admit the possibility of a woman independent of
masculine domination.

Wives and Daughters is less successful in eliminating alternative
possibilities from the gaze of its heroine. Molly, after all, has the
striking though ultimately ineffectual example of Cynthia before her
to show that women can choose self-assertion. Even before her stepsister's arrival Molly questions Roger's doctrine:

> Thinking more of others' happiness than of her own was very
> fine; but did it not mean giving up her very individuality,
> quenching all the warm love, the true desires, that made her
> herself? (169)

In time her thinking advances from regret at her own wasted potential to a more general discontent with her decision to give her stepmother a free field in the domestic sphere. "She knew that very often
she longed to protest, but did not do it, from the desire of sparing
her father any discord" (407); yet she wonders whether she is derelict

in a duty beyond that of subservience, "whether, as [people] are placed in families for distinct purposes, not by chance merely, there are not duties involved in this aspect of their lot in life" (416). She is on the verge of acknowledging the necessity of a well-ordered domestic sphere (run by a strong woman) for the successful operation of society, but she pulls back from the completion of her analysis. Molly's doubts do not change her behavior, which continues to be a model of submission: on behalf of her father and Roger she maintains a self-denying silence in the face of Mrs. Gibson's misuse of her household authority. She is not too far from attaining Amy Dorrit's ideal of being overlooked and forgotten, her own voice lost in her devotion to masculine notions of duty.

However, the final stage in the pacification of women involves a curious reactivation of them under new principles. Ultimately, the women of these novels internalize patriarchal codes so fully that the existing social structure can harness their energies. Sometimes women may be so totally absorbed by society that they become an archetypal embodiment of patriarchal forms of oppression. In *Little Dorrit* Mrs. General and Mrs. Clennam are the chief exponents of two ideologies that help keep woman in her place: propriety and religion. In the case of the latter, Dickens helpfully provides a genealogy of Mrs. Clennam's fanaticism, and we learn unsurprisingly that a repressive father is at the bottom of it (646). The heroines of *Wives and Daughters* and *Felix Holt* have not reached Mrs. Clennam's degree of moral unsightliness, but each demonstrates the extent of her cooptation by an act of bravery that is reminiscent of, but totally different in import from, the condition-of-England heroine's assumption of responsibility.

Molly Gibson performs her ultimate act of self-degradation in her recovery of Cynthia's letters from Mr. Preston. When she confronts him her unselfconsciousness is strikingly reminiscent of Sissy's attitude during her confrontation with Harthouse in *Hard Times*: Preston "perceived that Molly was as unconscious that he was a young man, and she a young woman, as if she had been a pure angel of heaven" (533). Yet this implacable angel is involved not, as Sissy was, in removing a source of shame but rather in taking another's shame upon herself. Acting to shield Cynthia for Roger's sake, Molly becomes the target of gossip and scorn in her community. She has fully learned the lessons he taught her: she has sacrificed herself for the sake of smoothing out the lives of others. Ironically, her action only delays the inevitable breakup of Cynthia and Roger's engagement; nevertheless, through this pointless test of loyalty Molly has removed the shadow cast by her earlier subversive doubts.

Felix Holt's test of loyalty evokes the courtroom scene of *Mary Barton*. Like Mary, Esther takes the stand to defend her accused lover from a charge of murder. However, Esther has not done anything beforehand to exonerate Felix (who is, in any event, technically guilty—there is no alibi to be chased down in Liverpool Harbor). Her testimony is less a self-willed action than a final submission to Felix's authority: she is indeed, as the clarity of her voice suggests, "making a confession of faith" (572). The effect of her testimony is not to reveal the truth or even clarify matters of fact: it is to impress upon the men like Sir Maximus Debarry who are in charge of the judicial system that Felix must be good because he has such evident power over "a modest, brave, beautiful woman" (576). She procures a pardon for Felix not by controlling the system's determination of guilt but by playing up to its sentimental paternalism. Esther's words are testimony to her irrevocable commitment to the social system Felix advocates, a world of continued class divisions and female subservience. Her reverence for him has created an unthinking response to his plight—"one irresistible impulse for her heart" (571). By taking the stand, she demonstrates that she has abandoned her independence and embraced the patriarchal role of Felix's submissive instrument.

These later novels, then, have so transformed the female role in social novels that even women's dramatic actions can serve only patriarchal ends. Post-condition-of-England fiction repeatedly advocates unselfishness and adherence to duty but not, as before, as a means of cloaking a subversive self-authorization. Under this new dispensation women are required to muffle their voices and bind their hands and feet in order to escape the fate of their disobedient sisters, such as Miss Wade and Mrs. Transome—women who have become powerless monsters without a cause. Sadly, the closest approach to female self-determination that these writers permit their heroines is the subservient public gesture of an Esther or Molly. Their actions evoke a more effectual female role that they themselves are unable to take: their social participation is the fictional equivalent of a vestigial tail.

This acceding to masculine definitions, to the status quo, is inevitable given these novels' changed notion of social structure. A feminocentric view of reality has given way to a belief in the supremacy of patriarchal ideologies and institutions. Social stasis has replaced the pervasive crisis of the earlier novels, and so there seems no point in searching for new sources of value; if society is a prison, as *Little Dorrit* repeatedly asserts, it is a prison from which no one can escape. Although the domestic sphere has not disappeared, it has been dramatically diminished, just as Amy is consistently diminished by her nicknames. Whereas the home was previously the all-encompassing basis of society, it is now a product of the masculine sphere of public affairs, circumscribed and constricted by the sort of law that limits the freedom of heroines.

The fatalism of these novels precludes revolutionary change, whether in class relations, economic behavior, or sex roles. Instead, there is an almost resigned acceptance of things as they are. One of the most distressing characteristics of these novels is their abandonment of the right to offer an imaginative transformation of reality that might point the way toward a different sort of world. It is especially sad to see Gaskell and Dickens, who had demonstrated in their earlier works the curative potential of womanly power, lose their faith in the possibility of even fictional change. But by the late 1850s, it seems, it was no longer possible to write a condition-of-England novel: writers could no longer envision significant change in the structure of industrial society, because that society had become less vulnerable to assault. Faced with a more peaceful and controlled English society, writers concerned with its injustice could respond only with complacency or despair.

The decline in the novel's ability to imagine a radical alteration of English society paralleled significant changes in English industrial life after mid-century. It is common, though dangerous, to identify the third quarter of the nineteenth century as a time of widespread national prosperity; as R. A. Church has pointed out, the unevenness of economic growth in the period makes it possible to offer such a generalization only very cautiously.[16] Nevertheless, the steady though unspectacular development of the economy may have played a role in a more striking phenomenon: a significant reduction in tensions in labor relations. With the demise of Chartism after 1848, England no longer possessed a unified national working-class political organization. Industrial laborers channeled their energies into the more formal institutions of self-help organizations and labor unions and concentrated on issues of local rather than national concern.[17] Describing the Lancashire cotton industry in the years following the Preston strike, Patrick Joyce has identified the attitude of trades unions as "conciliatory . . . , professing the identification of the interests of employer and operative."[18] On the other side of the class divide employers were changing their practice as well: Joyce observes that industrialists for their part came to embrace a new form of paternalism far removed from the indifference that characterized their attitudes in the 1830s and 1840s. Harold Perkin argues that English society was coming of age after the turbulent adolescence of early industrialism:

> The crucial factor in the rise of a viable class society was in fact the institutionalization of class, the creation, recognition and acceptance of the political, social and industrial institutions through which the classes could express themselves, safeguard or ameliorate their standards and conditions of life, and channel their conflicts out of the paths of violence into those of negotiation and compromise.[19]

Despite the continued cause for concern the condition of workers offered, the threat of violence that had suffused English society in the earlier decades of the century seemed to have passed.[20] Legislative reform would continue throughout the next decades but without the pressure of imminent revolution to motivate it. As Brantlinger has suggested, the spirit of the times was meliorative rather than transformative; people expected evolutionary progress rather than sudden change from the social organism.[21]

But it was not only the end of the condition-of-England crisis that may have sapped the particular feminist impulse of condition-of-England fiction. Just as there began to be institutionalized forms of expression for the concerns of the working class, formal structures for the advocacy of women's causes arose. Women's role in society became an explicit political issue in public discourse: some women (and men such as John Stuart Mill) began to clamor for women's property and suffrage rights. The decade of the 1850s saw the real beginnings of organized British feminism[22] as well as the first of the

legislative acts that would grant women greater personal independence.[23] British feminist activity found a formal focus with the foundation of the *English Woman's Journal* in 1858 and the Society for the
Promotion of the Employment of Women in 1859. The 1860s would
see the start of the suffrage movement.[24] Part, though not all, of the
force of the condition-of-England novel had come from the unspoken
grievances of women in English society that paralleled the situation
of workers. By the late 1850s a forum had arisen in which such grievances could be named: feminism became a distinctive political entity
rather than a shadow issue in the analysis of industrial patriarchy.
As early as 1855, the *Christian Remembrancer* noted the incursions of
American feminism (though with evident disbelief):

> [I]t may yet be a matter of surprise [to many cultivated women],
> that their own public position is becoming one of these great
> public questions; that their own grievances, their own disabili-
> ties, the oppressions and injustice to which they themselves are
> subject, are collectively, in the judgment of many of their sex
> [and politicians and reformers], the most crying evil of the day.[25]

By 1864 Justin McCarthy could describe the reconfiguration in the
genre of social-problem fiction that institutionalized feminism had
helped effect:

> The greatest social difficulty in the England of to-day is not that
> which is created by the relations between wealth and poverty.
> These, however painful, still are hardly any longer perplexed.
> They seem at least to be brought as directly in the way towards
> a gradual adjustment as human enlightenment and benevolence
> can place them for the present. . . . A much more complicated
> difficulty is found in the relations between man and woman. If
> we are to believe [published reports] . . . the social life of England
> to-day shows scarcely any improvement in this direction. . . .
> Now to this theme, or at least to some topic bearing on and
> connected with it, some novelists who write with a purpose to-
> day are boldly addressing themselves.[26]

The public awareness of a formal feminist discourse opened new
opportunities for the representation and analysis of injustice. How-

ever, the suppressed resentment that found compensatory expression in industrial fiction was no longer so readily available to fuel older forms of social-problem fiction.

Finally, with the establishment of new frameworks for class interaction and the expression of women's concerns, one old relationship that became obsolete was that between the charitable rich and the needy poor. According to Richard Evans, the growth of professionalism played a role in changing women's activities:

> [P]hilanthropy . . . became itself more organised and professionalised. . . . Untutored benevolence gave way to sociological investigation. The casual pattern of female charitable activity familiar from the days when it was dominated by the titled ladies of the aristocracy was no longer appropriate.[27]

In the interstice between the eras of patronage and class organization, the condition-of-England novel used traditional roles such as that of aristocratic patroness to enforce stability in a volatile political situation. But by mid-century the traditional philanthropic roles that condition-of-England heroines appropriated to subversive effect were falling out of currency.

The multifold institutionalization of English life thus created an intellectual climate that was inhospitable to the condition-of-England novel. National life no longer seemed in need of a new structure, for new institutions had arisen. The novelists of this genre had seized a unique opportunity for utopian feminism in the 1830s and 1840s—a moment in which society seemed to be drifting toward chaos and in which the most solid ideology at hand seemed to be newly ascendant domesticity. In conjunction with the century's mythic conception of womanhood, this ideology could be appropriated for the creation of powerful heroines. These fictional women could draw on female energies that society disallowed to offer an imaginative transformation of the fundamental terms of English society.

While it lasted, the vision of the condition-of-England novel provided a coherent alternative to a continuation of masculine power. But the novels' feminist prophecy could not become reality because patriarchal power had never really lost its grip on English society. Once the transition to a professionalized, ordered class system was made, writers could no longer imagine women's control over the private sphere as a vehicle for social transformation; instead, their fictions about women in problematic societies construct worlds, like those of *Felix Holt* and *Wives and Daughters,* in which change is illusory and women's options limited to a choice of male rulers.

Yet it is unfair to judge the condition-of-England genre on the basis of its ultimate failure to transform the world. The myth of powerful womanhood it helped perpetuate would continue throughout the century. Even as George Eliot was writing her unusually reactionary *Felix Holt,* John Ruskin published his ambiguous admonition to women to exercise the domestic power of their subservience.

> Vainly, as falsely, you blame or rebuke the desire of power!—For Heaven's sake, and for Man's sake, desire it all you can. But *what* power? . . . Power to heal, to redeem, to guide, and to guard. Power of the sceptre and shield. . . . Will you not covet such power as this, and seek such throne as this, and be no more housewives, but queens?[28]

Even at a moment of resurgent patriarchy, Ruskin appropriates the idea of separate spheres for purposes that are ultimately visionary rather than merely pragmatic and functional. The alternatives of housewife and queen that Ruskin offers his audience retain a curiously equivocal quality; they, like the domestic ideal itself, at once confine women and liberate them. The condition-of-England novel stakes out an imaginative territory within which this ideology realizes its most subversive possibilities—a region in which housewives *are* queens. The fictional realm that these novels created for them endures as testimony to the exceeding strength of a myth of womanhood that could propose alternative values at a time of relative patriarchal ineffectuality. If these novels ultimately fail to carve out a permanent role for women in the world of public affairs, surely they make a lasting contribution by inculcating into the British public the virtues of an egalitarian society it could not yet bring into being.

Notes

Introduction

1. Thomas Carlyle, *Past and Present* (London: Chapman, 1897; New York: AMS, 1969) 7, vol. 10 of *The Works of Thomas Carlyle*.
2. "On the whole . . . there was no general recognition of the social and political aspects of the new [industrial] economic order until the emergence of the Ten Hours Agitation and the Chartists in the 1830s and 1840s." A. D. Harvey, "First Public Reactions to the Industrial Revolution," *Études Anglaises* 31 (1978): 293.
3. J. T. Ward, *The Factory Movement, 1830–1855* (London: Macmillan, 1962) 81.
4. Dorothy Thompson, *The Chartists: Popular Politics in the Industrial Revolution* (New York: Pantheon, 1984) 16–17.
5. James Epstein, *The Lion of Freedom: Feargus O'Connor and the Chartist Movement, 1832–1842* (London: Croom Helm, 1982) 13.
6. Norman Gash, *Aristocracy and People: Britain, 1815–1865*, The New History of England (Cambridge: Harvard UP, 1979) 197, 209 ff.
7. [Henry Rogers], "Revolution and Reform," *Edinburgh Review* 88 (1848): 361.
8. Thomas Carlyle, *Chartism, Critical and Miscellaneous Essays in Five Volumes: Volume IV* (London: Chapman, 1899; New York: AMS, 1969) 118, vol. 29 of *The Works of Thomas Carlyle*.
9. Steven Marcus, *Engels, Manchester, and the Working Class* (New York: Random, 1974) 109.
10. He "was close to exchanging the role of the man of thought for that of the man of action. Carlyle was, I believe, the first English-speaking author to stake out this frontier for literature." Philip Rosenberg, *The Seventh Hero: Thomas Carlyle and the Theory of Radical Activism* (Cambridge: Harvard UP, 1974) vii.
11. Jules Paul Seigel, introduction, *Thomas Carlyle: The Critical Heritage*, ed. Jules Paul Seigel (London: Routledge, 1971) 12.
12. [George Eliot], rev. of *Passages Selected from the Writings of Thomas Carlyle: With a Biographical Memoir*, by Thomas Ballantyne, *Leader* 27 Oct. 1855: 1035.
13. [Peter LePage Renouf], rev. of *Past and Present*, by Thomas Carlyle, *Dublin Review* 15 (1843): 185.
14. Carlyle, *Past and Present* 17.
15. Carlyle, *Chartism* 118.
16. Philip Rosenberg notes that critical opinion has long been divided over whether

Carlyle's nostalgia for medieval life identifies *Past and Present* as a conservative work (anticipatory of his later thought) rather than a radical critique of English life. Rosenberg himself usefully questions "the assumption that there is something inherently reactionary in turning to the past for one's social models" and cites more or less contemporary readers who see Carlyle as radical (P. Rosenberg 148–49). John D. Rosenberg assesses the paradoxes of Carlyle's intellectual career and finds both "continuities and discontinuities"; he concludes that "the Carlyle who kindled the enthusiasm of Emerson and Engels and Whitman . . . is not another creature from the Carlyle who brought tears of hope to the eyes of Hitler" (*Carlyle and the Burden of History* [Cambridge: Harvard UP, 1985] 117).

17. Carlyle, *Past and Present* 36.
18. J. Rosenberg 95, 96.
19. While I have treated *Chartism* and *Past and Present* as two manifestations of a single critique, Chris Vanden Bossche draws a sharp distinction between them. *Chartism*, he argues, uses "arguments . . . dictated by the parameters of parliamentary debate," while *Past and Present* steps outside that framework to address "aristocratic landowners and middle-class industrialists" directly (*Carlyle and the Search for Authority* [Columbus: Ohio State UP, 1991] 96, 105).
20. Carlyle, *Past and Present* 264.
21. [William Sewell], "Carlyle's Works," *Quarterly Review* 66 (1840): 496.
22. J. Rosenberg 132. Vanden Bossche, on the other hand, while arguing for the superiority of *Past and Present* to *Chartism*, observes that the former "only partially succeeds in reuniting the domains of religion and economy, for it envisions an escape from the commercial world into the transcendental idyll" (113).
23. [William Henry Smith], rev. of *Past and Present*, by Thomas Carlyle, *Blackwood's Edinburgh Magazine* 54 (1843): 123.
24. P. Rosenberg 139.
25. Elliot Engel and Margaret F. King, *The Victorian Novel before Victoria: British Fiction during the Reign of William IV, 1830–37* (New York: St. Martin's, 1984) 6.
26. Richard D. Altick, *The Presence of the Present: Topics of the Day in the Victorian Novel* (Columbus: Ohio State UP, 1991) 52.
27. Patrick Brantlinger, *The Spirit of Reform: British Literature and Politics, 1832–1867* (Cambridge: Harvard UP, 1977) 28.
28. Because of the inherent fuzziness of literary categories, there is no generally accepted, scientifically precise definition of this genre, or even agreement on which novels belong to it. There does seem to be some degree of consensus on the seven novels I include: Catherine Gallagher observed in 1980 with good reason that they, *Felix Holt*, and "numerous minor works" are "generally understood" to constitute the industrial novel ("*Hard Times* and *North and South*: The Family and Society in Two Industrial Novels," *Arizona Quarterly* 36 [1980]: 70n). *Industrial novel* is indeed the term most commonly used for works that deal in some way with the human consequences of the Industrial Revolution at mid-century (give or take a decade). Throughout my study I will ordinarily use the less inclusive term *condition-of-England novel*, which is more precise for my purposes.
29. Philip Collins, "Dickens and Industrialism," *SEL* 20 (1980): 652. An almost equally scornful assessment can be found in J. M. Jefferson, "Industrialisation and Poverty:

In Fact and Fiction," *The Long Debate on Poverty: Eight Essays on Industrialisation and "the condition of England"* ([London]: Institute of Economic Affairs, 1972) 187–238. Compare Jerome Hamilton Buckley, *The Victorian Temper* (Cambridge: Harvard UP, 1951) 27–28; see as well Lionel Stevenson, *The English Novel: A Panorama* (Boston: Houghton, 1960) 279–82.

30. There are, however, a few examples of this sort of criticism. See the following: Bernard N. Schilling, *Human Dignity and the Great Victorians* (New York: Columbia UP, 1946); Herbert L. Sussman, *Victorians and the Machine: The Literary Response to Technology* (Cambridge: Harvard UP, 1968); Sijna de Vooys, *The Psychological Element in the English Sociological Novel of the Nineteenth Century* (Amsterdam: Paris, 1927); Arnold Kettle, "The Early Victorian Social-Problem Novel," *From Dickens to Hardy,* ed. Boris Ford, vol. 6 of The New Pelican Guide to English Literature, rev. ed. (Harmondsworth: Penguin, 1982) 164–81; Raimund Borgmeier, "Soziale Probleme zum Zeitvertreib?—Unterhaltung des Lesers und Gesellschaftskritik im viktorianischen Industrieroman," *Text-Leser-Bedeutung: Untersuchungen zur Interaktion von Text und Leser,* ed. Herbert Grabes (Grossen-Linden: Hoffman, 1977) 19–41; T. B. Tomlinson, *The English Middle-Class Novel* (London: Macmillan, 1976).

31. The classic example of course is F. R. Leavis's treatment of *Hard Times* in *The Great Tradition,* but see also Kathleen Tillotson, *Novels of the Eighteen-Forties* (Oxford: Clarendon, 1954). Tillotson sees *Mary Barton* as part of a genre—"the novel-with-a-purpose"—but chooses to discuss it independently of the rest of the genre.

32. See Arnold Hauser, *The Social History of Art,* 2 vols. (New York: Knopf, 1952) 2: 824–25; Irena Dobrzycka, *The Conditions of Living of the Working Class in the Social Novels of Charles Kingsley,* Poznańskie Towarzystwo Przyjaciół Nauk, Wydział Filologiczno-Filozoficzny, Prace Komisji Filologicznej, vol. 16, no. 2 (Poznań: [Państwowe Wydawn. Naukowe], 1955); William O. Aydelotte, "The England of Marx and Mill as Reflected in Fiction," *Journal of Economic History* Suppl. 8 (1948): 42–58.

33. Raymond Williams, *Culture and Society, 1780–1950* (New York: Columbia UP, 1958).

34. Another firm proponent of a class-based view is P. J. Keating, *The Working Classes in Victorian Literature* (New York: Barnes, 1971). Philippa Walsh Colella also offers a critical appraisal of Gaskell's middle-class limitations in "Elizabeth Gaskell as Social Commentator: Radical, Liberal, or Bourgeois Apologist?" *Studi dell'Istituto Linguistico* 4 (1981): 69–83.

    Deirdre David offers an interesting reading of *North and South* that bears only a partial resemblance to this line of criticism in *Fictions of Resolution in Three Victorian Novels* (New York: Columbia UP, 1981). While seeing the industrial novels as products of the middle class for the middle class, she emphasizes the self-consistent mythmaking of their resolutions.

35. John Lucas, "Mrs. Gaskell and Brotherhood," *Tradition and Tolerance in Nineteenth-Century Fiction: Critical Essays on Some English and American Novels,* ed. David Howard, John Lucas, and John Goode (London: Routledge, 1966) 143. Lucas's overall approach to the genre is very similar in his later book, *The Literature of Change: Studies in the Nineteenth-Century Provincial Novel* (New York: Barnes, 1977). The argument is not substantially different from that of Mary Eagleton and David Pierce, *Attitudes to Class in the English Novel from Walter Scott to David Storey* (Lon-

don: Thames, 1979): to take the case of one novelist, "Mrs. Gaskell's understanding of the reasons for class antagonism is at odds with the evidence of her own eyes" (38).

36. Gertrude Himmelfarb has observed with some justice that a term such as *middle class* is frequently used to signify "any position that falls short of the degree of militancy and alienation the critic may deem appropriate" (*The Idea of Poverty: England in the Early Industrial Age* [New York: Knopf, 1984] 518).

37. Louis Cazamian, *The Social Novel in England, 1830–1850*, trans. Martin Fido (first published in French, 1903; London: Routledge, 1973). Some critics concern themselves with tracing Victorian attitudes to particular subjects: Ivan Melada, *The Captain of Industry in English Fiction, 1821–1871* (Albuquerque: U of New Mexico P, 1970); Herman Jansonius, *Some Aspects of Business Life in Early Victorian Fiction* (Purmerend: Muusses, 1926).

38. Despite his appreciation for *Mary Barton*, John Colmer faults Gaskell's "process of making the characters and plot conform to a pre-established view of man and society, a view based on social and religious assumptions, rather than any coherent political philosophy" (*Coleridge to Catch-22: Images of Society* [New York: St. Martin's, 1978] 76). Ivanka Kovačević, in *Fact into Fiction: English Literature and the Industrial Scene, 1750–1850* (Leicester: Leicester UP; Belgrade: Faculty of Philology, U of Belgrade, 1975), makes a similar point in ascribing the aesthetic failures of industrial fiction to their confusing social philosophies (109).

39. Joseph Kestner, *Protest and Reform: The British Social Narrative by Women, 1827–1867* (Madison: U of Wisconsin P, 1985).

40. However, a precedent was set as early as 1929 by Wanda Fraiken Neff's use of fictional material to support her analysis of the role of working women in Victorian society: *Victorian Working Women: An Historical and Literary Study of Women in British Industries and Professions, 1832–1850* (1929; New York: AMS, 1966).

   There are numerous examples of the documentary critical approach, many exhibiting as well a history-of-ideas orientation: Monica Correa Fryckstedt, *Elizabeth Gaskell's* Mary Barton *and* Ruth: A Challenge to Christian England, Studia Anglistica Upsaliensia 43 (Uppsala: Acta Universitatis Upsaliensis, 1982); David Smith, "*Mary Barton* and *Hard Times*: Their Social Insights," *Mosaic* 5.2 (1972): 97–112; Raymond Chapman, *The Victorian Debate: English Literature and Society, 1832–1901* (New York: Basic, 1968); Helena Bergmann, *Between Obedience and Freedom: Woman's Role in the Mid-Nineteenth Century Industrial Novel*, Gothenburg Studies in English 45 (Göteborg: Acta Universitatis Gothoburgensis, 1979); David Craig, *The Real Foundations: Literature and Social Change* (New York: Oxford UP, 1974). At least one economic historian uses an industrial novel as a slightly flawed case study: James P. Henderson, "Charles Dickens's *Hard Times* and the Industrial Revolution," *Cresset* 43.5 (1980): 13–17.

41. Sheila M. Smith, *The Other Nation: The Poor in English Novels of the 1840s and 1850s* (Oxford: Clarendon, 1980).

42. Kettle 179.

43. Joan Kirkby, "The Unaesthetic Poor," rev. of *Proper Stations*, by Richard Faber, and *The Working Classes in Victorian Fiction*, by P. J. Keating, *Southern Review* (Australia) 5 (1972): 259.

44. Catherine Gallagher, *The Industrial Reformation of English Fiction: Social Discourse and Narrative Form, 1832–1867* (Chicago: U of Chicago P, 1985) xiii.

45. Rosemarie Bodenheimer, *The Politics of Story in Victorian Social Fiction* (Ithaca: Cornell UP, 1988) 3, 18. Ruth Yeazell, in "Why Political Novels Have Heroines: *Sybil, Mary Barton,* and *Felix Holt*" *Novel* 18 (1985): 126–44, also addresses the issue of heroinism in several industrial novels and notes the striking juxtaposition of heroines and political analysis. However, the conclusions she draws from this collocation are directly opposite to my own. In her view courtship plots are used to conceal male violence and disarm the potential force of depictions of the working class: heroines and radical analysis work in opposition, not in tandem. Where I see powerful, active female protagonists, she sees psychologically regressive girls. In this argument, as in the earlier assessments of critics like Williams, women bring us back to conventionality and the private sphere after the genre's brief excursion into truly political issues.

46. Roger P. Wallins, "Victorian Periodicals and the Emerging Social Conscience," *Victorian Periodicals Newsletter* 8 (1975): 49.

47. George Levine, *The Realistic Imagination: English Fiction from Frankenstein to Lady Chatterley* (Chicago: U of Chicago P, 1981) 12.

48. Charlotte Elizabeth [Tonna], *Helen Fleetwood, The Works of Charlotte Elizabeth,* 2 vols. (New York: Dodd, 1847) 1: 519.

49. Thomas Carlyle, "Biography," *Critical and Miscellaneous Essays in Five Volumes: Volume III* (London: Chapman, 1899; New York: AMS, 1969) 49, vol. 28 of *The Works of Thomas Carlyle.* W. R. Greg offered a similar complaint while objecting to social-purpose fiction in the course of a review of *Alton Locke:* "[T]he novelist *makes his facts* as well as his reasonings. He *coins* the premises from which his conclusions are deduced; and he may coin exactly what he wants" ("English Socialism, and Communistic Associations," *Edinburgh Review* 93 [1851]: 31).

50. Kenneth Burke, "Literature as Equipment for Living," *The Philosophy of Literary Form,* 3rd ed. (Berkeley: U of California P, 1973) 296.

51. Kenneth Burke, "The Philosophy of Literary Form," Burke 3.

52. Winfried Fluck, "Literature as Symbolic Action" *Amerikastudien/American Studies* 28 (1983): 364–65.

53. Fluck 371.

54. The phrase is Claude Lévi-Strauss's, although used in a somewhat different context. *Structural Anthropology,* trans. Claire Jacobson and Brooke Grundfest Schoepf (New York: Basic, 1963) 213.

55. Their first joint book has been of greatest use to me: Sandra M. Gilbert and Susan Gubar, *The Madwoman in the Attic: The Woman Writer and the Nineteenth-Century Literary Imagination* (New Haven: Yale UP, 1979). However, Gilbert and Gubar have continued to explore many of the same fundamental issues in the first two volumes of *No Man's Land: The Place of the Woman Writer in the Twentieth Century.*

56. Nina Auerbach, *Woman and the Demon: The Life of a Victorian Myth* (Cambridge: Harvard UP, 1982).

57. Burke, "The Philosophy of Literary Form" 67.

58. For the development of domestic ideology in this period, see Leonore Davidoff and Catherine Hall, *Family Fortunes: Men and Women of the English Middle Class,*

1780–1850 (Chicago: U of Chicago P, 1987) 180–92. Nancy Armstrong has also argued for the importance of this period as the time in which the gendering of subjectivity took on political significance (*Desire and Domestic Fiction: A Political History of the Novel* [Oxford: Oxford UP, 1987] 20).

59. James A. Epstein offers a valuable discussion of the Chartist appropriation of the language of constitutionalism, an apparently conservative discourse, for revolutionary ends. While Epstein describes a conscious political strategy, his insight into the value for radicals of occupying shared "cultural and political terrain" is useful here as well ("The Constitutional Idiom: Radical Reasoning, Rhetoric and Action in Early Nineteenth-Century England," *Journal of Social History* 23 [1990]: 553–74).

Chapter 1

1. Elizabeth Gaskell, *North and South*, ed. Dorothy Collin (1855; Harmondsworth: Penguin, 1970). Page references to this and all other condition-of-England novels will be provided parenthetically in the text. The editions cited are as follows: Charles Dickens, *Hard Times*, ed. George Ford and Sylvère Monod (1854; New York: Norton, 1966); Benjamin Disraeli, *Sybil; or, The Two Nations*, ed. Sheila M. Smith (1845; Oxford: Oxford UP, 1981); Elizabeth Gaskell, *Mary Barton: A Tale of Manchester Life*, ed. Stephen Gill (1848; Harmondsworth: Penguin, 1970); Charles Kingsley, *Alton Locke, Tailor and Poet: An Autobiography*, ed. Elizabeth A. Cripps (1850; Oxford: Oxford UP, 1983); Charlotte Elizabeth [Tonna], *Helen Fleetwood, The Works of Charlotte Elizabeth*, vol. 1 (1841; New York: Dodd, 1847); 2 vols.; Frances Trollope, *The Life and Adventures of Michael Armstrong, the Factory Boy* (London: Colburn, 1840).

2. Not all critics would state as strongly as I do that Margaret is successfully assuming public power here. Bodenheimer, for instance, considers Margaret's action to be ambiguous but sees it as most significantly an expression of purely personal feeling for Thornton, "not an abstract mediation between classes" (*Politics of Story* 64). Gallagher argues that its social impact is negligible because of "the moral blindness of those who witness it" (*Industrial Reformation* 173). To the extent that Margaret has power, Gallagher suggests, its "source and nature remain . . . mysterious," and Margaret's conviction that her power is moral in origin remains problematic (178).

3. Barbara Leah Harman treats the riot scene at some length in "In Promiscuous Company: Female Public Appearance in Elizabeth Gaskell's *North and South*," *Victorian Studies* 31 (1988): 351–74. Harman argues that Margaret's attempts to desexualize her actions are futile, since female entry into the public arena is inevitably compromising. Gaskell, however, according to Harman, accepts this sexual taint and endorses women's participation in a public life that domestic virtues do not change. Deborah Epstein Nord offers another view of Margaret's sexual maturation in "The Urban Peripatetic: Spectator, Streetwalker, Woman Writer," *Nineteenth-Century Literature* 46 (1991): 351–75. Nord, in the course of identifying "a distinctively female urban vision" (365) that locates a path to subjecthood only through sexual objectification, suggests that for Gaskell "sexual self-consciousness" (370) and "class-consciousness" (371) are connected.

4. Davidoff and Hall 313.

5. Mary Poovey has argued for the crucial importance of "the unevenness within the

construction and deployment of mid-Victorian representations of gender" that simultaneously enabled "conservative ideological work" and "a genuinely—although incompletely articulated—oppositional voice" (*Uneven Developments: The Ideological Work of Gender in Mid-Victorian England* [Chicago: U of Chicago P, 1988] 4).

6. Anna Clark, "The Rhetoric of Chartist Domesticity: Gender, Language, and Class in the 1830s and 1840s," *Journal of British Studies* 31 (1992): 62–88. However, Clark goes on to observe that such a politicized use (particularly by Chartist women) of domesticity eventually gave way to entrapment by the middle-class depoliticization of the private sphere.

    Marianna Valverde, in the course of pointing out the "distinctively masculinist cast" of the early self-definition of the British working class, offers additional evidence for Clark's final point—that working-class men as well as the middle class made use of the ideology of separate spheres. If her example reveals that the ideology of domesticity was appropriated for the benefit of men within a specifically working-class situation, it nonetheless underlines the pervasiveness of domestic ideology in early-Victorian Britain. Valverde, " 'Giving the Female a Domestic Turn': The Social, Legal and Moral Regulation of Women's Work in British Cotton Mills, 1820–1850," *Journal of Social History* 21 (1988): 619–34. See also Sally Alexander, "Women, Class and Sexual Differences in the 1830s and 1840s: Some Reflections on the Writing of a Feminist History," *History Journal* 17 (1984): 125–49.

7. Davidoff and Hall 33, 149.

8. Sarah Stickney Ellis, *The Women of England* (1839; Philadelphia: Herman Hooker, 1841) 23. Davidoff and Hall interestingly note that Ellis's pragmatic approach struck her contemporaries as "a radical departure, an attempt to break with the unhappy state of affairs in the middle-class homes of England, where gentility had been winning too many victories over practicality" (182).

9. Barbara Corrado Pope, "Angels in the Devil's Workshop: Leisured and Charitable Women in Nineteenth-Century England and France," *Becoming Visible: Women in European History,* ed. Renate Bridenthal and Claudia Koontz (Boston: Houghton, 1977) 304.

10. Ellis 33.

11. [Catharine Maria Sedgwick], *Means and Ends, or Self-Training* (1839; New York: Harper, 1845) 275. Sedgwick is consciously steering a course between women's rights activists and those who would relegate women to a very narrowly defined domestic sphere. Mary Bond is her recurrent figure of an exemplary young woman.

12. The significance of domestic ideology for women and nineteenth-century society has long been a subject of critical scrutiny. For a sketch of the ideology and a consideration of the early stages of the debate in the American context, in which the notion of "domestic feminism" first emerged, see Nancy F. Cott, *The Bonds of Womanhood: "Woman's Sphere" in New England, 1780–1835* (New Haven: Yale UP, 1977), esp. 197–206. For an example of literary criticism that views the ideology of domesticity as confining, see Judith Lowder Newton, *Women, Power, and Subversion: Social Strategies in British Fiction, 1778–1860* (Athens: U of Georgia P, 1981). Newton compares *North and South* unfavorably with *Villette* and *The Mill on the*

Floss because of "the radical limitations, politically and aesthetically as well, of [Gaskell's] conservative relation to ideology" (168).

More recent critics have offered fresh considerations of the domestic sphere that emphasize its complicity with middle-class hegemony. Elizabeth Langland argues that middle-class women's control of the household gave them great political power—"bourgeois women had become fully invested and centrally significant in the discursive practices that consolidated middle-class power." As Langland observes, her analysis usefully "complicate[s] the portrait of middle-class women by identifying their complicity in the power systems that oppress them" ("Nobody's Angels: Domestic Ideology and Middle-Class Women in the Victorian Novel," *PMLA* 107 [1992]: 303). Anita Levy sees the discourse of domesticity as a means for the exercise of social control by the middle class over the working class (particularly working-class women) in *Other Women* (Princeton: Princeton UP, 1991).

13. Daniel Scott Smith, "Family Limitation, Sexual Control, and Domestic Feminism in Victorian America," *Feminist Studies* 1.3–4 (1973): 40–57.

14. Mary P. Ryan, *The Empire of the Mother: American Writing about Domesticity, 1830–1860*, Women and History, no. 2/3 (New York: Institute for Research in History; Haworth Press, 1982) 5. For a consideration of the lives American women could forge for themselves within an oppressive culture, see Carroll Smith-Rosenberg, *Disorderly Conduct: Visions of Gender in Victorian America* (New York: Knopf, 1985).

15. Barbara Welter, "The Cult of True Womanhood: 1820–1860," *American Quarterly* 18 (1966): 174. Davidoff and Hall make note of both the contradictions between cultural ideals English women experienced and the pervasiveness of male fears of female independence; see in particular 451. Poovey explores at length the inherent instability of the notion of separate spheres. She notes that "the domestic ideal always contained an aggressive component" (170), which could be represented as sexual aggression or capability (163).

16. Jane Tompkins, *Sensational Designs: The Cultural Work of American Fiction, 1790–1860* (Oxford: Oxford UP, 1985) 161. Tompkins also asserts a proposition to which I will return in chapter 3 when I consider the solutions condition-of-England novels offer: "[T]he popular domestic novel of the nineteenth century represents a monumental effort to reorganize culture from the woman's point of view" (124). Gillian Beer offers a useful caution in her own assessment of domesticity in American literature: since domestic ideology is bound up with the ideology of possessive individualism, "[t]o think of the domestic as reformist or revolutionary . . . is to register only one of its operations" (*Domestic Individualism: Imagining Self in Nineteenth-Century America* [Berkeley: U of California P, 1990] 7).

Another recent and influential account of domestic fiction is Nancy Armstrong's *Desire and Domestic Fiction*. Armstrong argues that, far from offering a truly oppositional principle to middle-class ideology, domestic fiction was responsible for the creation of middle-class subjectivity and the maintenance of middle-class social control. In her view the ostensible apoliticism of domestic fiction ensured the displacement of older political contests and the containment of political resistance.

17. I refer to "novels" rather than "novelists" here because I am not suggesting that individual writers found psychological or political satisfaction in the vicarious exercise of feminist power. For all I know they could have done so, but my point is distinct from concerns of authorial motivation (whether conscious or subconscious): domestic ideology contained within itself, however self-contradictorily, the legitimation of a female authority that could provide a way out of the cultural dilemma the condition-of-England crisis posed to industrial novelists. Such "a way out" was available for, and taken by, those novelists who constructed the crisis in the Carlylean terms my introduction delineated.

18. Gallagher, in *Industrial Reformation*, also considers extensively the connections industrial novels make between the public and private spheres. Gallagher argues that this connection is paradoxical: the reforming potential of the family is predicated upon the continued separation of the family from society. However, this conclusion is based on Gallagher's earlier assertion that "because private problems are unlike public problems, because they seem responsive to individual efforts of will, whereas public problems do not, novelists often 'solve' social conflicts by first translating them into private conflicts" (114). It seems to me that Gallagher's argument rests on the assumption that social conflicts must always initially be conceived of as events in the public sphere. I argue below that condition-of-England novels represent the public sphere as a subset of the private sphere, and social conflict therefore as an essentially domestic question. I would suggest that by beginning with the text rather than the extratextual act of "translating" we see a domesticized social conflict that is consistent with the domesticized solutions offered. Consequently, I would locate paradox within the definition of the ideology of separate spheres rather than in the novels themselves. I certainly agree with Gallagher that this ideology *was* inherently self-contradictory; however, I would not agree that all appropriations of domestic ideology inevitably remained (like Ellis's [*Industrial Reformation* 119]) mired in paradox. My suggestion is that the condition-of-England novelists were able to short circuit the ideology's self-contradiction by redefining the public sphere.

19. Bodenheimer, *Politics of Story* 111; she is not specifically referring to domestic feminism here, but to the potential that is inherent in women's marginality.

20. Angus Easson, *Elizabeth Gaskell* (London: Routledge, 1979) 90.

21. Gallagher stresses the importance of Richard Green, whom she calls "the hero of *Helen Fleetwood*" (*Industrial Reformation* 41) because of his role in confronting the providential and antiprovidential determinisms of M. My analysis sees the novel as primarily concerned with the exploration of painful and triumphant industrial martyrdom rather than with tensions between free will and determinism; in this light Helen herself is the hero of the novel.

22. For supposedly shifting her focus by moving from the initially conceived *John Barton* to *Mary Barton*, Gaskell's apparently bourgeois emphasis on her heroine has been deplored, notably by Raymond Williams—most recently in *Writing in Society* (London: Verso, 1983) 160. However, Brian Crick argues interestingly that there is no evidence that Gaskell's preference for the title of *John Barton* reflects an earlier conception of the novel in which Mary's story played a less prominent role. I think Crick is right to conclude that Mary's tale was always seen by Gaskell as

an integral part of her industrial tale ("The Implications of the Title Changes and Textual Revisions in Mrs. Gaskell's *Mary Barton: A Tale of Manchester Life,*" *Notes and Queries* 225 [1980]: 514–19).

23. In this paragraph, as I move to novels with a less exclusive focus on the central female character(s), I am also moving to fiction written by men. Bodenheimer interestingly distinguishes men's and women's industrial fiction. Men's novels, she observes, "do not in the same way hang their plots on the development of their heroines" (*Politics of Story* 16). While acknowledging these differences, I believe that they do not significantly impinge upon the notion of feminocentrism I advance here.

    Part of what I find remarkable about the condition-of-England genre is the similarity of fictional analysis by both male and female writers. As I suggested in the introduction, I would in part attribute this relative uniformity to the similar middle-class ideologies of class and gender that informed all these writers' experiences, however unevenly. But I am also intrigued by Armstrong's suggestion that "any use of language was considered essentially female if sufficiently detached from the contentious ways of the marketplace and rooted instead in the values of the heart and home" (41). Perhaps an identification of condition-of-England novels with a female position within fictional discourse can help account for the surprising unanimity of male and female writers. See also Jean Ferguson Carr, "Writing as a Woman: Dickens, *Hard Times,* and Feminine Discourses," *Dickens Studies Annual* 18 (1989): 161–78. Carr finds Dickens's appropriation of a female discourse only ambiguously successful.

24. Deborah Kaplan has made the interesting point that Tonna's second novel, *The Wrongs of Woman*—an examination of the exploitation of women in four different occupations—is distinguished from *Mary Barton* and *Hard Times* by its focus on working conditions rather than domestic life ("The Woman Worker in Charlotte Elizabeth Tonna's Fiction," *Mosaic* 18.2 [1985]: 59–60).

25. Terry Lovell, *Consuming Fiction,* Questions for Feminism (London: Verso, 1987) 88. Likewise, Bodenheimer observes that "an astonishing and hitherto unemphasized proportion of the novel is devoted to the depiction of domestic scenes: family life, neighborly help, and the apparently irrelevant small talk that humanizes private and daily life" ("Private Grief and Public Acts in *Mary Barton,*" *Dickens Studies Annual* 9 [1981]: 196). Gallagher also notes that "reality is always domestic in *Mary Barton*" (*Industrial Reformation* 81). However, she argues that the chief effect domestic narrative has here is that it "formally authorizes the suppression of tragic causality," exemplified by John Barton's history (78).

    My argument about *Mary Barton* sees the novel's reliance on the ideology of separate spheres as crucial to its delineation of the industrial situation. For a different view, see Marjorie Stone, "Bakhtinian Polyphony in *Mary Barton:* Class, Gender, and the Textual Voice," *Dickens Studies Annual* 20 (1991): 175–200. Stone emphasizes the polyvocality of *Mary Barton* that engages readers "in a complex series of interlocking debates and encounters with conflicting languages and ideologies" (196). Consequently, she argues, such polyphony "undermine[s] conventional alignments of gender and sphere" (183).

26. The issue of what went on during working hours was evidently a subsidiary one to Frances Trollope herself, for she did not feel obligated to see a factory with her own eyes before starting her book. She visited a mill for the first time only after writing several chapters of *Michael Armstrong* (W. H. Chaloner, "Mrs. Trollope and the Early Factory System," *Victorian Studies* 4 [1960]: 159–66).

27. Although Gallagher also notes the partial reformation of the Gradgrind family, she emphasizes that "their family cohesion is itself fragile and ambiguous" (*Industrial Reformation* 158). I agree, but I would focus on the positive changes that have taken place as a result of Sissy's intervention.

28. Gallagher discusses at some length how the members of the circus "dramatize the social paternalists' trope: the family-society metaphor. The unrelated individuals of the circus society come together and behave like a loyal family" (*Industrial Reformation* 160). However, Gallagher goes on to explore the resemblance of the circus people to Bounderby, which she argues undermines the circus's metaphorical usefulness (and the value of metaphor itself).

29. Bodenheimer, "Private Grief" 204. However, Bodenheimer argues that "the implicit pattern is an apolitical one." In contrast, Hilary M. Schor sees that the private story, specifically Mary's story, has a political import, but she identifies this as "The heroine's movement toward speech" (*Scheherezade in the Marketplace: Elizabeth Gaskell and the Victorian Novel* [Oxford: Oxford UP, 1992] 15).

30. In contrast, Bodenheimer suggests that the crudeness of Trollope's design obviates any effective social critique. "Trollope is incapable of systemic analysis: every one of these incidents [of Dowling's evil activity] is atypical, a special form of personal evil rather than an effect of social condition or philosophy" (*Politics of Story* 131). I would argue that if Dowling is understood as exemplary of the genre's characteristic miniaturization of reality (which I discuss later in this chapter), Trollope's analysis stands revealed as systemic in its own idiosyncratic way.

31. For Gallagher's discussion of Dickens's metaphoric connection of public and private, see *Industrial Reformation* 149–66.

32. Martin Dodsworth, introduction, *North and South*, by Elizabeth Gaskell (Harmondsworth: Penguin, 1970) 10–11.

33. Easson 93.

34. Amelia Z. in *Helen Fleetwood* provides a similar though less extensively developed example of a well-meaning daughter whose obedience to her father prevents her from making any difference in the treatment of mill workers (560).

35. David Roberts, *Paternalism in Early Victorian England* (New Brunswick: Rutgers UP, 1979) 22.

36. For discussion of an example of complicity between domestic ideology and paternalism, see Judy Lown, "Not so much a Factory, More a Form of Patriarchy: Gender and Class during Industrialisation," *Gender, Class and Work*, ed. Eva Gamarnikow et al. (London: Heinemann, 1983) 28–45.

37. Gallagher offers a valuable discussion of paternalism and domestic ideology that identifies the first as metaphoric and the second as metonymic. She goes on to argue that the two ideologies are connected by the similarity of their self-contradictions, and to observe that they were "wedded" by factory reformers' rhetoric in the 1840s (*Industrial Reformation* 125). Two remarks at this point may clarify my

own approach. I emphasize the significance of the distinctions between paternalism and domestic ideology, for instance in their differing conceptions of the nature of the family. I would also underscore the susceptibility of domestic ideology to divergent appropriations: Tory reformers used it to serve their own (paternalist) ends, but, as I observe above, so did Chartists and domestic feminists. One appropriation does not enforce a permanent connection or preclude others.

38. In chapter 1 of *Politics of Story*, Bodenheimer argues that *Michael Armstrong, Jessie Phillips, Shirley*, and *North and South* progressively engage the issue of paternalism by employing an interventionist heroine in a social-problem narrative that is also a romantic melodrama. In this view female paternalist intervention is inherently paradoxical because it can only be authorized by passive acquiescence in the paternal order. (Bodenheimer sees *Michael Armstrong* as particularly problematic in Mary Brotherton's final reconstitution of the powerless domestic sphere, while she suggests that *North and South* transforms paternalism in part by refusing to associate Margaret Hale with a sphere of domestic purity.) I would argue that the interventions that Bodenheimer identifies as paternalist (particularly Mary Brotherton's) are authorized by an appropriation of domesticity separate from those paternalism offered. Consequently, I believe that female intervention is not necessarily dependent upon an acceptance of women's subordination to men. I would also argue that throughout the book Margaret Hale has a closer affiliation with the domestic sphere than Bodenheimer would grant.

39. Bodenheimer, *Politics of Story* 58. In this context, Bodenheimer's entire discussion of *North and South* in this section (53–68) is very useful.

40. Gallagher brilliantly delineates the inconsistencies that lie within Dickens's use of metaphor in *Hard Times*. However, I am uncomfortable with her assumption that Dickens's use of a metaphorical organization for his novel necessarily implies some endorsement of paternalism as a social ideology (*Industrial Reformation*, esp. 148, 153–56). I suggest here that Dickens is explicitly critical of paternalism; I explore more fully in chapter 3 how Sissy Jupe offers the genuine social alternative to Coketown's problems. Gallagher also recognizes Sissy's role, but has less confidence than I do in the strength of her "slight shoulders" (159).

41. Auerbach.

Chapter 2

1. Auerbach 34.
2. Catherine Barnes Stevenson, "'What Must Not Be Said': *North and South* and the Problem of Women's Work," *Victorian Literature and Culture* 19 (1991): 68. Stevenson cites the statistic that females over age thirteen constituted 55.8 percent of the factory work force at Preston.
3. Rev. of *The Life and Adventures of Michael Armstrong, the Factory Boy*, by Frances Trollope, nos. I to VI, *Athenaeum* no. 615 (10 Aug. 1339): 590. The novel consisted of twelve numbers in all. It seems only fair to add that in the first part of the novel Michael provides a singularly unthreatening example of victimhood. Boys, however, grow up to be men, as Trollope herself realized.

4. "Mary Barton," rev. of *Mary Barton*, by Elizabeth Gaskell, *New Monthly Magazine* 84 (1848): 407.

5. Rev. of *Mary Barton*, by Elizabeth Gaskell, *Athenaeum* no. 1095 (21 Oct. 1848): 1050. On the whole, though, this review is highly favorable.

6. [J. W. Croker], "Revolutionary Literature," *Quarterly Review* 89 (1851): 528. For an overview of contemporary reactions to Kingsley's social thought, see John C. Hawley, "Responses to Charles Kingsley's Attack on Political Economy," *Victorian Periodicals Review* 19 (1986): 131–37.

7. Trollope goes on to insist upon the impossibility of misprisioning the meaning of her child victims. Her perception of the need for such a disclaimer suggests instead the possibility of such a reading.

8. F. R. Leavis, *The Great Tradition* (London: Chatto, 1948) 235.

9. Anne Smith, "The Martyrdom of Stephen in *Hard Times*," *Journal of Narrative Technique* 2 (1972): 165.

10. A. Smith 167.

11. Gallagher attributes the incongruity of the novel's elements to the incompatibility of providential and antiprovidential causalities (*Industrial Reform* 50).

12. Interestingly enough, the *Athenaeum* reviewer singled out the illustration that accompanied this very scene as particularly liable to inflame the lower classes (Rev. of *Michael Armstrong* 590).

13. Karen Sánchez-Eppler, "Bodily Bonds: The Intersecting Rhetorics of Feminism and Abolition," *Representations* 24 (1988): 28–59. Sánchez-Eppler also tends to hold a negative view of domesticity as complicit with oppressive social power.

14. Stephen Gill, introduction, *Mary Barton*, by Elizabeth Gaskell (Harmondsworth: Penguin, 1970) 27.

15. Raymond Williams, for instance, locates the novel's failure in the incompleteness of Gaskell's sympathy with the working class. The moment at which this sympathy ceases is Barton's murder of Harry Carson; afterwards, Williams says, sympathy is "diverted to the less compromising figure of the daughter" and her "familiar and orthodox plot . . . of little lasting interest" (*Culture and Society* 89). Tomlinson, who assesses Gaskell's political views as quite conservative, deplores the insipid conventionality of Mary's love story and argues that when Gaskell focuses on it, "[t]he conditions that caused Carson's murder are left gradually behind" (73).

16. Gallagher, *Industrial Reformation* 151. Gallagher sees this connection as part of Dickens's establishment of a family-society metaphor that eventually disintegrates.

17. See Marjorie Cohen, "Changing Perceptions of the Impact of the Industrial Revolution on Female Labour," *International Journal of Women's Studies* 7 (1984): 292. For a general overview of women's work in this period, see Ivy Pinchbeck, *Women Workers and the Industrial Revolution, 1750–1850* (New York: Crofts, 1930). Gallagher discusses the implications of the Ten Hours movement's preoccupation with little girls and the subsequent growth of reform's concern with women. She points out the self-contradiction inherent in describing women workers as especially representative yet insisting that work interfered with true womanhood (*Industrial Reformation* 127–29).

18. For the continuation of these attitudes into the early years of social science re-

search, see Dorothy C. Wertz, "Social Science Attitudes towards Women Workers, 1870–1970," *International Journal of Women's Studies* 5 (1982): 161–71.

19. Sally Mitchell, *The Fallen Angel: Chastity, Class and Women's Reading, 1835–1880* (Bowling Green: Bowling Green U Popular P, 1981) 51.

20. Valverde, passim.

21. Patricia Meyer Spacks, *The Female Imagination* (New York: Knopf, 1975) 88.

22. See, for instance, Ellen Moers, *Literary Women* (New York: Doubleday, 1976), esp. 18–30. Kestner has a consistent though not exclusive affinity for this issue.

23. Auerbach 64. My discussion of female angels and demons, as well as my earlier discussion of the superior strength of female victimhood, is deeply indebted to *Woman and the Demon*. Auerbach's comments about Victorian society's underlying myth of womanhood form the foundation of much of my analysis in this chapter, but my argument moves in a somewhat different direction from hers. Whereas politics do not figure in Auerbach's study at all, the politics of industrialism so pervade the condition-of-England genre that they are crucial to the definition of victimhood. To be effective victims of the contemporary age, characters must be at once injured by the industrial social order and clearly exonerated from complicity in it. The result (in all but one novel) of the centrality of industrial politics is the separation of the roles of victim and heroine. While Auerbach's women can be both oppressed and triumphant, the condition-of-England victim has generally been so distanced from possible sources of political power that she is unable to conquer her society. Political action must be left to another, less battered woman— the heroine, who can make use of the attar of subversive power released by the crushed victim.

24. Bodenheimer, "Private Grief" 209.

25. Tillotson 213. Tillotson generally finds Mary a disappointing character; she argues that "her relation to [the novel's] theme seems too weakly developed" (213).

26. Gilbert and Gubar 78.

27. Auerbach 75.

28. Auerbach 75.

29. For a discussion of fire imagery, see William J. Palmer, "*Hard Times*: A Dickens Fable of Personal Salvation," *Dalhousie Review* 52 (1972): 72–74.

30. Auerbach 150.

Chapter 3

1. Tillotson 213.

2. Coral Lansbury, *Elizabeth Gaskell: The Novel of Social Crisis* (New York: Barnes, 1975) 23.

3. Kestner 57.

4. Gallagher acknowledges that in the conclusion of *North and South* Gaskell "intertwine[s] her social and familial themes and plots so thoroughly that the very conventional resolution of the novel's love plot appears to be a partial solution to industrial social problems" (*Industrial Reformation* 170). However, she argues that the novel ultimately reveals the self-contradiction of its own ideology and method (184). This chapter of Gallagher's first appeared in an earlier version that I found

very useful in the development of my argument. In this version Gallagher expressed greater confidence in the symbolic success of the novel's resolution (Gallagher, "*Hard Times* and *North and South*").

Schor sees the marriage of Margaret and Thornton not as a resolution of larger social problems but as part of a pattern of maintaining invigorating oppositions (Schor, esp. 144–50).

5. Thom Braun, *Disraeli the Novelist* (London: Allen, 1981) 108.
6. Bodenheimer, *Politics of Story* 3.
7. Williams, *Culture and Society* 91.
8. Bodenheimer in contrast argues that "[t]he nature of the changes recorded" in *Hard Times* initially appears "so private that it hardly seems to bear on the question of social change" (*Politics of Story* 205). However, she ultimately locates a kind of radicalism in Dickens's utter nihilism.
9. Brantlinger, *Spirit of Reform* 137.
10. Lansbury 31.
11. Auerbach is again useful in this context. For a considerably earlier treatment of such cultural "percolation," see Patricia Thomson, *The Victorian Heroine: A Changing Ideal, 1837–1873* (London: Oxford UP, 1956) 7.
12. Tompkins 142–43. *Uncle Tom's Cabin* differs from the texts I cover in its emphasis on motherhood and child rearing. Yet, similarly, it looks forward with a millenarian sensibility to the abolition of competition and force.
13. Barbara Taylor, *Eve and the New Jerusalem: Socialism and Feminism in the Nineteenth Century* (New York: Pantheon, 1983).
14. Taylor 160.
15. For an account of millenarianism, see J. F. C. Harrison, *The Second Coming: Popular Millenarianism, 1780–1850* (New Brunswick: Rutgers UP, 1979). Harrison interestingly discusses the presence of female messiahs such as Joanna Southcott and Ann Lee within the tradition of popular millenarianism. Here again we find a kind of cultural precedent for the feminist imaginings of the condition-of-England novel.
16. Kestner 57.
17. Bodenheimer observes that "Love and gratitude between persons untainted by capitalism create an ideal family with a woman's social and economic power at its head" (*Politics of Story* 30). However, she goes on to argue that this household reinstates a restrictive vision of female domesticity.
18. Brantlinger, *Spirit of Reform* 104. See Disraeli 173.
19. This spirit seems to have suffused much of Tonna's other work as well. Kovačević and Kanner characterize her as "a more prolific polemicist in the cause of millenarianism than in that of social reform." Ivanka Kovačević and S. Barbara Kanner, "Blue Book into Novel: The Forgotten Industrial Fiction of Charlotte Elizabeth Tonna," *Nineteenth-Century Fiction* 25 (1970): 155. Interestingly, these critics also see Tonna as a precursor to Maurice and Christian Socialism (160).
20. Brantlinger, *Spirit of Reform* 57.
21. Carol Pearson, "Coming Home: Four Feminist Utopias and Patriarchal Experience," *Future Females: A Critical Anthology*, ed. Marleen S. Barr (Bowling Green: Bowling Green State U Popular P, 1981) 64–65.

Chapter 4

1. Charlotte Brontë, *Shirley*, ed. Herbert Rosengarten and Margaret Smith (1849; Oxford: Clarendon, 1979) 386. Future references will be to this edition, with page references cited parenthetically in the text.
2. Bodenheimer argues that *Shirley*'s salient feature is its adherence to and exploration of paternalist models of social organization. This inability to imagine an alternative model becomes precisely the strength of the novel: Brontë winds up revealing the gaps and inadequacies within paternalism (*Politics of Story* 36–53).
3. Terry Eagleton, *Myths of Power: A Marxist Study of the Brontës* (New York: Barnes, 1975) 45. Eagleton and Pierce state that "[i]ts relation to the 'condition of England' novelists [*sic*] . . . [is] clear" (47). Tillotson observes that Brontë's "novels about the past are still novels for [her] present" (98).
4. For an argument that Brontë actually endorses industrialism for the new possibilities it opens up for women, see Susan Zlotnick, "Luddism, Medievalism and Women's History in *Shirley*: Charlotte Brontë's Revisionist Tactics," *Novel* 24 (1991): 282–95.
5. Helene Moglen, *Charlotte Brontë: The Self Conceived* (New York: Norton, 1976) 167.
6. Eagleton and Pierce 49.
7. This is part of what Arnold Shapiro identifies as the novel's total separation of male and female worlds in "Public Themes and Private Lives: Social Criticism in *Shirley*," *Papers on Literature and Language* 4 (1968): 77.
8. Gilbert and Gubar 376.
9. See Auerbach, chap. 4.
10. Marxist Feminist Literature Collective, "Women's Writing: *Jane Eyre, Shirley, Villette, Aurora Leigh*," *1848: The Sociology of Literature*, ed. Francis Barker et al., Proc. of the Essex Conference on the Sociology of Literature, July 1977 ([Colchester]: U of Essex, 1978) 194.
11. Gilbert and Gubar 384, 379.
12. Spacks 88.
13. Robert Godwin-Jones, "George Sand, Charlotte Brontë, and the Industrial Novel," *George Sand Papers: Conference Proceedings, 1978*, ed. Natalie Datlof et al., Hofstra U Cultural and Intercultural Studies 2 (New York: AMS, 1982) 167.
14. Roslyn Belkin, "Rejects of the Marketplace: Old Maids in Charlotte Brontë's *Shirley*," *International Journal of Women's Studies* 4 (1981): 50.
15. Marxist Feminist Literature Collective 194.
16. Elaine Showalter, *A Literature of Their Own: British Women Novelists from Brontë to Lessing* (Princeton: Princeton UP, 1977) 28.
17. Interestingly enough, according to the notes to the Clarendon edition, Brontë seems here to have been specifically distinguishing her work from *Michael Armstrong* (752–53). Bodenheimer offers some interesting contrasts between Brontë's and Trollope's fictional procedures (*Politics of Story* 36–38, 48–49, 52).
18. Belkin 64. See Brontë 367.
19. Gilbert and Gubar 384.
20. For a more extended discussion of how feminist dissent offers a challenge to the

novel's superficial embrace of orthodox Christianity, see Kate Lawson, "The Dissenting Voice: *Shirley*'s Vision of Women and Christianity," *SEL* 29 (1989): 729–43.

21. Bernadette Bertrandias, "*Shirley:* le double apprivoisé," *Le double dans le romantisme anglo-américain,* Centre du romantisme anglais ns fasc. 19 (Clermont-Ferrand: Faculté des lettres et sciences humaines de l'Université de Clermont-Ferrand II, 1984) 167. See also Gilbert and Gubar 382–83.

22. Auerbach 94.

23. For a discussion of moon imagery, see Robert B. Heilman, "Charlotte Brontë, Reason, and the Moon," *Nineteenth-Century Fiction* 14 (1960): 283–302.

24. Linda C. Hunt, "Sustenance and Balm: The Question of Female Friendship in *Shirley* and *Villette*," *Tulsa Studies in Women's Literature* 1 (1982): 58.

25. Gilbert and Gubar 382.

26. Hunt 58. Hunt sees the myth at the heart of *Shirley* as one of female friendship, but she makes a general statement with which I can agree: "the excursion to Nunnwood cannot take place because, as an answer to how to be a woman in the middle of the nineteenth century, such a vision offers no solutions that are useful in the real world of 'Monday morning'" (59).

27. Gilbert and Gubar 392.

28. Moglen detects an autobiographical impulse (of which I am somewhat skeptical) behind the depiction of the "deeply flawed" relationship between Shirley and Caroline and credits the failure of female friendship to class barriers as well as to competition for men. "[W]hen women are not drawn together by the indissoluble ties which bound Charlotte to Anne and Emily . . . sexual competition and social differences prove more divisive than the unifying influence of shared concerns" (181).

29. Moglen 180. See also Gilbert and Gubar 394.

30. Bertrandias 175.

31. Margaret Miller, "Happily Ever After: Marriage in Charlotte Brontë's Novels," *Massachusetts Studies in English* 8.2 (1982): 25.

32. Gilbert and Gubar identify this as part of her "almost cynical excess of concession to narrative conventions" (396).

33. Robert Bernard Martin, in *The Accents of Persuasion: Charlotte Brontë's Novels* (New York: Norton, 1966), does not employ a feminist perspective, but even after pointing out the advantages of the two marriages he reaches the same conclusion. "Nowhere does the novel seem more sober, more disillusioned than in the conventional 'happy' ending" (135).

34. Jacob Korg, "The Problem of Unity in *Shirley*," *Nineteenth-Century Fiction* 12 (1957): 135.

Chapter 5

1. Page references to these novels will be given parenthetically in the text. The following editions are cited: Charles Dickens, *Little Dorrit*, ed. Harvey Peter Sucksmith (1857; Oxford: Oxford UP, 1982); George Eliot, *Felix Holt, The Radical*, ed. Peter Coveney (1866; Harmondsworth: Penguin, 1972); Elizabeth Gaskell, *Wives and Daughters*, ed. Frank Glover Smith (1866; Harmondsworth: Penguin, 1969).

2. Gallagher sees *Felix Holt* in the context of the English debate in the 1860s over political representation; she explores Eliot's use of Felix as an embodiment of Arnoldian pure political value who ultimately points to problems within the discourse of culture itself (*Industrial Reformation*, chap. 3). Bodenheimer argues that in *Felix Holt* Eliot attempts to demonstrate the possibility of effecting political change through a reliance on the suprahistorical power of consciousness. By facing his own determinants and creating his own authentic personal narrative Felix manages to transcend his own conditions and ensure transindividual continuity through his conversion of Esther (*Politics of Story* 207–30).

3. In her chapter on *Wives and Daughters*, Margaret Homans describes Molly's encounter with symbolic and presymbolic languages, both of which ultimately prove to be contained by patriarchal power (*Bearing the Word: Language and Female Experience in Nineteenth-Century Women's Writing* [Chicago: U of Chicago P, 1986] chap. 10).

4. Bodenheimer, however, argues for the radicalism of *Felix Holt* in "refusing to fantasize about virtuous arrangements of power within conventional structures of social order." By resisting such structures Felix and Esther "will survive in a kind of moral guerrilla warfare with gentility" (*Politics of Story* 108). To my mind this underestimates the significance of the conventional gender relations the novel enforces.

5. Brantlinger, *Spirit of Reform* 5.

6. Bonnie Zimmerman has opened up the possibility that in this novel Eliot may have been directly responding to the emergence of organized feminism. In *Felix Holt*, Zimmerman argues, an Eliot fearful of the social consequences of emancipation "firmly draws the curtain between the male sphere of activity and the female sphere of passivity" (446–47), and harks back to the domestic ideology of a book (*Woman's Mission*) she read in her youth ("*Felix Holt* and the True Power of Womanhood," *ELH* 46 [1979]: 432–51). I would add that Eliot is clearly appropriating the most self-abnegating form of domestic ideology, not the powerful potential condition-of-England novelists embrace.

7. Deirdre David, *Intellectual Women and Victorian Patriarchy* (Ithaca: Cornell UP, 1987) 200–201. David sees in this an implicit critique of the limited possibilities open to women in Eliot's society; I am more inclined, in light of Zimmerman's article, to read this as distrust of women unsubdued by self-sacrifice.

8. Sally Shuttleworth insightfully examines the parallel between Eliot's organicist model of society and her severely constricted definition of woman's place, in part by drawing comparisons between *Felix Holt* and *Shirley* (*George Eliot and Nineteenth-Century Science: The Make-Believe of a Beginning* [Cambridge: Cambridge UP, 1984]). Shuttleworth sees Eliot's vision as quite conservative on both counts: "The sexual division to which Esther submits is directly correlated with the preservation of a traditional form of hierarchical community" (140). Only the unhappy Mrs. Transome "stands as a challenge to all ideals of unity, continuity, and organic harmony" (141).

9. Schor in contrast challenges any hard-and-fast separation of the natural-historical masculine world from the female domestic world. Employing the insights of Michel Foucault, she argues that "what Roger's scientific experiments suggest again is at once the prefixedness, and the always-invented quality of his

own . . . culture. Roger's 'museum' is never that far from the world of . . . disrupted (female) every-day life" (197).

10. Langland offers a more sympathetic reading of Hyacinth that emphasizes her ability to master social codes and manage resources to gain status (300–301).

11. For an argument that *Felix Holt* has a disguised feminist content both in its abundance of female protest and in Eliot's sense of the interdependency of public and private life, see Alison Booth, *Greatness Engendered: George Eliot and Virginia Woolf*, Reading Women Writing (Ithaca: Cornell UP, 1992) chap. 6.

12. In contrast, Alison Booth argues that Little Dorrit, along with Dorothea Brooke of *Middlemarch*, attains a spiritual triumph through her transcendent purity ("Little Dorrit and Dorothea Brooke: Interpreting the Heroines of History," *Nineteenth-Century Literature* 41 [1986]: 190–216).

13. For a discussion of how Amy's service to others, her "emotions work," ultimately "covers patriarchy's tracks" by deferring the need for any substantial change, see Sarah Winter, "Domestic Fictions: Feminine Deference and Maternal Shadow Labor in Dickens' *Little Dorrit*," *Dickens Studies Annual* 18 (1989): 243–54.

14. Indeed, Richard A. Currie has recently argued that Amy is practically a psychological case study of narcissism, with her evident self-hatred and her protection of a beloved object (her father) ("'As if She Had Done Him a Wrong': Hidden Rage and Object Protection in Dickens's *Little Dorrit*," *English Studies* 72 [1991]: 368–76).

15. Kestner 207.

16. R. A. Church, *The Great Victorian Boom, 1850–1873*, Studies in Economic and Social History (London: Macmillan, 1975) 76. John Saville also helps put the issue in perspective by pointing out that the 1840s themselves, far from being uniformly a time of economic downturn, had witnessed almost unbroken growth after 1842 (*1848: The British State and the Chartist Movement* [Cambridge: Cambridge UP, 1987] 59).

17. Saville stresses the continuity between such later forms of working-class expression and the institutions present in previous years: "the institutional and sociological foundations of reformism were established before the final years of Chartism" (226).

18. Patrick Joyce, *Work, Society and Politics: The Culture of the Factory in Later Victorian England* (New Brunswick: Rutgers UP, 1980) 65. Joyce distinguishes Lancashire from the West Riding, where industrialism was less developed and class relations were considerably more tense.

19. Harold Perkin, *The Origins of Modern English Society, 1780–1880* (London: Routledge, 1969) 346.

20. A perusal of the year-end summaries of the *Illustrated London News* (*ILN*) from the early 1840s to the late 1860s reveals a marked increase in cheerfulness about English society beginning around 1851. Two examples will serve to exhibit the striking change in mood: in 1844, "far down in the depths of society lie restless, unquiet, and dangerous elements" ("The New Year," *ILN* 4 Jan. 1845: 1); in 1862, even economic hard times "have begotten no fierce discontent, and no deep-mouthed objurgations on the institutions under which we live" ("The Coming Year," *ILN* 3 Jan. 1863: 2). I find it interesting that the Preston strike, which seems to have convinced Dickens and Gaskell that the condition-of-England crisis was

still at hand, rates only an allusion in the summary for 1853 ("The Old and the New Year," *ILN* 31 Dec. 1853: 589–90); the *ILN* places greater weight on the relative prosperity of Britain as a whole.

21. Brantlinger, *Spirit of Reform* 4–8.
22. For a useful summary of the early days of the British feminist movement, see Richard J. Evans, *The Feminists: Women's Emancipation Movements in Europe, America and Australasia 1840–1920* (London: Croom Helm, 1977) 63–69.
23. That is, the Matrimonial Causes Act of 1857.
24. Olive Banks, *Faces of Feminism: A Study of Feminism as a Social Movement* (1981; Oxford: Blackwell, 1986) 34.
25. "The Rights of Women," *Christian Remembrancer* ns 30 (July 1855): 1.
26. [Justin McCarthy], "Novels with a Purpose," *Westminster Review* 82 (1864): 18–19.
27. Evans 29–30.
28. John Ruskin, "Of Queens' Gardens," *Sesame and Lilies,* ed. E. T. Cook and Alexander Wedderburn (London: Allen, 1905) 137, vol. 18 of *The Works of John Ruskin.*

Bibliography

Primary Sources

Brontë, Charlotte. *Shirley*. Ed. Herbert Rosengarten and Margaret Smith. 1849. Oxford: Clarendon, 1979.

Carlyle, Thomas. "Biography." *Critical and Miscellaneous Essays in Five Volumes: Volume III. The Works of Thomas Carlyle*. Vol. 28. London: Chapman, 1899. New York: AMS, 1969. 30 vols.

———. *Chartism. Critical and Miscellaneous Essays in Five Volumes: Volume IV. The Works of Thomas Carlyle*. Vol. 29. London: Chapman, 1899. New York: AMS, 1969. 30 vols.

———. *Past and Present. The Works of Thomas Carlyle*. Vol. 10. London: Chapman, 1897. New York: AMS, 1969. 30 vols.

"The Coming Year." *Illustrated London News* 3 Jan. 1863: 1–2.

[Croker, J. W.] "Revolutionary Literature." *Quarterly Review* 89 (1851): 491–543.

Dickens, Charles. *Hard Times*. Ed. George Ford and Sylvère Monod. 1854. New York: Norton, 1966.

———. *Little Dorrit*. Ed. Harvey Peter Sucksmith. 1857. Oxford: Oxford UP, 1982.

Disraeli, Benjamin. *Sybil; or, The Two Nations*. Ed. Sheila M. Smith. 1845. Oxford: Oxford UP, 1981.

Eliot, George. *Felix Holt, The Radical*. Ed. Peter Coveney. 1866. Harmondsworth: Penguin, 1972.

———. Rev. of *Passages Selected from the Writings of Thomas Carlyle: With a Biographical Memoir*, by Thomas Ballantyne. *Leader* 27 Oct. 1855: 1034–35.

Ellis, Sarah Stickney. *The Women of England*. 1839. Philadelphia: Herman Hooker, 1841.

Gaskell, Elizabeth. *Mary Barton: A Tale of Manchester Life*. Ed. Stephen Gill. 1848. Harmondsworth: Penguin, 1970.

———. *North and South*. Ed. Dorothy Collin. 1855. Harmondsworth: Penguin, 1970.

———. *Wives and Daughters*. Ed. Frank Glover Smith. 1866. Harmondsworth: Penguin, 1969.

[Greg, W. R.] "English Socialism, and Communistic Associations." *Edinburgh Review* 93 (1851): 1–33.

Kingsley, Charles. *Alton Locke, Tailor and Poet: An Autobiography*. Ed. Elizabeth A. Cripps. 1850. Oxford: Oxford UP, 1983.

———. Rev. of *Mary Barton*, by Elizabeth Gaskell. *Fraser's Magazine* 39 (1849): 429–32.

[McCarthy, Justin]. "Novels with a Purpose." *Westminster Review* 82 (1864): 11–23.

"Mary Barton." Rev. of *Mary Barton*, by Elizabeth Gaskell. *New Monthly Magazine* 84 (1848): 406–8.

"The New Year." *Illustrated London News* 4 Jan. 1845: 1.

"The Old and the New Year." *Illustrated London News* 31 Dec. 1853: 589–90.

[Renouf, Peter LePage]. Rev. of *Past and Present*, by Thomas Carlyle. *Dublin Review* 15 (1843): 182–200.

Rev. of *The Life and Adventures of Michael Armstrong, the Factory Boy*, by Frances Trollope, nos. I to VI. *Athenaeum* no. 615 (10 Aug. 1839): 587–90.

Rev. of *Mary Barton*, by Elizabeth Gaskell. *Athenaeum* no. 1095 (21 Oct. 1848): 1050–51.

"The Rights of Women." *Christian Remembrancer* ns 30 (July 1855): 1–47.

[Rogers, Henry]. "Revolution and Reform." *Edinburgh Review* 88 (1848): 360–403.

Ruskin, John. "Of Queens' Gardens." *Sesame and Lilies. The Works of John Ruskin.* Ed. E. T. Cook and Alexander Wedderburn. Vol. 18. London: Allen, 1905. 39 vols. 1903–12.

[Sedgwick, Catharine Maria]. *Means and Ends, or Self-Training.* 1839. New York: Harper, 1845.

[Sewell, William]. "Carlyle's *Works*." *Quarterly Review* 66 (1840): 446–503.

[Smith, William Henry]. Rev. of *Past and Present*, by Thomas Carlyle. *Blackwood's Edinburgh Magazine* 54 (1843): 121–38.

[Tonna], Charlotte Elizabeth. *Helen Fleetwood.* 1841. *The Works of Charlotte Elizabeth.* Vol. 1. New York: Dodd, 1847. 2 vols.

Trollope, Frances. *The Life and Adventures of Michael Armstrong, the Factory Boy.* London: Colburn, 1840.

Secondary Sources: Literary Studies

Altick, Richard D. *The Presence of the Present: Topics of the Day in the Victorian Novel.* Columbus: Ohio State UP, 1991.

Armstrong, Nancy. *Desire and Domestic Fiction: A Political History of the Novel.* Oxford: Oxford UP, 1987.

Auerbach, Nina. *Woman and the Demon: The Life of a Victorian Myth.* Cambridge: Harvard UP, 1982.

Aydelotte, William O. "The England of Marx and Mill as Reflected in Fiction." *Journal of Economic History* Suppl. 8 (1948): 42–58.

Beer, Gillian. *Domestic Individualism: Imagining Self in Nineteenth-Century America.* Berkeley: U of California P, 1990.

Belkin, Roslyn. "Rejects of the Marketplace: Old Maids in Charlotte Brontë's *Shirley*." *International Journal of Women's Studies* 4 (1981): 50–66.

Bergmann, Helena. *Between Obedience and Freedom: Woman's Role in the Mid-Nineteenth Century Industrial Novel.* Gothenburg Studies in English 45. Göteborg: Acta Universitatis Gothoburgensis, 1979.

Bertrandias, Bernadette. "*Shirley:* le double apprivoisé." *Le double dans le romantisme anglo-américain.* Centre du romantisme anglais ns fasc. 19. Clermont-Ferrand: Faculté des lettres et sciences humaines de l'Université de Clermont-Ferrand II, 1984.

Bodenheimer, Rosemarie. "North and South: A Permanent State of Change." *Nineteenth-Century Fiction* 34 (1979): 281–301.

———. *The Politics of Story in Victorian Social Fiction*. Ithaca: Cornell UP, 1988.

———. "Private Grief and Public Acts in *Mary Barton*." *Dickens Studies Annual* 9 (1981): 195–216.

Booth, Alison. *Greatness Engendered: George Eliot and Virginia Woolf*. Reading Women Writing. Ithaca: Cornell UP, 1992.

———. "Little Dorrit and Dorothea Brooke: Interpreting the Heroines of History." *Nineteenth-Century Literature* 41 (1986): 190–216.

Borgmeier, Raimund. "Soziale Probleme zum Zeitvertreib?—Unterhaltung des Lesers und Gesellschaftskritik im viktorianischen Industrieroman." *Text-Leser-Bedeutung: Untersuchungen zur Interaktion von Text und Leser*. Ed. Herbert Grabes. Grossen-Linden: Hoffman, 1977.

Brantlinger, Patrick. "Bluebooks, the Social Organism, and the Victorian Novel." *Criticism* 14 (1972): 328–44.

———. *The Spirit of Reform: British Literature and Politics, 1832-1867*. Cambridge: Harvard UP, 1977.

Braun, Thom. *Disraeli the Novelist*. London: Allen, 1981.

Buckley, Jerome Hamilton. *The Victorian Temper*. Cambridge: Harvard UP, 1951.

Burke, Kenneth. *The Philosophy of Literary Form*. 3rd ed. Berkeley: U of California P, 1973.

Carr, Jean Ferguson. "Writing as a Woman: Dickens, *Hard Times*, and Feminine Discourses." *Dickens Studies Annual* 18 (1989): 161–78.

Cazamian, Louis. *The Social Novel in England, 1830–1850*. Trans. Martin Fido. First published in French, 1903. London: Routledge, 1973.

Chaloner, W. H. "Mrs. Trollope and the Early Factory System." *Victorian Studies* 4 (1960): 159–66.

Chapman, Raymond. *The Victorian Debate: English Literature and Society, 1832–1901*. New York: Basic, 1968.

Colella, Philippa Walsh. "Elizabeth Gaskell as Social Commentator: Radical, Liberal or Bourgeois Apologist?" *Studi dell'Istituto Linguistico* 4 (1981): 69–83.

Collins, Philip. "Dickens and Industrialism." *SEL* 20 (1980): 651–73.

Colmer, John. *Coleridge to Catch-22: Images of Society*. New York: St. Martin's, 1978.

Cooke, Michael. "Trying to Understand Victorians." Rev. of *Laughter and Despair: Readings in Ten Novels of the Victorian Era*, by U. C. Knoepflmacher; *The Working Classes in Victorian Fiction*, by P. J. Keating; and *Drink and the Victorians: The Temperance Question*, by Brian Harrison. *Yale Review* ns 61 (1972): 433–41.

Cott, Nancy F. *The Bonds of Womanhood: "Woman's Sphere" in New England, 1780–1835*. New Haven: Yale UP, 1977.

Craig, David. *The Real Foundations: Literature and Social Change*. New York: Oxford UP, 1974.

Crick, Brian. "The Implications of the Title Changes and Textual Revisions in Mrs. Gaskell's *Mary Barton: A Tale of Manchester Life*." *Notes and Queries* 225 (1980): 514–19.

Currie, Richard A. "'As if She Had Done Him a Wrong': Hidden Rage and Object Protection in Dickens's *Little Dorrit*." *English Studies* 72 (1991): 368–76.

David, Deirdre. *Fictions of Resolution in Three Victorian Novels*. New York: Columbia UP, 1981.

———. *Intellectual Women and Victorian Patriarchy*. Ithaca: Cornell UP, 1987.

Dobrzycka, Irena. *The Conditions of Living of the Working Class in the Social Novels of Charles Kingsley*. Poznańskie Towarzystwo Przyjaciół Nauk, Wydział Filologiczno-Filozoficzny. Prace Komisji Filologicznej. Vol 16. No. 2. Poznań: [Państwowe Wydawn. Naukowe], 1955.

Dodsworth, Martin. Introduction. *North and South*. By Elizabeth Gaskell. Harmondsworth: Penguin, 1970.

Eagleton, Mary, and David Pierce. *Attitudes to Class in the English Novel from Walter Scott to David Storey*. London: Thames, 1979.

Eagleton, Terry. *Myths of Power: A Marxist Study of the Brontës*. New York: Barnes, 1975.

Easson, Angus. *Elizabeth Gaskell*. London: Routledge, 1979.

Engel, Elliot, and Margaret F. King. *The Victorian Novel before Victoria: British Fiction during the Reign of William IV, 1830–37*. New York: St. Martin's, 1984.

Fluck, Winfried. "Literature as Symbolic Action." *Amerikastudien/American Studies* 28 (1983): 361–71.

Fryckstedt, Monica Correa. *Elizabeth Gaskell's* Mary Barton *and* Ruth: *A Challenge to Christian England*. Studia Anglistica Upsaliensia 43. Uppsala: Acta Universitatis Upsaliensis, 1982.

Gallagher, Catherine. "*Hard Times* and *North and South:* The Family and Society in Two Industrial Novels." *Arizona Quarterly* 36 (1980): 70–96.

———. *The Industrial Reformation of English Fiction: Social Discourse and Narrative Form, 1832–1867*. Chicago: U of Chicago P, 1985.

Gilbert, Sandra M., and Susan Gubar. *The Madwoman in the Attic: The Woman Writer and the Nineteenth-Century Literary Imagination*. New Haven: Yale UP, 1979.

Gill, Stephen. Introduction. *Mary Barton*. By Elizabeth Gaskell. Harmondsworth: Penguin, 1970.

Godwin-Jones, Robert. "George Sand, Charlotte Brontë, and the Industrial Novel." *George Sand Papers: Conference Proceedings, 1978*. Ed. Natalie Datlof et al. Hofstra U Cultural and Intercultural Studies 2. New York: AMS, 1982.

Harman, Barbara Leah. "In Promiscuous Company: Female Public Appearance in Elizabeth Gaskell's *North and South*." *Victorian Studies* 31 (1988): 351–74.

Hauser, Arnold. *The Social History of Art*. 2 vols. New York: Knopf, 1952.

Hawley, John C. "Responses to Charles Kingsley's Attack on Political Economy." *Victorian Periodicals Review* 19 (1986): 131–37.

Heilman, Robert B. "Charlotte Brontë, Reason, and the Moon." *Nineteenth-Century Fiction* 14 (1960): 283–302.

Henderson, James P. "Charles Dickens's *Hard Times* and the Industrial Revolution." *Cresset* 43.5 (1980): 13–17.

Homans, Margaret. *Bearing the Word: Language and Female Experience in Nineteenth-Century Women's Writing*. Chicago: U of Chicago P, 1986.

Hunt, Linda C. "Sustenance and Balm: The Question of Female Friendship in *Shirley* and *Villette*." *Tulsa Studies in Women's Literature* 1 (1982): 55–66.

Jansonius, Herman. *Some Aspects of Business Life in Early Victorian Fiction*. Purmerend: Muusses, 1926.

Kaplan, Deborah. "The Woman Worker in Charlotte Elizabeth Tonna's Fiction." *Mosaic* 18.2 (1985): 51–63.

Keating, P. J. *The Working Classes in Victorian Literature.* New York: Barnes, 1971.

Kestner, Joseph. *Protest and Reform: The British Social Narrative by Women, 1827–1867.* Madison: U of Wisconsin P, 1985.

Kettle, Arnold. "The Early Victorian Social-Problem Novel." *From Dickens to Hardy.* Ed. Boris Ford. Vol. 6 of The New Pelican Guide to English Literature. Rev. ed. Harmondsworth: Penguin, 1982.

Kirkby, Joan. "The Unaesthetic Poor." Rev. of *Proper Stations,* by Richard Faber; and *The Working Classes in Victorian Fiction,* by P. J. Keating. *Southern Review* (Australia) 5 (1972): 255–59.

Korg, Jacob. "The Problem of Unity in *Shirley.*" *Nineteenth-Century Fiction* 12 (1957): 125–36.

Kovačević, Ivanka. *Fact into Fiction: English Literature and the Industrial Scene, 1750–1850.* Leicester: Leicester UP; Belgrade: Faculty of Philology, U of Belgrade, 1975.

Kovačević, Ivanka, and S. Barbara Kanner. "Blue Book into Novel: The Forgotten Industrial Fiction of Charlotte Elizabeth Tonna." *Nineteenth-Century Fiction* 25 (1970): 152–73.

Langland, Elizabeth. "Nobody's Angels: Domestic Ideology and Middle-Class Women in the Victorian Novel." *PMLA* 107 (1992): 290–304.

Lansbury, Coral. *Elizabeth Gaskell: The Novel of Social Crisis.* New York: Barnes, 1975.

Lawson, Kate. "The Dissenting Voice: *Shirley*'s Vision of Women and Christianity." *SEL* 29 (1989): 729–43.

Leavis, F. R. *The Great Tradition.* London: Chatto, 1948.

Lévi-Strauss, Claude. *Structural Anthropology.* Trans. Claire Jacobson and Brooke Grundfest Schoepf. New York: Basic, 1963.

Levine, George. *The Realistic Imagination: English Fiction from Frankenstein to Lady Chatterley.* Chicago: U of Chicago P, 1981.

Levy, Anita. *Other Women.* Princeton: Princeton UP, 1991.

Lovell, Terry. *Consuming Fiction.* Questions for Feminism. London: Verso, 1987.

Lucas, John. *The Literature of Change: Studies in the Nineteenth-Century Provincial Novel.* New York: Barnes, 1977.

———. "Mrs. Gaskell and Brotherhood." *Tradition and Tolerance in Nineteenth-Century Fiction: Critical Essays on Some English and American Novels.* Ed. David Howard, John Lucas, and John Goode. London: Routledge, 1966.

Martin, Robert Bernard. *The Accents of Persuasion: Charlotte Brontë's Novels.* New York: Norton, 1966.

Marxist Feminist Literature Collective. "Women's Writing: *Jane Eyre, Shirley, Villette, Aurora Leigh.*" *1848: The Sociology of Literature.* Ed. Francis Barker et al. Proc. of the Essex Conference on the Sociology of Literature, July 1977. [Colchester]: U of Essex, 1978.

Melada, Ivan. *The Captain of Industry in English Fiction, 1821–1871.* Albuquerque: U of New Mexico P, 1970.

Miller, Margaret. "Happily Ever After: Marriage in Charlotte Brontë's Novels." *Massachusetts Studies in English* 8.2 (1982): 21–38.

Mitchell, Sally. *The Fallen Angel: Chastity, Class, and Women's Reading, 1835–1880*. Bowling Green: Bowling Green U Popular P, 1981.

Moers, Ellen. *Literary Women*. New York: Doubleday, 1975.

Moglen, Helene. *Charlotte Brontë: The Self Conceived*. New York: Norton, 1976.

Neff, Wanda Fraiken. *Victorian Working Women: An Historical and Literary Study of Women in British Industries and Professions, 1832–1850*. 1929. New York: AMS, 1966.

Newton, Judith Lowder. *Women, Power, and Subversion: Social Strategies in British Fiction, 1778–1860*. Athens: U of Georgia P, 1981.

Nord, Deborah Epstein. "The Urban Peripatetic: Spectator, Streetwalker, Woman Writer." *Nineteenth-Century Literature* 46 (1991): 351–75.

Palmer, William J. "Hard Times: A Dickens Fable of Personal Salvation." *Dalhousie Review* 52 (1972): 67–77.

Pearson, Carol. "Coming Home: Four Feminist Utopias and Patriarchal Experience." *Future Females: A Critical Anthology*. Ed. Marleen S. Barr. Bowling Green: Bowling Green State U Popular P, 1981.

Poovey, Mary. *Uneven Developments: The Ideological Work of Gender in Mid-Victorian England*. Chicago: U of Chicago P, 1988.

Rosenberg, John D. *Carlyle and the Burden of History*. Cambridge: Harvard UP, 1985.

Rosenberg, Philip. *The Seventh Hero: Thomas Carlyle and the Theory of Radical Activism*. Cambridge: Harvard UP, 1974.

Sánchez-Eppler, Karen. "Bodily Bonds: The Intersecting Rhetorics of Feminism and Abolition." *Representations* 24 (1988): 28–59.

Schilling, Bernard N. *Human Dignity and the Great Victorians*. New York: Columbia UP, 1946.

Schor, Hilary M. *Scheherezade in the Marketplace: Elizabeth Gaskell and the Victorian Novel*. Oxford: Oxford UP, 1992.

Seigel, Jules Paul. Introduction. *Thomas Carlyle: The Critical Heritage*. Ed. Jules Paul Seigel. London: Routledge, 1971.

Shapiro, Arnold. "Public Themes and Private Lives: Social Criticism in *Shirley*." *Papers on Literature and Language* 4 (1968): 74–84.

Showalter, Elaine. *A Literature of Their Own: British Women Novelists from Brontë to Lessing*. Princeton: Princeton UP, 1977.

Shuttleworth, Sally. *George Eliot and Nineteenth-Century Science: The Make-Believe of a Beginning*. Cambridge: Cambridge UP, 1984.

Smith, Anne. "The Martyrdom of Stephen in *Hard Times*." *Journal of Narrative Technique* 2 (1972): 159–70.

Smith, David. "*Mary Barton* and *Hard Times*: Their Social Insights." *Mosaic* 5.2 (1972): 97–112.

Smith, Sheila M. *The Other Nation: The Poor in English Novels of the 1840s and 1850s*. Oxford: Clarendon, 1980.

Spacks, Patricia Meyer. *The Female Imagination*. New York: Knopf, 1975.

Stevenson, Catherine Barnes. "'What Must Not Be Said': *North and South* and the Problem of Women's Work." *Victorian Literature and Culture* 19 (1991): 67–84.

Stevenson, Lionel. *The English Novel: A Panorama*. Boston: Houghton, 1960.

Stone, Marjorie. "Bakhtinian Polyphony in *Mary Barton*: Class, Gender, and the Textual Voice." *Dickens Studies Annual* 20 (1991): 175–200.

Sussman, Herbert L. *Victorians and the Machine: The Literary Response to Technology.*
    Cambridge: Harvard UP, 1968.
Thomson, Patricia. *The Victorian Heroine: A Changing Ideal, 1837–1873.* London: Oxford
    UP, 1956.
Tillotson, Kathleen. *Novels of the Eighteen-Forties.* Oxford: Clarendon, 1954.
Tomlinson, T. B. *The English Middle-Class Novel.* London: Macmillan, 1976.
Tompkins, Jane. *Sensational Designs: The Cultural Work of American Fiction, 1790–1860.*
    Oxford: Oxford UP, 1985.
Vanden Bossche, Chris R. *Carlyle and the Search for Authority.* Columbus: Ohio State
    UP, 1991.
Vooys, Sijna de. *The Psychological Element in the English Sociological Novel of the Nineteenth
    Century.* Amsterdam: Paris, 1927.
Wallins, Roger P. "Victorian Periodicals and the Emerging Social Conscience." *Victorian
    Periodicals Newsletter* 8 (1975): 47–59.
Williams, Raymond. *Culture and Society, 1780–1950.* New York: Columbia UP, 1958.
———. *Writing in Society.* London: Verso, 1983.
Winter, Sarah. "Domestic Fictions: Feminine Deference and Maternal Shadow Labor
    in Dickens' *Little Dorrit.*" *Dickens Studies Annual* 18 (1989): 243–54.
Yeazell, Ruth. "Why Political Novels Have Heroines: *Sybil, Mary Barton,* and *Felix
    Holt.*" *Novel* 18 (1985): 126–44.
Zimmerman, Bonnie. "*Felix Holt* and the True Power of Womanhood." *ELH* 46 (1979):
    432–51.
Zlotnick, Susan. "Luddism, Medievalism and Women's History in *Shirley:* Charlotte
    Brontë's Revisionist Tactics." *Novel* 24 (1991): 282–95.

Secondary Sources: Historical and Sociological Studies

Alexander, Sally. "Women, Class and Sexual Differences in the 1830s and 1840s: Some
    Reflections on the Writing of a Feminist History." *History Journal* 17 (1984): 125–49.
Banks, Olive. *Faces of Feminism: A Study of Feminism as a Social Movement.* 1981. Oxford:
    Blackwell, 1986.
Church, R. A. *The Great Victorian Boom, 1850–1873.* Studies in Economic and Social
    History. London: Macmillan, 1975.
Clark, Anna. "The Rhetoric of Chartist Domesticity: Gender, Language, and Class in
    the 1830s and 1840s." *Journal of British Studies* 31 (1992): 62–88.
Cohen, Marjorie. "Changing Perceptions of the Impact of the Industrial Revolution
    on Female Labour." *International Journal of Women's Studies* 7 (1984): 291–305.
Davidoff, Leonore, and Catherine Hall. *Family Fortunes: Men and Women of the English
    Middle Class, 1780–1850.* Chicago: U of Chicago P, 1987.
Epstein, James A. "The Constitutional Idiom: Radical Reasoning, Rhetoric and Action
    in Early Nineteenth-Century England." *Journal of Social History* 23 (1990): 553–74.
———. *The Lion of Freedom: Feargus O'Connor and the Chartist Movement, 1832–1842.*
    London: Croom Helm, 1982.
Evans, Richard J. *The Feminists: Women's Emancipation Movements in Europe, America and
    Australasia 1840–1920.* London: Croom Helm, 1977.

Gash, Norman. *Aristocracy and People: Britain, 1815–1865.* The New History of England. Cambridge: Harvard UP, 1979.

Harrison, J. F. C. *The Second Coming: Popular Millenarianism, 1780–1850.* New Brunswick: Rutgers UP, 1979.

Harvey, A. D. "First Public Reactions to the Industrial Revolution." *Études Anglaises* 31 (1978): 273–93.

Himmelfarb, Gertrude. *The Idea of Poverty: England in the Early Industrial Age.* New York: Knopf, 1984.

Hughes, J. R. T. "Problems of Industrial Change." *1859: Entering an Age of Crisis.* Ed. Philip Appleman, William A. Madden, and Michael Wolff. Bloomington: Indiana UP, 1959.

Jefferson, J. M. "Industrialisation and Poverty: In Fact and Fiction." *The Long Debate on Poverty: Eight Essays on Industrialisation and "the condition of England."* [London]: Institute of Economic Affairs, 1972.

Joyce, Patrick. *Work, Society and Politics: The Culture of the Factory in Later Victorian England.* New Brunswick: Rutgers UP, 1980.

Lown, Judy. "Not so much a Factory, More a Form of Patriarchy: Gender and Class during Industrialisation." *Gender, Class and Work.* Ed. Eva Gamarnikow et al. London: Heinemann, 1983.

Marcus, Steven. *Engels, Manchester, and the Working Class.* New York: Random, 1974.

Perkin, Harold. *The Origins of Modern English Society, 1780–1880.* London: Routledge, 1969.

Pinchbeck, Ivy. *Women Workers and the Industrial Revolution, 1750–1850.* New York: Crofts, 1930.

Pope, Barbara Corrado. "Angels in the Devil's Workshop: Leisured and Charitable Women in Nineteenth-Century England and France." *Becoming Visible: Women in European History.* Ed. Renate Bridenthal and Claudia Koontz. Boston: Houghton, 1977.

Roberts, David. *Paternalism in Early Victorian England.* New Brunswick: Rutgers UP, 1979.

Ryan, Mary P. *The Empire of the Mother: American Writing about Domesticity, 1830–1860.* Women and History. No. 2/3. New York: Institute for Research in History; Haworth Press, 1982.

Saville, John. *1848: The British State and the Chartist Movement.* Cambridge: Cambridge UP, 1987.

Smith, Daniel Scott. "Family Limitation, Sexual Control, and Domestic Feminism in Victorian America." *Feminist Studies* 1.3–4 (1973): 40–57.

Smith-Rosenberg, Carroll. *Disorderly Conduct: Visions of Gender in Victorian America.* New York: Knopf, 1985.

Taylor, Barbara. *Eve and the New Jerusalem: Socialism and Feminism in the Nineteenth Century.* New York: Pantheon, 1983.

Thompson, Dorothy. *The Chartists: Popular Politics in the Industrial Revolution.* New York: Pantheon, 1984.

Valverde, Marianna. "'Giving the Female a Domestic Turn': The Social, Legal and Moral Regulation of Women's Work in British Cotton Mills, 1820–1850." *Journal of Social History* 21 (1988): 619–34.

Ward, J. T. *The Factory Movement, 1830–1855.* London: Macmillan, 1962.

Welter, Barbara. "The Cult of True Womanhood: 1820–1860." *American Quarterly* 18 (1966): 151–74.

Wertz, Dorothy C. "Social Science Attitudes towards Women Workers, 1870–1970." *International Journal of Women's Studies* 5 (1982): 161–71.

Wolff, Michael. "The Uses of Context: Aspects of the 1860s." *Victorian Studies* 9 (1965): Suppl., 47–63.

Index

Analogy, 36, 49–50, 60–62, 64, 127–29
Angels. *See* Supernatural power
Apocalyptic sensibility, 4, 70, 99, 108, 110–12, 150. *See also* Millenarianism
Aristocracy, 40, 42, 62, 87, 98–99, 153, 168
Armstrong, Nancy, 176n.58, 178n.16, 180n.23
Ashley, Lord, 91
Auerbach, Nina, 15, 46, 47, 64, 69, 71, 135, 184n.23, 185n.11, 186n.9

Bodenheimer, Rosemarie, 12, 21, 33, 43, 66, 99, 176n.2, 180nn. 23, 25, 181n.30, 182nn. 38, 39, 185nn. 8, 17, 186nn. 2, 188nn. 2, 4
Brantlinger, Patrick, 6, 10, 102, 111, 112, 150, 166
Brontë, Charlotte, 116–17, 121, 147; *Shirley*, 8, 115–45, 147, 150, 159
Burke, Kenneth, 13, 15

Carlyle, Thomas, 1–8, 13; "Biography," 13; *Chartism*, 1–5; *Past and Present*, 1, 3–5
Chartism, 2, 6, 18, 165–66, 176n.59, 177n.6: in fiction, 25, 42, 48, 59, 61, 91, 92, 93, 96, 98
Christian Remembrancer, 167
Christian Socialism (in *Alton Locke*), 25, 27, 49, 94, 102, 111
Church. *See* Religion
Class relations, proposed restructuring of, 44–45, 109–10, 113

Condition-of-England question, 1–8, 12–16, 147, 165–66, 168
Croker, J. W., 49

Davidoff, Leonore: and Catherine Hall, 18, 177n.8, 178n.15
Demons. *See* Supernatural power
Dickens, Charles, 7, 23, 147, 154, 165; *Great Expectations*, 154, 158; *Hard Times*, 7; chap. 1, esp. 24, 28, 32–33, 38, 40, 43; chap. 2, esp. 50–55, 60, 62, 68–69, 71–72; chap. 3, esp. 85–88, 101–2, 108–9, 110–11; 119, 120, 126–27, 144, 148, 149, 154, 158, 163; *Little Dorrit*, 8, 148–51, 153–55, 157–58, 163–65; *Our Mutual Friend*, 154
Disraeli, Benjamin: *Coningsby*, 7; *Sybil*, 7; chap. 1, esp. 24, 27–28, 34, 38, 42, 44; chap. 2, esp. 60, 61–62, 63; chap. 3, esp. 76, 91, 95–99, 102–3, 105–6, 111; 119, 136, 139, 144, 156, 159
Domestication of reality. *See* Feminocentrism
Domestic feminism, 20–21, 41, 45
Domestic ideology, 15, 18–21, 41, 153, 168–69, 179nn. 17, 18, 181n.37, 182n.38

Edinburgh Review, 2
Eliot, George, 3, 147, 169; *Felix Holt*, 8, 148–57, 160–65, 169
Ellis, Sarah Stickney, 19–20
Emigration, 5, 99–101, 141–42
English Woman's Journal, 167
Evangelical Christianity. *See* Religion, in *Helen Fleetwood*

DH

823.
809
352
042
HAR